POVERTY AND POLICY IN TUDOR AND STUART ENGLAND

THEMES IN BRITISH SOCIAL HISTORY

edited by Dr J. Stevenson

This series covers the most important aspects of British social history from the renaissance to the present day. Topics include education, poverty, health, religion, leisure, crime and popular protest, some of which are treated in more than one volume. The books are written for undergraduates, postgraduates and the general reader, and each volume combines a general approach to the subject with the primary research of the author.

* already published

POVERTY AND POLICY IN TUDOR AND STUART ENGLAND

Paul Slack

LONGMAN
London and New York

LONGMAN GROUP UK LIMITED
Longman House, Burnt Mill, Harlow,
Essex CM20 2JE, England
and Associated Companies throughout the world.

Published in the United States of America
by Longman Inc., New York

First published 1988

BRITISH LIBRARY CATALOGUING IN PUBLICATION DATA
Slack, Paul
    Poverty and policy in Tudor and Stuart
    England.——(Themes in British social
    history)
    1. Poor——Government policy——England——
    History
    I. Title   II. Series
    362.5′8′0942   HC260.P6
    ISBN 0-582-48965-2

LIBRARY OF CONGRESS CATALOGING-IN-PUBLICATION DATA
Slack, Paul.
    Poverty and policy in Tudor and Stuart England.
    (Themes in British social history)
    Bibliography: p.
    Includes index.
    1. Great Britain——Economic policy.   2. Great
Britain——Economic conditions.   3. Great Britain——
Social policy.   4. Great Britain——Social conditions.
5. Poor——Great Britain——History.   I. Title.
II. Series.
HC254.4.S42   1988   362.5′561′0942   87–2657
ISBN 0-582-48965-2 (alk. paper)

Set in 10/11pt Times Comp/Edit 6400
Produced by Longman Group (FE) Limited
Printed in Hong Kong

CONTENTS

PREFACE

This book is an introduction to a very large topic, and one whose interest has been considerably enhanced by recent historical research. I have profited at various points from the work of other scholars, and in particular from the questions and insights of A. L. Beier, John Hadwin, Timothy Hitchcock, Stacy Hoffhaus, Joanna Innes, Sarah Lloyd, Stephen Macfarlane and Timothy Wales. None of these, of course, is responsible for any errors or oversimplifications in the arguments which follow. My undergraduate pupils also helped more than they knew, by showing me what was important and interesting in the subject and where I had gone wrong. Parts of the argument were rehearsed at a seminar at the Shelby Cullom Davis Center in Princeton in April 1985 and I learnt a good deal from the comments of Lawrence Stone and the other participants. A grant from the Economic and Social Research Council enabled me to gather some of the local material employed in Chapter 8. Finally, John Stevenson has been amazingly patient and unfailingly encouraging; and my wife has helped most of all.

The Publishers would like to thank the Open University Press for permission to use Figure 2 from A322, Unit 11, Figure 7 (copyright reserved).

Exeter College, Oxford   P.A.S.

(N.B. In all notes and references, place of publication is London unless otherwise stated. UP refers to University Press.)

LIST OF TABLES AND FIGURES

Chapter 1

INTRODUCTION: COMPARATIVE PERSPECTIVES

It is one of the commonplaces of English social history that the sixteenth century witnessed a radical transformation in attitudes towards the poor, and in the means of dealing with them. The Elizabethan Poor Law of 1601, based on precedents stretching back into Henry VIII's reign, established the principles and strategies of poor relief in England until 1834, and many of the assumptions on which it rested have persisted into the twentieth century. The state had accepted responsibility for the social welfare of its citizens, and had begun to erect a complex apparatus through which to realise it. Poor rates, outdoor relief, compulsory apprenticeship of poor children, and savage punishment of vagrants, were all characteristic of English social policy after 1600. By the middle of the seventeenth century they were well established, and thereafter their history and implications were widely commented on. These mechanisms formed the subject-matter of seventeenth-century tracts on the duties of justices of the peace and local authorities. They were discussed at length in the eighteenth century, when some revision of the machine was suggested, and again in the early nineteenth century when reform was embarked upon.[1] Finally, in the years around 1900, another reconsideration of Elizabethan principles inspired the histories of E. M. Leonard and of Sidney and Beatrice Webb; and these remain the standard accounts of what was by then termed the 'Old Poor Law'.[2]

Although its first historians tended to concentrate on legislation and its implementation, however, the sixteenth-century achievement was not a simple one-sided process of new attitudes and new mechanisms being imposed on a recalcitrant nation by an enlightened government and parliament. It was the product of deep-seated changes spread more widely through society. Leonard showed that innovation in legislation had often been preceded by independent experiments in the localities, and more recent work on English towns and counties has amply confirmed that local governors were quick to seize on new methods of controlling one of their most pressing problems, and to publicize them. Not only that: W. K. Jordan's researches into philanthropy have

1

demonstrated that the sixteenth and early seventeenth centuries also saw a remarkable investment of private wealth in endowed charities for the relief and rehabilitation of the poor.[3] Although his statistics have been much criticized (and reservations about them will be noted in a later chapter), they demonstrate that the new awareness of social problems and the new determination to provide lasting solutions to them were not confined to public authorities. All sorts and conditions of benefactors founded almshouses and hospitals, funds for pauper apprenticeships and loans for poor tradesmen, doles and other forms of outdoor relief; and again many of them survived into the twentieth century.

This book is intended to describe these multifarious changes, to investigate their origins and purpose and to measure their effects. It will seek to show how, for the first time, poverty came to be a central concern of the property-owning and governing class; how they interpreted and responded to it; and what sort of an impact their response had, both on the poor minority who were its target, and – perhaps even more important – on the relatively prosperous majority who were not. Parts of the story will be familiar from previous histories: the Tudor poor law rightly has a place in every textbook. But some prolonged reconsideration of the whole topic is justified on several grounds. There is the work by recent local historians which was not available to Miss Leonard and the Webbs, and for which more recent and much shorter surveys have had little space[4]: it needs to be fully incorporated in a rounded account. There are simple questions of fact which still remain to be answered, some of them of a surprisingly basic and obvious kind: What was the scale and nature of poverty in this period? How many people were categorized as poor and what sort of people were they? When were poor rates generally established over the country? Who paid them? Who received outdoor relief and how generous was it?

Above all, a reappraisal of the early history of the English poor law is necessary because modern investigations into the concepts and practices of social welfare at various points in the past have raised questions of a more theoretical and comparative kind. They concern three aspects of our subject: definitions of poverty; their relationship to economic and social realities; and the place of English developments in a European context. This introduction will look briefly at each of these in turn.

DEFINITIONS

The problem of definition follows from the obvious fact that poverty is a relative and not an absolute concept. Perceptions of it change as assumptions about what is an adequate standard of living change. Hence there can be no universally applicable measure of poverty which is unadulterated by changing social expectations.

Efforts have been made to define an absolute poverty line, and they have usually been based on the supposed minimum requirements for physical subsistence. They have involved the calculation of a subsistence level. In his famous study of poverty in York in 1899, B. S. Rowntree drew an absolute poverty line determined by the income needed 'to obtain the minimum necessaries for the maintenance of merely physical efficiency'.[5] He calculated the minimal cost of an adequate diet, using contemporary theories of nutrition, and he compared it with incomes in late Victorian York. Influential though Rowntree's approach has been, there are many difficulties involved in it. Nutritional assessments of diet, and definitions of 'physical efficiency' and even physical subsistence, are imprecise tools, involving complex variables and subjective judgment: they do not pinpoint a single objective level of human need. Moreover, they bear little relationship to the real world, where diets vary widely and consumers exercise preferences based on criteria other than the merely nutritional. Rowntree himself found many families which had adequate incomes by his physical efficiency standard, but which chose to employ part of their earnings in what he considered non-essential and therefore 'wasteful' forms of expenditure (on drink, for example). He argued that these people were in 'secondary' as distinct from 'primary' poverty, and they formed two-thirds of his class of poor. They evidently, and understandably, did not judge their standard of living simply in the cold terms of 'physical efficiency'.

Similar reservations may be made about historians' attempts to copy Rowntree's method. Comparisons between wages and the cost of essentials such as food and housing have proved fruitful. They can tell us whether real wages were rising or falling; and whether average wage-earners had more or less than a given, supposedly sufficient, level of income.[6] But they involve problems. Neither expenditure nor income is easily assessed, since consumer habits were elastic and employment varied from season to season and from week to week; and there remains the difficulty of deciding where to set the poverty line. As Adam Smith recognized, some societies will regard as necessities what others see as luxuries – linen shirts or leather shoes, for example. Necessaries, according to Smith, must be defined as 'not only the commodities which are indispensably necessary for the support of life, but whatever the custom of the country renders it indecent for creditable people, even of the lowest order, to be without.'[7]

Smith's point about the 'custom of the country' has been driven home in the twentieth century by the recognition of poverty in rich, developed societies such as those of Britain and the USA. Here poverty is seen to exist, although people do not starve and the real incomes of the poor are well above the average in, for example, contemporary India or China. It is now generally accepted, therefore, that 'a poverty line is necessarily defined in relation to social conventions and the contemporary living standards of a particular society'.[8] Consequently, economists and

3

sociologists have in practice come to accept nationally agreed definitions of poverty, such as the Supplementary Benefit scale in the United Kingdom, and they employ them to judge a country's social achievements in its own terms. The utility of such measures for comparative purposes is, of course, limited. They may be used to show changes over short periods of time, between the 1950s and 1960s in England, for example, although even that poses conceptual problems; but they cannot be taken much further. We can deduce little from the information that the proportion of the population in poverty was 28 per cent in York in 1899, 12 per cent in the United Kingdom in 1954, and 20 per cent in the USA in the 1960s.[9] Figures like these tell us only how far each society was meeting its own objectives at a particular moment in time.

There are obvious lessons here for the historian of poverty. He must pay attention to contemporary definitions. There was, of course, no nationally agreed assistance level anywhere in early modern Europe. But the welfare reforms of the sixteenth century led to the compiling of listings and surveys of the poor which implied at least a locally accepted standard. From them we can calculate the proportion of the population defined as poor in different places at different times. The variations were very great. We shall see in Chapter 4 that censuses of the poor in English towns reveal between 5 and 22 per cent of the population in poverty. The proportions covered a similar range in continental Europe. In part of Ghent 18 per cent of families were receiving assistance in 1492; in Lyons 5 per cent of the population were receiving alms in the 1550s; in Genoa 17 per cent of the population similarly depended on poor relief in 1625. Sometimes it is clear that high figures are due to exceptional economic circumstances when the surveys were taken. Thus no less than 57 per cent of the population of Genoa depended on charity during the plague of 1580, and up to 20 per cent of the population of Lyons may have needed relief in the harvest crisis of 1596–97.[10] But not all the variations can be accounted for in this way. They suggest different perceptions of poverty in different places, and warn us of the danger of making straight quantitative comparisons across space and time without first investigating their foundations.

There is one further difficulty which is less pronounced in modern Europe. Modern definitions of poverty aim to be economic in foundation, to assess a family's income according to some agreed, objective measure of its adequacy. Although they do not always succeed, as Rowntree's comments on wasteful expenditure show, they generally try to exclude value judgements about character or behaviour. This was far from the case in the sixteenth and seventeenth centuries, when moral status was as important as economic status and often confused with it. As a result it is all the more important that we should examine the criteria by which poverty was defined. We cannot properly interpret such records as listings of the poor, for example, until we know what their authors set out to describe. The changing perception of poverty in early modern England therefore forms the foundation of our inquiry, and it will occupy our attention in Chapter 2.

ECONOMIC AND SOCIAL REALITIES

The problem of definition is connected with our second area of uncertainty, the economic background. Having examined contemporary conceptions, we shall need to ask how far they conformed to reality. Were the new anxieties about poverty, the new and ambitious social policies and the lengthening lists of paupers on the dole, a product of worsening economic circumstances? This might seem *prima facie* plausible. It was not necessarily so, however. There was no inevitable one-to-one correlation between social need and social response. Elaborate provision for the relief of the poor could even be a sign of relative wealth.

This important point was forcefully made by Alexis de Tocqueville, after a visit to England in 1833 – on the eve of the reform of the Old Poor Law. With his characteristic agility in identifying a paradox, he noted that England was the richest country in Europe and the one with the largest proportion of its population dependent on organized charity; and he took up Smith's observation about social expectations in order to explain this:

> In a country where the majority is ill-clothed, ill-housed, ill-fed, who thinks of giving clean clothes, healthy foods, comfortable quarters to the poor? The majority of the English, having all these things, regard their absence as a frightful misfortune; society believes itself bound to come to the aid of those who lack them, and cures evils which are not even recognised elsewhere. In England, the average standard of living man can hope for in the course of his life is higher than in any other country of the world. This greatly facilitates the extension of pauperism in that kingdom.[11]

Tocqueville's analysis poses a challenge to the historian of the origins of the English poor law as well as to those seeking to account for its later development. In his view, rising expectations explain the public relief of a mass of paupers. As material circumstances improved, changing definitions of what was a minimum acceptable standard of living led to an expansion in the number of people classed as 'poor'. This expansion was the result of pressure from both directions: the poor themselves had a heightened sense of what we would now call relative deprivation; the comfortably off recognized new needs among the lower orders and had the wealth and moral inclination to try to meet them. Once a public machinery of relief – a poor law – was available, both groups came to

5

view the obligation to provide for changing wants as a moral principle, and to accept that poor relief was an entitlement. If this was so in the later eighteenth and early nineteenth centuries, might it not also have been the case in the sixteenth and seventeenth? New structures of poor relief would then be the result, not of deteriorating circumstances for the mass of the population, but of new assumptions about adequate standards of living and a sharper sense of benevolence (or perhaps guilt) on the part of the comfortably off.

This problem has been given added force by recent attempts to revise the standard picture of the social and economic history of Tudor and Stuart England. Attacks have been mounted from several directions on the familiar view that the century or so before the Civil War saw sharply declining living standards for the majority of the population, the break-up of a feudal system which offered security if not comfort to the lower orders, and the rise of a harshly competitive market economy which involved the growth of wage-labour and widespread unemployment and under-employment. Some historians have stressed the evidence of real economic growth in the century before 1640, and questioned the evidence for declining living standards.[12] It has been argued more broadly that the whole notion of a radical social and economic transition in this period is misplaced: in the later Middle Ages Englishmen were already individualists, heavily engaged in a market economy, mobile, and, by comparison with other societies, economically advanced.[13] Closer to our own subject, energetic and elaborate provision for the poor in the early seventeenth century has been seen as the expression of a stable, concerned and relatively prosperous society, not as an urgent, belated and inadequate response to mounting social and economic pressures.[14]

The revisionist case, or rather cases, can be taken too far; but they cannot be ignored. The old picture cannot survive unamended, and a fresh look at the poor law must respond to the provocation and incorporate the real insights of recent scholarship. Chapter 3 will therefore examine the economic background in an effort to determine whether economic and social changes were in fact producing new social problems or aggravating old ones. It will be argued that there was change, and that, as far as the poorer sections of society were concerned, it was change for the worse for much of our period. Living standards declined for a century after 1520, and an optimistic view of the English economy at the end of the sixteenth century runs counter to all the available evidence. Moreover, economic growth in the seventeenth century rested on developments which involved costs as well as benefits. Yet we shall also see that that is not the whole story. By the end of the seventeenth century standards of living had certainly improved, although expenditure on poor relief continued to grow; and even in 1550 or 1600 living standards were higher in England than in many other parts of Europe. Tocqueville's observation retains its force in comparative terms. We must look beyond economic distress in order to explain new trends in English social welfare.

The same conclusion emerges from the consideration of the poor themselves which is undertaken in Chapters 4 and 5 below. The discussion there shows that there was no close fit between the attitudes described in Chapter 2 and the results of the economic and social developments surveyed in Chapter 3. Some perceptions of poverty matched the facts but others plainly did not. The poor were neither so desperate nor so disorderly as was commonly supposed. Yet perceptions proved remarkably resilient, changing only slowly in the face of the facts. In some respects, indeed, they altered social realities as much as they were affected by them. The interaction worked both ways.

Something of the quantity and quality of poverty in early modern England will, it is hoped, be clear from Chapters 4 and 5. It should be stressed, however, that they do not attempt to provide a full history of the poor, if by that is meant a history of the lower classes as a whole. This is partly because of the limitations of the sources, and partly because the subject is too large and amorphous. The sources seldom allow the poor to speak for themselves. They organize them in categories and according to stereotypes shaped by the preconceptions of the elite. It is possible to correct for this distortion to some degree, in order to glimpse the underlying reality. But what is revealed is a jumble of social groups and individuals with little in common besides their poverty. This is not to deny that the poor sometimes expressed a consciousness of their collective status, usually in opposition to 'the rich'; but it was normally a transient and vague sense of identity. People moved into and out of poverty in the course of a life-time, and they had other, more precise means of defining their social position. To write their real history, in their own terms, would therefore be to do little less than write the history of the English people, or more accurately the history of many of its sub-groups: of artisans, rural labourers, single women, children and old people who were often, but not always and not always for a life-time, destitute.

Our concern is narrower and more manageable than that. It lies with that section of the poor which did have a distinct group identity, albeit an identity imposed on it from above – the dependent poor, the paupers. In a very real sense they were *created* by the social and political elite. It was not only that those in authority in church and state defined a concept or concepts of poverty. They also forced individuals into the roles they had prescribed for them. They made them rogues and vagabonds by punishing them and giving them passports; they established their identity as deserving poor by putting them into almshouses or giving them outdoor relief. Again there was transience: people moved into and out of these groups. But while they were in them their status was evident and unquestioned, openly proclaimed by welfare payments, institutions and the law. The stereotypes and

elites and the poor

categories evident in the sources thus did more than distort contemporary and later images of the poor as a whole; they moulded the
social existence of some of them.

Our central theme will therefore be the ways in which intractable
social realities were viewed, defined, made palatable and to a degree
shaped by people in authority; and the second half of this book will be
largely concerned with the machinery of social welfare, its purposes and
its effects. It is written in the conviction that institutions – as social
constructs and social agents – matter; and that the institution of the poor
law had an importance in the seventeenth century which has still to be
fully recognized. Not only did it affect the lives of the poor who received
relief. It reflected and influenced the attitudes of those who administered
and paid for it. Pensioners and rate-payers between them formed a half of
all householders by 1700: the impact of the Old Poor Law was far from
narrow. In order to appreciate the nature of the institution fully,
however, we require another comparative perspective. We must look at
our third and final introductory topic: the European context.

THE EUROPEAN SETTING

The innovations to be discussed in later chapters were not unique to
England. They were part of a movement common to the whole of
western Europe. This fact was well known to the Webbs and others who
wrote at the beginning of this century about the development of English
social welfare. It was obscured by some later writers who sought to
identify a distinct 'Protestant ethic'. They found in English attitudes to
poor relief and in English charity a Protestant revulsion against Catholic
almsgiving, which was said to be indiscriminate, clerically controlled,
and oriented towards the salvation of the donor rather than the
objective relief of the recipient.[15] More recent work has shown this to be
much too rigid a distinction, however, and revealed more similarities
than contrasts between Catholic and Protestant countries. Although the
comparative history of poor relief in the sixteenth and seventeenth
centuries still needs more attention before a balanced picture can be
drawn, some consideration of this continental background is essential if
we are to gauge the significance of English developments.

Between 1520 and 1550 many European towns and governments
produced new ordinances for the relief and regulation of the poor.
Experiments in poor relief were initiated in Nuremberg in 1522, in
Strasbourg and Leisnig in 1523–24, in Zurich, Mons and Ypres in 1525,
in Venice in 1528–29, in Lyons, Rouen and Geneva between 1531 and
1535, and in Paris, Madrid, Toledo and London in the 1540s; and there
were laws and decrees promulgated by central governments on the same

subject in the Netherlands in 1531, in England in 1531 and 1536, in Brandenburg and Castile in 1540 and in France in 1536 and 1566.[16] This is not an exhaustive list, but it is long enough to persuade us that we are dealing with a European phenomenon.

Although the details of the various schemes and regulations were not identical, most of them had several features in common. First, they tried to reduce the amount of begging and often banned it entirely; and in doing so, they carefully discriminated between those paupers who were worthy of relief and those able-bodied rogues who had to be punished and forced to work. Secondly, they signified the forceful introduction of secular authority into the field of social welfare and placed at least part of the responsibility for organizing relief in lay hands. Thirdly, the majority of them centralized control of a miscellany of existing charitable institutions and mechanisms. Sometimes, as in Geneva, this was achieved through the erection of a General Hospital, a single all-purpose institution; more often it was done by pooling different sources of alms in one centrally directed fund. Discrimination, an increase in lay control, and greater centralization were the hallmarks of innovations in social welfare in much of western Europe.

It must be admitted that some of the first towns to adopt these innovations were early Protestant centres. Strasbourg was one, and Leisnig, where Luther was personally responsible for the new initiative, was another. Neither can it be denied that some Catholic theologians were deeply suspicious of these new departures, and resisted their introduction, occasionally – as in Spain – with some success.[17] They feared secular competition with the established claims and authority of the Church in this area, and they recognized that attacks on begging threatened old traditions of voluntary almsgiving and holy poverty which formed one of the *raisons d'être* for the mendicant religious orders. Yet these suspicions were overcome in Catholic towns such as Ypres, Lyons and Venice; and in Protestant towns welfare reform often came very early indeed, as one of the harbingers of religious reform, rather than as its consequence.

In fact, two more pervasive forces than Protestantism lay behind the movement. One was the Christian humanism of the Renaissance, which stressed the responsibility of governors for the social welfare of all their subjects. It found precise exposition in Juan Luis Vives's *De Subventione Pauperum* of 1526, and it moulded educated opinion across Europe, as in England and the Netherlands where Vives had influential contacts. The second force was the social and economic environment of Renaissance towns: poverty was becoming a pressing social problem there, and secular institutions were already competing with ecclesiastical authorities and eager to take over where they had conspicuously failed. In the fifteenth century there were already signs in the most heavily urbanized areas of Europe, in Flanders and northern Italy, of the new developments in social welfare which became commonplace after

1520.[18] We need to push the sources of welfare reform back beyond Protestantism, therefore: to humanism and the urban environment, which might indeed provide fertile ground for the Reformation in some parts of Europe, but which could equally well coexist with Catholicism, albeit Catholicism in one of its newer, Counter-Reformation, guises.

There remained differences of emphasis between Protestant and Catholic societies. They were rooted in real theological divergences, particularly on the question of good works. But we should not exaggerate their social importance or their practical consequences. One powerful impetus behind Catholic charity was undoubtedly a quest for salvation, a drive towards self-sanctification through the practice of mercy. Yet preachers in England were obsessively anxious to counteract any inclination among Protestants to let doctrines of grace and justification by faith discourage good works: rather, they argued that charitable generosity should be seen as 'firm and evident proof' that a man was a 'true and not a false Christian'.[19] Catholic concentration on the donor rather than the recipient of alms ought in theory to have inclined men to be less discriminating in their charity and more tolerant of beggars in Catholic countries; and there is some evidence that this was the case, especially in the sixteenth century.[20] By the seventeenth century, however, distinctions between different categories of poor were stressed no less in France and Italy (and even in parts of Spain) than in England, while English preachers, as we shall see, were quick to warn their audience against allowing an overscrupulous definition of the deserving poor to limit their liberality.

Even pious concern for the soul as well as the body of the pauper, which has been seen as characteristic of Catholic charitable activity,[21] can find its parallels in Protestant countries. Those Puritan reformers whose activities we shall later describe may have employed a different religious terminology from that of their Catholic counterparts on the continent; but they were no less concerned with demonstrating their own religious faith and worth, and with bringing the lower orders of society to a realization of the same ideals and an enjoyment of the same spiritual benefits. Certainly, when we move from theory to practice, such manifestations of prevalent ambitions as hospitals and workhouses spread across Europe in the later sixteenth and seventeenth centuries without regard to confessional boundaries.

We must conclude that we can point to few clear-cut or lasting distinctions between Catholic and Protestant approaches to social welfare. If one is seeking to distinguish the forces promoting and resisting change all over western Europe, a contrast between urban and rural attitudes makes more sense than one between Protestant and Catholic ethics. That does not mean, however, that developments in England were in all respects similar to those on the continent. It is possible to illuminate some of the special characteristics of English poor relief by comparing England with *ancien régime* France, whose welfare institutions have been fully explored.[22] By the later seventeenth century, when each system was well developed, there appear to have been three important points of divergence.

First, England was set apart from France, and indeed from the rest of Europe, by its poor rate – the compulsory tax raised on a parochial basis after 1572 and distributed in cash as a form of outdoor relief. By 1660, as we shall see, rates were probably being raised in the majority of English parishes, and they were undoubtedly the chief formal mechanism for relieving the poor. In France this was not the case. Compulsory taxes for the poor were raised on occasion, but they were spasmodic and usually emergency devices, a reaction to crisis circumstances.[23] The main burden of relief fell elsewhere. Many villages and towns had a *bureau de charité*, a pool of alms from different sources (most of them voluntary), which provided outdoor relief, often in kind as well as in cash. But this basic provision was supplemented in the larger towns by the more ambitious *hôpital général*: an institution for the punishment of rogues, relief of the sick and orphans and employment of the idle, which spread through France in the later seventeenth century.[24] It embodied something of the character of the English workhouses and houses of correction; but it was much larger, numbering its inmates in hundreds and thousands rather than in dozens, and it served a multitude of purposes. In France the most striking embodiment of formal poor relief in the later seventeenth century was the large institution; in England it was the poor rate.

Secondly, the rigour and precision of the English settlement laws were absent from France and most of the rest of Europe. There were many attempts in French towns to exclude strange beggars; there were decrees that local communities should be responsible for their own poor, and regular expulsions of vagrants from particular provinces. But there was no attempt at so narrow a definition of settlement and of parochial responsibility for the unfortunate as was present in the English vagrancy statutes, in the procedure by which vagrants were moved from parish to parish back to their birth- or dwelling-place, and finally in the Act of Settlement of 1662.

The third difference is less marked and less easily defined. It lies in the character of charitable effort. If the poor rate and parish settlement were two pillars of English poor relief, a third was the endowed charity – the almshouse, apprenticeship fund or annual dole, often bearing the founder's name. Such charities existed throughout Europe: the Dutch Republic, for example, was famous for the number of its almshouses. They existed also in France, but they seem to have been less numerous than in England. There were charitable *fonds* based on legacies in several villages, but they were small and they were far from universal: only 40 per cent of French parishes had *fonds* in the 1770s, compared with the 60 per cent or so of English parishes which seem to have been moderately well equipped with charities for the poor by 1660.[25]

11

Unfortunately, a proper comparative survey is impeded by the fact that we know most about English charity in the early seventeenth century and about French charity in the early eighteenth. There were certainly similarities between them: in each case many legacies for the poor took the form of once-for-all doles. It would appear, however, that in France other charitable benefactions generally went to existing institutions – to the *hôpitaux*, to confraternities for the care of the poor, or to parish *bureaux*, where they existed – rather than to separate individual foundations. It may be that as a result charitable endowments were even more unevenly distributed in France than in England, and also more collective in character, more the achievement of groups and communities than of wealthy individual donors.[26]

Each of these distinctions between England and France has been broadly defined. Each requires some qualification, and the third might even be overturned by further detailed research. They rest on historical work which may have been biased by historians' interests and by the uneven survival of records; and they denote differences in policy which may have been more marked in theory than in practice. In the actual relief of the poor, for example, outdoor relief was undeniably important in France, despite the size of hospital institutions and the hopes attached to them.[27] Similarly, the precision of the English vagrancy laws should not be allowed to conceal the fact that they usually failed in practice, as we shall see. Neither should we forget one important, undocumented area of poor relief which was common to all countries and possibly of greater practical import than all the rest: the informal charity given to the begging poor at men's doors or in the streets. Nevertheless, the distinctions suggested above help us to identify some of the salient features of English social welfare as it had evolved by 1700.

The course of that evolution will be described in later chapters, and their detailed argument need not be anticipated here. The comparative perspective does, however, allow us to suggest some of the more general reasons why the English welfare apparatus was different from that of France by the end of our period. One important determinant was the degree of political and legal centralization, and the relative lack of provincial autonomy in England. This made it possible for a uniform system of poor rates and uniform settlement regulations to be imposed there, when similar ambitions failed in France. It also meant that parliamentary statutes encouraging charitable trusts, and Chancery proceedings protecting them, had an effect all over England.[28]

Secondly, we might point to the lack of major towns in England as compared with its neighbour. Large poor relief institutions were the mark of great cities in France, of Lyons, Rouen and Paris, for example, where neither decentralized charity nor parish authorities could adequately cope with the problems. England's urban centres were small by comparison, none outside London having a population of more than 15,000 in 1600. Although the parochial system of poor relief was often found wanting in small towns such as Ipswich or Salisbury, it did not require major surgery to enable it to limp along, and it never wholly broke down. As we shall see, London is the exception which proves the rule: only there were institutions for the care of the poor comparable in size with continental foundations.

A third factor of importance was the Reformation: not because of its theological undermining of the doctrine of good works, but through its practical impact on the provision of resources for the poor. The dissolution of monasteries, chantries, religious gilds and fraternities in the 1530s and 1540s radically reduced existing sources of charity. The real aid which they had provided for the poor was no doubt concentrated geographically, but it was more substantial than has often been supposed, and its destruction left a real vacuum. It has been estimated that monasteries alone provided £6,500 a year in alms before 1537; and that sum was not made good by private benefactions until after 1580.[29] Moreover, whatever the amounts involved, their removal inevitably affected attitudes and expectations. Contemporaries were quick to bemoan the loss, to demand new endowments to fill the gap, and to complain of the failure of the Chantries Act of 1547 to guarantee in practice the continuation of charitable works.[30] The result may well have been a greater readiness to countenance a compulsory poor rate, and a more decisive movement of private benefactions towards the relief of the poor, than would have occurred if the religious foundations had remained. Their dissolution meant that reform of poor relief in sixteenth-century England was not a matter simply of reorganizing or supplementing existing provision, as it was in France, Italy and Spain. It required intervention by secular authorities and individual donors to replace what had been lost and thus, it must often have seemed, to rebuild a system of social welfare from scratch.

All these are partial explanations for the differences between England and France. There is also a fourth possibility which merits consideration. It may well be that the problem of poverty was in important respects less severe in England than in France. In the later seventeenth century, when new welfare institutions were being founded in French towns, endowed charities and poor rates may have sufficed in England because the number of absolutely destitute paupers begging in the streets was significantly smaller. Settlement legislation may have been easier to define in Restoration England because there were not so many impoverished vagrants on the roads.[31] This brings us back, of course, to Tocqueville's point. The relative wealth of England did not prevent the development of complex strategies of social welfare, far from it. But it may have helped to determine what sort of strategies they would be.

Despite the problems of definition and of context which make comparative assessments so difficult, these preliminary remarks perhaps suffice to show the range of factors bearing on the policies and institutions we shall be describing – from social and economic realities and expectations to political and religious events and assumptions. In order to understand the interaction between poverty and society, we shall need to take all of them into account.

NOTES AND REFERENCES

1.   See, for example, **Matthew Hale**, *A Discourse Touching Provision for the Poor* (1683); [Samuel Carter], *Legal Provisions for the Poor* (1710); **R. Burn**, *The History of the Poor Laws* (1764); **F. M. Eden**, *The State of the Poor*, 3 vols (1797); **J. H. Poynter**, *Society and Pauperism. English Ideas on Poor Relief 1795–1834* (Routledge and Kegan Paul, 1969); **S. G. and E. A. O. Checkland** (eds), *The Poor Law Report of 1834* (Penguin Books, Harmondsworth, 1974), pp. 72–81; **G. Nicholls**, *A History of the English Poor Law*, 2 vols (1854).

2.   **E. M. Leonard**, *The Early History of English Poor Relief* (Cambridge UP, 1900); **S. and B. Webb**, *English Poor Law History. Part I: The Old Poor Law* (Longmans, Green and Co., 1927).

3.   **W. K. Jordan**, *Philanthropy in England 1480–1660* (Allen and Unwin, 1959); idem, *The Charities of London 1480–1660* (Allen and Unwin, 1960); idem, *The Charities of Rural England 1480–1660* (Allen and Unwin, 1961); and the other works cited in note 25 below.

4.   **J. Pound**, *Poverty and Vagrancy in Tudor England* (Longman, 1971); **A. L. Beier**, *The Problem of the Poor in Tudor and Early Stuart England* (Methuen, 1983). There is also a good account in **P. Williams**, *The Tudor Regime* (Oxford UP, 1979), Ch. VI.

5.   **B. S. Rowntree**, *Poverty. A Study of Town Life* (Macmillan, 1901), p. 86.

6.   Cf. **E. H. Phelps Brown** and **S. V. Hopkins**, 'Seven Centuries of the Prices of Consumables compared with Builders' Wage-Rates', in **E. M. Carus-Wilson** (ed.), *Essays in Economic History*, 2 vols (Arnold, 1962), ii, 179–96; **W. P. Blockmans** and **W. Prevenier**, 'Poverty in Flanders and Brabant from the Fourteenth to the Mid-Sixteenth Century: Sources and Problems', *Acta Historiae Neerlandicae*, x (1978), 22–7.

7.   Quoted in **G. Himmelfarb**, *The Idea of Poverty. England in the Early Industrial Age* (Faber and Faber, 1984), p. 61.

8.   **A. B. Atkinson**, *The Economics of Inequality* (Oxford UP, 1975), p. 186. For good modern discussions of the problem of definition, see *ibid.*, Ch. 10; **P. Townsend** (ed.), *The Concept of Poverty* (Heinemann, 1970), Chs 1 and 2; **W. Beckerman**, 'The Measurement of Poverty', in **T. Riis** (ed.), *Aspects of Poverty in Early Modern Europe* (European University Institute Publications, 10, Florence, 1981), pp. 47–63.

9.   **Rowntree**, *Poverty*, p. 298; **Atkinson**, *Economics of Inequality*, p. 194; **Townsend** (ed.), *Concept of Poverty*, p. 1.

10.   **Blockmans** and **Prevenier**, 'Poverty in Flanders and Brabant', p. 33; **N. Z. Davis**, *Society and Culture in Early Modern France* (Duckworth, 1975), pp. 63–4; **C. Wilson** and **G. Parker**, *An Introduction to the Sources of European Economic History 1500–1800* (Weidenfeld and Nicolson, 1977), p. 29; **R. Gascon**, 'Économie et pauvreté aux XVIe and XVIIe siècles: Lyon, ville

exemplaire et prophetique', in **M. Mollat** (ed.), *Études sur l'Histoire de la Pauvreté (Moyen Age-XVIe siècle)*, 2 vols (Publications de la Sorbonne, Paris, 1974), ii, pp. 755–6.

11. Quoted and discussed in **Himmelfarb,** *Idea of Poverty,* pp. 147–52.

12. Cf. **D. M. Palliser,** 'Tawney's Century: Brave New World or Malthusian Trap?', *Econ. Hist. Rev.*, 2 ser., xxxv (1982), 339–53; idem, *The Age of Elizabeth* (Longman, 1983), *passim*; and the emphasis on economic growth in **J. Thirsk,** *Economic Policy and Projects* (Oxford UP, 1978).

13. **A. Macfarlane,** *The Origins of English Individualism* (Blackwell, Oxford, 1978), espec. pp. 195–202.

14. **V. Pearl,** 'Social Policy in Early Modern London', in **H. Lloyd-Jones, V. Pearl** and **B. Worden** (eds), *History and Imagination. Essays in honour of H. R. Trevor-Roper* (Duckworth, 1981), pp. 115–31. Cf. the same author's 'Change and Stability in Seventeenth-Century London', *London Journal*, v (1979), 3–34.

15. For elaboration of this view, see **Jordan,** *Philanthropy,* pp. 146–7, 151–4; **C. Hill,** *Society and Puritanism in Pre-Revolutionary England* (Secker and Warburg, 1964), pp. 270–7.

16. **J. P. Gutton,** *La société et les pauvres en Europe (XVIe–XVIIIe siècles)* (Presses Universitaires de France, Paris, 1974), pp. 102–8; **R. M. Kingdon,** 'Social Welfare in Calvin's Geneva', *American Historical Review*, lxxvi (1971), 67–8; **F. R. Salter** (ed.), *Some Early Tracts on Poor Relief* (Methuen, 1926), pp. 80–1, 104, 106; **S. and B. Webb,** *Old Poor Law*, pp. 31–4; **B. Pullan,** *Rich and Poor in Renaissance Venice* (Blackwell, Oxford, 1971), Part II, Ch. 3; **L. Martz,** *Poverty and Welfare in Habsburg Spain* (Cambridge UP, 1983), pp. 19–20, 119–23; **R. A. Dorwart,** *The Prussian Welfare State before 1740* (Harvard UP, Cambridge, Mass., 1971), p. 96. On England and London, see Ch. 5, and for other examples, **C. Lis** and **H. Soly,** *Poverty and Capitalism in Pre-industrial Europe* (Harvester, Hassocks, 1979), pp. 87–9.

17. **Salter,** *Early Tracts on Poor Relief,* pp. 32–3, 76–8; **B. Pullan,** 'Catholics and the Poor in Early Modern Europe', *Trans. Roy. Hist. Soc.*, 5th ser., xxvi (1976), p. 16; **Martz,** *Poverty and Welfare,* pp. 7–13, 23–9, 32–3.

18. **Blockmans** and **Prevenier,** 'Poverty in Flanders and Brabant', p. 48; **B. Geremek,** 'Renfermement des Pauvres en Italie (XIV–XVII siècles)', *Mélanges en l'Honeur de Fernand Braudel* (Privat, Toulouse, 1973), pp. 207–8.

19. **William Whately,** *The Poore Mans Advocate* (1637), p. 21. Cf. **Henry Bedel,** *A Sermon exhorting to pitie the poore* (1573), sig. Aiii; **Jordan,** *Philanthropy,* p. 170.

20. Cf. **Martz,** *Poverty and Welfare,* p. 26 and Ch. 2; and below, pp. 120–1 for the attitude of Marian authorities in England.

21. **W. J. Pugh,** 'Social Welfare and the Edict of Nantes: Lyon and Nîmes', *French Historical Studies*, viii (1973–74), 351–2; **Pullan,** 'Catholics and the Poor', pp. 28–30. The latter contains a wide-ranging account of these comparative problems.

22. Especially by **O. Hufton,** *The Poor of Eighteenth-Century France 1750–1789* (Oxford UP, 1974); **J. P. Gutton,** *La société et les pauvres: L'exemple de la généralité de Lyon 1534–1789* (Les Belles Lettres, Paris, 1971).

23. **M. Fosseyeux,** 'La taxe des pauvres au XVIe siècle', *Revue d'histoire de*

l'Église de France, xx (1934), 407–32; **Hufton**, *Poor of Eighteenth-Century France*, p. 133. For an exception, see **P. Deyon**, *Amiens, Capitale Provinciale* (Mouton, Paris, 1967), p. 238.

24.   **Hufton**, *Poor of Eighteenth-Century France*, pp. 139–73 *passim*.

25.   **Hufton**, *Poor of Eighteenth-Century France*, pp. 137–9; **Jordan**, *Philanthropy*, p. 257, and cf. **Jordan**, *Charities of Rural England*, pp. 76, 196, 410; idem, *Social Institutions in Kent 1480–1660* (Archaeologia Cantiana, lxxv, 1961), pp. 130–1; idem, *Social Institutions of Lancashire* (Chetham Soc., 3 ser., xi, 1962), p. 97. Nearly two thirds of the parishes in Somerset, however, seem to have been poorly endowed: idem, *The Forming of the Charitable Institutions of the West of England* (Trans. American Philosophical Soc., N.S., 50, 1960), p. 77.

26.   In addition to the works of **Jordan** for England and **Hufton** for France, see **M. Vovelle**, *Piété Baroque et Déchristianisation en Provence au XVIIIe siècle* (Plon, Paris, 1973), Ch. VII. The few major English foundations, like the London hospitals, naturally received additional bequests, but it was not until the eighteenth century that group subscription to charities seems to have become common, and the endowment of individual trusts to have declined in England: **D. Owen**, *English Philanthropy 1660–1960* (Harvard UP, Cambridge, Mass., 1964), pp. 71–2. Cf. below, p. 206.

27.   See, for example, **C. C. Fairchilds**, *Poverty and Charity in Aix-en-Provence 1640–1789* (Johns Hopkins UP, Baltimore, 1976), pp. 34, 77, 94. The importance of outdoor relief vitiates some of the extreme claims about the 'Great Confinement' of the poor put forward by **M. Foucault**, *Madness and Civilization* (Tavistock, 1965), Ch. 2.

28.   **E. Chill**, 'Religion and Mendicity in Seventeenth-Century France', *International Review of Social History*, vii (1962), pp. 401–2; **Jordan**, *Philanthropy*, pp. 112–17. On the law, see **G. Jones**, *History of the Law of Charity 1532–1827* (Cambridge UP, 1969).

29.   **J. F. Hadwin**, 'Deflating Philanthropy', *Econ. Hist. Rev.*, 2nd ser., xxxi (1978), p. 113. On the charitable importance of gilds and fraternities, see **J. J. Scarisbrick**, *The Reformation and the English People* (Blackwell, Oxford, 1984), Ch. 2.

30.   **W. R. D. Jones**, *The Tudor Commonwealth 1529–1559* (Athlone, 1970), pp. 112–13, 118–19; **Jordan**, *Philanthropy*, pp. 161–5; Scarisbrick, *Reformation*, Ch. 6.

31.   See below, pp. 44–55, 194–5.

Chapter 2

PERCEPTIONS OF POVERTY

Those who wrote about 'the poor' in the sixteenth and seventeenth centuries did not spend much time examining their economic credentials. Neither did they worry very much about the fact that the term was an elastic one, used in different ways in different contexts. A poor man might be described as one who was 'ready to starve for want of bread' or as 'one that wants things needful for him' – rather different things; but these were incidental remarks rather than definitions.[1] In the seventeenth century 'alms-takers' or 'paupers', people who received public relief, were sometimes distinguished from the poor in general.[2] That might appear to have economic implications, but in practice it was an administrative distinction imposed by the selective and inconsistent hand of the poor-law authorities. It was not until the end of the eighteenth century that some writers drew a clear line between poverty on the one hand and indigence on the other: between those whose only property was their labour, and those plainly in 'want, misery and distress' who needed public or private alms in order to survive.[3]

In our period the economic station of the poor was taken for granted. They were broadly and simply the opposite numbers of the rich, who were an equally mixed bag. Attention focused rather on the ways in which these two groups were related, and the image of the poor was determined by their supposed role in the relationship. It is possible to discern three distinct views of it. In the first place, the poor could be seen as objects of charity: targets for the pity, sympathy, generosity and sometimes admiration of their betters. Secondly, they might appear as a threat: they must be excluded from sympathy and aid, if not eliminated altogether, in order to preserve public order, public morality and public health. Thirdly, they might be viewed as a potentially productive resource: needing only proper training in labour to yield profits for the general good.

These three attitudes co-existed in the sixteenth and seventeenth centuries, as they still do in the twentieth. To an extent, indeed, they naturally go together in a logical sequence. The bestowal of charity leads to inquiries into the merits of the recipients, to the identification of some who are undeserving and threatening, and to speculation about how they can usefully be reformed. In the sixteenth and seventeenth centuries it was easy to find different groups of people who fitted the three images. There were in reality worthy widows and orphans, dangerous rogues, and under-employed labourers, whom we may classify – using contemporary or near-contemporary terminology – as the impotent, the idle and the labouring poor. The three attitudes also tended to be the public property and preoccupation of different groups of observers: the first of the clergy, the second of governments and magistrates, the third of secular writers and economic projectors. The different viewpoints competed and interacted with one another.

Nevertheless, we shall see that a chronological sequence can be identified in them too. Between 1500 and 1700 emphasis shifted from the first through the second to the third, from charity to threat and finally to opportunity. Governments and magistrates set the tone for roughly a century after 1530, bringing the danger of the idle poor into prominence; in the later seventeenth century economic writers directed public attention to the economic potential of the labouring poor; and other social commentators, like the clergy, were infected to a greater or lesser degree by the prevailing fashion. Neither of the first two attitudes was jettisoned as another occupied the limelight, but it was pushed into the background and reshaped. Moreover, although the images of the impotent, the idle and the labouring poor could appropriately be applied to different people, concentration successively on one rather than the others helped to determine the perception and treatment of the poor as a whole.

TRIBUTE

In traditional societies, it has been asserted, 'poverty is not a certain small amount of goods, nor is it just a relation between means and ends; above all it is a relation between people . . . a tributary relation'.[4] Much the same applied in early modern England. It was commonplace in the sixteenth and early seventeenth centuries to compare the lot of rich and poor, of Dives and Lazarus, in order to determine the ideal type of each, and hence their reciprocal obligations.[5] The poor man's duties were the easier since, according to Scripture, he was already closer to the kingdom of heaven. He must simply be patient, hard-working and honest. He could count his blessings: he should thank God that he was not subject to the temptations of the prosperous, and he should welcome his earthly tribulations as a purification in preparation for the life to come. The rich man, on the other hand, must beware the danger of eternal torment if he was covetous or took pride in his wealth, for his wealth was not his own. He held it in trust for the poor, and he must be generous in returning it to them: 'The rich man is no more than God's steward and the poor man's treasurer.' It was a tributary relationship and tribute was paid by both sides: 'The rich men by their alms uphold the poor . . . and the poor men again overshadow the rich men with their prayers'.[6]

The obligations of the rich were often summed up under the headings of charity and hospitality. These Christian virtues were as ill-defined as poverty itself, partly because there should ideally be no bounds to them. Charity encompassed love of God and love of all one's neighbours; hospitality should be extended widely, to neighbours and strangers alike. The Sermon on the Mount was not socially exclusive. The poor were singled out as particular objects of charity, however, because they were Christ's special representatives: 'whatsoever is given for their comfort, is given to Christ himself', as the Royal Injunctions of 1547 put it. That gave a powerful impulse throughout our period to the acts of mercy which Christ himself had recommended.[7] It explains the philanthropic endowments and annual doles which provided aid for poor prisoners, or food, clothing and almshouses for the hungry, naked and homeless. It also underlay the practice of hospitality to the poor. That was not normally given under a rich man's roof, although the inmates of William Cecil's almshouse at Stamford were to dine at Burghley House once every quarter.[8] But it was given, in food or cash, at a man's gates. Funeral sermons praised men like Sir Edward Lewkenor, whose house 'was full of hospitality, and there was always a great crowd at his gate'; and vagrants were indeed supported in this way on their travels.[9]

The poor were thus an integral part of a Christian commonwealth, necessary stimuli if the rich were to practise virtue, and useful examples of humility in themselves. In this view there was no place for anxiety about their needs or their numbers. Charity would provide for them; and they should be welcomed and admired as people nearer to God than the rest. 'Blessed are the poor' was often quoted and elaborated on. 'Hear the voice of the people, especially of the poor, the people of God', urged Charles Fitz-Geffrey in 1631. 'God is the poor man's God', sang the children of Christ's Hospital in 1655. 'Then this is to be learned, that none contemn or despise the poor', Henry Bedel concluded in 1573.[10]

By 1573, however, as Henry Bedel well knew and as we shall shortly see, condemnation of the poor was becoming respectable; and the refusal of alms to a substantial proportion of them was widely regarded as legitimate. Homilies on charity therefore acquired a self-consciously defensive tone in their appeal to old ideals which seemed to be under threat. The suspicion that charity is in decline, as compared with some past golden age, is no doubt perennial, but it was particularly keenly felt in the later sixteenth and early seventeenth centuries.[11] Although it did not entirely accord with the facts, it appeared to be justified by new social and intellectual fashions. Local hospitality seemed to be threatened by the growth of towns, and particularly of London, with its 'season' which took landowners away from their estates; hence the government's proclamations in times of bad harvest ordering gentlemen to leave the capital and return home to care for their tenants and neighbours. At the same time, old notions of unlimited charity were directly attacked by sixteenth-century poor laws and the propaganda behind them, which condemned begging and the giving of alms to any but the obviously deserving.[12]

It was easier for preachers to castigate modes of behaviour which inhibited charity altogether than to resist the trend towards discrimination which had the voice of authority behind it. As might be expected, some of the strongest defences of the traditional concept of the harmonious commonwealth were published after years of dearth, particularly in the later 1590s and early 1630s. Then there was general agreement than the mutual obligations of rich and poor must be reiterated, and that the sins of the former were greater than those of the latter. People who neglected charity, wasted their wealth on extravagant fashions, hoarded corn and engaged in usury were the 'poor-makers', the causes of misery and indigence. There is a profound sense of guilt in much of this literature. Yet there was also an acknowledgement that the poor themselves might sin; they too might depart from the ideal. If they did not suffer humbly and in silence, if they were tempted to 'be impatient, and ... revenge [their] wrongs with execrations and curses', they broke the reciprocal relationship between rich and poor.[13] They excluded themselves from charity. From the middle of the sixteenth century onwards, the implications of this view were grudgingly accepted even by homilists who defended almsgiving most vociferously. When so many were poor, all available help should as far as possible be concentrated on those who deserved it.

'Cease not to give to all, without any regard', Robert Crowley urged in the 1550s: 'Though the beggars be wicked thou shalt have thy reward.' Later writers and preachers were much more cautious. In 1592 Henry Smith lamented the decline of almsgiving, but he also noted that 'to give unto such as we know of lewd behaviour, thereby to continue them in their wickedness, were very offensive'.[14] In his *Treatise of Christian Beneficence* of 1600 Robert Allen was closer to Crowley. Some of the poor were 'a monstrous and sottish multitude', but if charity were offered to them, 'their evil can no whit diminish thy goodness': 'Better is it ... that alms should be cast away, than any creature should perish for want of relief'. Even so, Allen's generosity had a sting in its tail: 'It is no sin for a merciful man to relieve any that be presently in urgent necessity, be they idle or be they worse, provided ... that with the outward relief admonition be given'. While disagreeing with writers like Peter Martyr who wished to ban private almsgiving altogether, Allen also conceded that organized poor relief might allow private charity to be restricted to those whose persons and worth one knew: 'It must needs be a great ease unto every one, touching persons unknown to them, in that they may with good conscience leave them to those who have the charge of the public distribution'.[15]

According to Allen and several other writers, poor relief should be given above all to those who were 'of the household of faith'. This Pauline prescription appealed to Puritans as a justification for restricting alms to the godly, and it was regarded by some of their opponents as encouraging an unwarranted concentration on a 'particular sect'.[16] Yet it also had a much wider appeal, as a reminder that the image of the holy poor depended on their being visibly and in fact holy. The reprobate could have no indisputable claim to charity. Ralph Josselin cannot have been alone in his unease when he helped the poor in the hard times at the end of the 1640s: 'I constrained myself to do more than ordinary for our poor: it is better to give than to receive: and yet poor people were never more regardless of God than nowadays.' The same uncertainty can be found in seventeenth-century sermons on liberality in almsgiving which took 'Cast thy bread upon the waters' as a text, while also recognizing the unworthiness of some of the recipients and the unlikelihood of any return.[17]

The suddenness and the extent of the decline of old charitable ideals should not be exaggerated. They had always needed defenders, and, as the above citations make clear, there was never any lack of troops manning the barricades of private charity and private almsgiving. In practice too, informal and relatively indiscriminate almsgiving continued throughout the seventeenth century. Although it now had to be defended by those who practised it, it could be justified so long as public relief remained inadequate. 'When so many thousands in this hard time seek and desire work, and yet have not to eat, how can we want fit objects of our bounty and liberality?', asked a preacher in 1631. At the end of our period, Richard Baxter was ready to disobey the laws against indiscriminate charity if overseers failed to relieve all the poor: 'I will take myself as guilty of their death, if I relieve them not when I am able.'[18]

Old attitudes were also employed to sanction new projects for organized poor relief in the later seventeenth century. In the 1670s Thomas Firmin paid more than lip-service to the notion of hospitality, albeit only for the deserving poor, when he described those who were licensed to beg food at men's doors not as beggars but as 'invited guests'. Later still, the Quaker John Bellers saw the same poor as 'living temples'; they were the holy poor still.[19] Sir Matthew Hale, author of the most influential discourse on the poor laws in the later seventeenth century, was famous for his practical charity 'even among street beggars', which he defended on much the same grounds as Baxter; and he began his tract with a classic exposition of the traditional view. Care of the poor was

> an act of great piety towards Almighty God, who requires it of us. He hath left the poor as his pupils, and the rich as his stewards to provide for them. It is one of those great tributes that he justly requires from the rest of mankind; which, because they cannot pay to him, he hath scattered the poor amongst the rest of mankind as his substitutes and receivers.[20]

Persistent and powerful as the concept of charity was, however, it was subtly but substantially modified in the course of our period. Discrimination and public relief made it necessary to define private charity, and in the process it became exclusive, calculating and deliberate. In its ideal form charity was a state: a condition of harmony between equally valuable individuals and social groups, all of them 'in charity' one with another. Its replacement was 'beneficence': a series of discrete actions with particular purposes and particular objects, excluding some potential recipients while embracing others. From the later sixteenth century onwards most commentators agreed that some of the poor should be denied tribute, the benefits of beneficence, and a place in Christian society altogether.

MARGINALITY

It should be stressed that discrimination between different categories of poor was not new in sixteenth-century England. It had behind it a tradition stretching back at least as far as the thirteenth century. Medieval canon lawyers had argued that 'we ought not to show ourselves generous indiscriminately to all who come', and they had cited scriptural authority for the refusal of alms to idle beggars, since, 'If a man will not work, neither shall he eat'.[21] This attitude was given formal expression in English labour legislation in the fourteenth century. The Statute of Labourers of 1349 forbade the giving of alms to able-bodied beggars, so that they might be forced 'to labour for their necessary living'; and a further statute against mobility of labour in 1388 separated beggars 'able to serve or labour' from beggars 'impotent to serve' who merited relief.[22] It was not only lawyers and legislators who praised the virtues of work. The same assumptions have been detected in later medieval literature, where the contrast between sloth or idleness and useful labour was an increasingly popular theme.[23]

By 1500, therefore, the distinction between the worthy and unworthy poor had already been formulated. It can be found in the first printed tract relevant to our theme, *Dives and Pauper*, which was published in 1493 but written at the very beginning of the fifteenth century. Although the author noted that 'Christ biddeth thee that thou give to each that asketh thee', he stressed that 'we must keep order in giving and taking heed to the cause'. Some were poor 'against their will', including victims of sickness and misfortune. Others were poor 'by their will', and they could be divided into two groups: those virtuous men such as friars who sought poverty 'for the love of God', and the rest who were poor for the love of sin and 'the world'. The sinful poor should be helped when in 'utter need', but the poor by virtue and by misfortune should be relieved first.[24]

Although present in the later Middle Ages, however, there can be no doubt that the dichotomy between the deserving and undeserving poor acquired much greater force in the sixteenth century. Hammered home in tracts, statutes and proclamations, it became a commonplace concept through which contemporaries organized their view of the social order. One reason for this was the destruction and discrediting of a section of the wilful poor described in *Dives and Pauper*. The abolition of the religious orders at the Reformation removed the need to admit the holiness of voluntary poverty altogether; and Protestant invective against monks and friars insisted that poverty must never be actively sought. The mendicant clergy were themselves branded as 'strong, puissant and counterfeit holy, and idle beggars and vagabonds' who took alms away from the 'impotent' poor. The wilful poor could therefore be blamed without qualification, and the victims of misfortune, sickness, old age, fire or shipwreck, accepted as 'the true poor indeed'. Writers could now articulate a simpler and more appealing classification than that of *Dives and Pauper*: 'All whom God, not their idleness, makes poor, must be relieved.'[25]

Still more important in reinforcing this distinction were the emotions of fear and disgust which mounted in the early sixteenth century. Wandering rogues came to be viewed as a social danger of unlimited proportions. Vives remarked in the 1520s that 'in a state the poorer members cannot be neglected without danger to the powerful ones'; and he was not thinking only of the threat from popular risings. The disorders of the poor included infectious diseases and equally infectious moral corruption. English writers shared his alarm. William Marshall was amazed at the 'multitude of poor and needy folks' in 1535, and horrified by their wandering 'idly, lasciviously and dissolutely' about, by their 'sundry and diverse diseases, contagions and infections', and by their 'heinous deeds, detestable sins, crimes and offences'.[26] The same message was propounded in Tudor proclamations. There the problem of poverty was invariably presented as the problem of wandering beggars and vagabonds: men who were 'suspect persons', embodiments of 'idleness, mother and root of all vices', people of 'vile, wretched and filthy purposes', and originators of 'all vices and enormities to the high displeasure of God and disturbance of the King's peace and his subjects'.[27] This strident reaction was quite different from that which greeted the honest widow and orphan, or the genuine victim of fire or theft. There is no mistaking the pervasive sense of an escalating threat.

The Tudor identification of the dangerous poor had diverse roots. There was no doubt a long-established fear of the beggars coming to town, although one may wonder whether they had always been the bogymen they clearly were by the seventeenth century, when mothers and nurses used them to silence naughty children: 'Take him, Beggar, take him!', they would cry.[28] Equally instinctive, perhaps, was that sense of outraged propriety which made testators in the early sixteenth century insist that 'common beggars' and 'mighty vagabonds' be kept away from their funerals and funeral feasts.[29] One new factor, as we shall see in the next chapter, was an increase in the number of beggars in the sixteenth century, which must have intensified feelings of revulsion. Important too were the new, or newly virulent, infectious diseases of the early sixteenth century: syphilis and the sweating sickness. They help to explain the horror at the 'incurable diseases and filthiness of body' and the 'maladies tedious, loathsome or abhorrible to be looked upon' which were now associated with the poor.[30]

Yet more than this seems to be involved in the aura of dirt, pollution and peril which was firmly attached to the Tudor poor. Similarly, it perhaps requires more than an increase in the number of beggars, and the recent arrival of gipsies on the wayfaring scene, to explain why people, who had once been tolerated as an integral and even attractive part of wayfaring life, should be proscribed and carefully listed in Tudor vagrancy statutes: tinkers, pedlars, minstrels and jugglers, for example.[31] It is as if social boundaries were being redrawn and proper, respectable society being newly and more tightly defined. The same process is suggested by other intellectual and social developments in the later sixteenth and early seventeenth centuries. There was the increasing use of the paradigm of the body politic, not to bind together a varied social whole, but to show the damage which untreated disease, disorder or decay in any one member might do to the rest: the diseased members should be cut off. We might point also to the growing interest in civility and refinement of manners which can be traced in the same period.[32] Behind all this, it may be argued, lay a general sense of insecurity at a time of rapid political, religious, social and economic change.

The exploration of this theme would take us beyond the confines of this book. But it perhaps helps to explain the widespread conviction that many of the poor were 'enemies to the commonwealth'.[33] The simplest way of defending virtue and order was by defining vice and disorder; and the identification of an external menace protected the essence of a body politic threatened with dissolution. This seems to have been the imperative behind the perception that the poor were outside rather than inside society, that they were marginal men and women. It was a perception which was not confined to England, and wherever it occurred in early modern Europe the treatment of the poor as peripheral beings had implications for people on both sides of the social boundaries which were created by it.[34]

The use of the poor as a yardstick, against which approved social norms could be measured out, may be seen most clearly in the representation of vagrants and idle paupers as the complete obverse of all that was acceptable. They were 'lawless beasts'. They 'lived and delighted themselves in a most barbarous and beastly confusion'. They were 'a promiscuous generation, who ... know no kindred, no house or home, no law but their sensual lust, ... men without religion, church, baptism, faith or God in the world'. They were 'the very filth and vermin of the common wealth ... the very Sodomites of the land, children of Belial, without God, without magistrate, without minister; dissolute, disobedient, and reprobate to every good work'.[35] Vagrants belonged to the animal realm, and could be defined in human terms only by negatives. They belonged in fact to the World Turned Upside Down. William Marshall's translation of the scheme of poor relief used in Ypres noted that 'all things [were] turned upside down' in the behaviour of idle beggars.[36]

If we wish to examine the function of the stereotype of the idle pauper, it would not be far-fetched, therefore, to compare it with other forms of inversion, of the World Turned Upside Down, in early modern Europe.[37] Many of them – from carnivals to fools and boy bishops – were ambivalent. They were conservative in that they reinforced by contrast contemporary notions of right order. Yet they were also a relatively harmless outlet for criticism of that order and for the open presentation of alternatives. Much of the rogue literature as it developed in the later sixteenth century served a similar purpose. Combining fact and fiction, writers from Thomas Harman onwards dramatized the dangerous rogue, exaggerated his eccentricity, and even romanticized him. They portrayed vagabonds as men enjoying a unique freedom, no less attractive for the fact that it was condemned as licence.[38] According to one writer, beggars were indeed the 'only freemen of a Commonwealth';[39] and in fiction they were allowed – rather like Court fools – to gull, outwit and occasionally criticize their betters.[40] These subversive potentialities were carefully controlled within the framework of the ballad and 'merry tale', however. In sixteenth-century reality, as statutes and local records show, they justified savage repression.

The condemnation of some of the poor led logically to the idealization of others: the deserving, impotent poor. This also produced a satisfying conceptual polarity, which appealed to a society accustomed to articulating its view of the world in terms of binary opposites. One class of poor was the inversion of the other, as contemporary labels make clear. They were respectively impotent and able, diligent and idle, tractable and incorrigible, willing and wilful, godly and godless. 'Of poor there are two sorts', said one writer in summary: 'God's poor and the Devil's'[41] God's poor were also now set on the margins of society, however. Widows, orphans and the disabled were no less incomplete members of the social order than rogues and vagabonds with no fixed abode; and they might sometimes need manipulating to make them conform to the ideal type. They were no longer simply accepted. They could be compelled to attend church, to renounce their sins, and to 'correct . . . their manners'.[42]

There was much common ground between these attitudes and Puritan aspirations, particularly with regard to the reformation of manners, in the later sixteenth and seventeenth centuries. For many ministers and magistrates religious and social reform were inextricably intertwined and the poor were obvious raw material for both, as we shall see.[43] Insistence on the culpability of the poor was not the exclusive property of Puritan enthusiasts, however. One of Charles I's chaplains, Henry Hammond, thought that 'it will hardly be found that any man is left . . . destitute who hath not first been wanting to himself'; and many observers would have agreed with John Gore that, while not all beggars were ungodly, it was 'a rare unusual thing to see a righteous body come to beggary'. By the 1640s Peter Chamberlen thought it necessary to state plainly that neither 'poverty and honesty, nor poverty and godliness are always at odds'.[44]

In these various ways powerful social stereotypes were created which justified the categorization of individuals as social problems, and produced clear prescriptions for policy and action. The deserving and undeserving could be distinguished by their behaviour and moral worth, and while the first were relieved by alms, or later by public rates, the second could be whipped without compunction, sent back to their home parishes and compelled to work there. This was the principle adopted in the poor law of 1531 and its successors. All that was needed was a close local examination of those who were needy, and the discovery of the true, worthy poor would be easy. They would prove to be few and their support would be no great financial burden.[45] The programme was simple.

It also seemed practicable, because there was in fact no lack of examples of worthy paupers and genuine rogues around. We can see typical instances in two local records compiled in the 1580s. The deserving poor are well represented by the people taken into an almshouse in Ipswich in 1588–89: 'an aged and impotent wench of this town, in respect of her poverty, age and lameness'; 'an old, aged and impotent wench of this town, who hath been a dweller in the same by the space of 70 years, in respect of her poverty, lameness and age'; 'a poor old woman, who was born in this town, being of honest fame and report'; 'a poor man of this town whom God hath visited with sickness'. A total contrast was presented by the suspicious wanderers examined in Warwick a few years earlier. They included six people found together in an alehouse, three of whom falsely claimed to be brother and sisters. One of them alleged that he was a Scholar of Magdalen College, Oxford, like the counterfeit wandering students mentioned in some of the statutes. There were several thieves, a man who wandered round the country doing cures, and a suspicious Yorkshireman whose father had been executed after the Rising in the North of 1569.[46] It was not difficult to find the two classes of marginal poor once one looked for them.

LABOUR   The "laboring" poor.

Other kinds of poor could also be discovered without difficulty, however. As we shall see in detail in Chapter 4, those who undertook surveys of the poor in the later sixteenth and early seventeenth centuries found more than they bargained for. They uncovered people who did not fit neatly into either the impotent or the idle category: men and women who were able and willing to work but who could find none, or not enough to pay for the upkeep of their families – the 'labouring poor', in fact. The discovery occasioned as great a shock as the similar revelation of submerged poverty made by Rowntree and others in the later nineteenth century, and by Townsend and his colleagues in the mid-twentieth; and it was equally unwelcome. One observer of Tudor censuses and surveys acidly concluded that 'to inquire after poor is the next way to procure poor'.[47] Yet these inquiries revealed conditions which all contemporaries agreed amounted to destitution. The rags and tatters of the labouring poor were less often on view than those of impotent and idle beggars; but once revealed, they seemed to contemporary sensibilities as plain a manifestation of intolerable, if relative, deprivation.

Although the term 'labouring poor' seems not to have been used before the eighteenth century, several observers came close to it in the seventeenth century and it would have been appropriate even in the sixteenth. The initial emphasis was on the moral worth of the hidden poor, on their self-respect which prevented begging and kept them at work. In early sixteenth-century Coventry, as in early sixteenth-century Spain, they were described as people who were 'ashamed to ask or beg openly': 'poor householders which be ashamed to beg and be no common beggars'.[48] Attention was also directed to the causes of their poverty, however, and in particular to the burden of supporting large families. One of the first urban surveys of the poor, undertaken in London in 1552, had to admit the existence of other groups besides the idle and the impotent. Having counted in turn 'idle vagabonds', 'aged persons', 'fatherless children', and 'sore and sick persons' – all of them predictable – the investigators were confronted by numbers of 'decayed householders' and of 'poor men overburdened with their children'.[49] By the end of the century labouring householders unable to make ends meet

27

had become familiar figures in analyses of the poor, sometimes earning a sub-heading of their own as the 'poor by casualty'.[50]

Not surprisingly, the existence of this group was recognized most often in crisis years when high food prices made casualties inevitable. A volume of officially approved homilies, published to 'move compassion to the poor' during the dearth of 1596, pointed out that there were many besides the impotent to be cared for. They might not be conspicuous, for they were often ashamed to beg, but they were numerous and needy:

> Though they do labour and take pains in their vocation and trade, yet by reason of the extremity of the world, for that their rents are so great, the prices of all necessaries so dear, and the hearts of men so hardened, they cannot live by their labour, nor maintain their charge, but suffer want and are poor.[51]

The same people were categorized more precisely in some of the parish surveys of the poor which were undertaken in 1597 and 1598. After the names of the impotent, of widows and the disabled, there were lists of 'poor able labouring folk', or 'labouring persons not able to live off their labour'.[52] From then on such phrases were commonplace. The poor were no longer marginal people. They were much closer to the mainstream of society. They included 'artificers or handicraftsmen, labouring diligently', 'the honest labourer and the poor householder', and 'persons who partly may live by labour and partly have need of relief and comfort'.[53] These were Allen's 'poor labouring householders' in 1600, Hartlib's 'laborious poor' in 1646, and Child's 'poor labouring people' twenty years later.[54]

The discovery of the labouring poor was a necessary consequence of the attempt to thrust the poor onto the margins which has just been described. There was a mismatch between that ideological impulse and the facts, and the ideology had to change in order to accommodate untidy reality. It changed only slowly, and it was never wholly transformed; but the two images of marginal people had somehow to be stretched to incorporate less socially eccentric categories of pauper. In the process, the assumption that the poor were a small group beyond the pale had to be abandoned.

The able-bodied poor fell traditionally among the idle: if they could not support themselves it was their own fault. From the beginning, therefore, Tudor vagrancy statutes cast a net wide enough to embrace almost all of them. After listing the marginal tricks and trades of vagrants, the 1598 Vagrancy Act specified two residual and very broad classes of rogue: 'all wandering persons and common labourers, being persons able in body, using loitering and refusing to work ... not having living otherwise to maintain themselves'. The two alternative qualifications of 'wandering' and 'loitering and refusing to work' could hardly be more imprecise, and they caused some confusion about methods of treatment. In the years after 1598 the Council and the judges had to gloss the law, making it clear that only wanderers were to be whipped back to their parishes of birth; those loitering in their parish of residence were to be punished and set to work there. The judges' insistence that 'none must be enforced to turn vagrant' was an open confession that the statutory definition of a rogue was unacceptably and impractically wide.[55] Yet the accent on punishment remained. There was no recognition here that people wandering or loitering might be trying to find work, not to avoid it. A statute of 1610, providing for houses of correction in every county, saw these as places of punishment and compulsory labour both for 'rogues' and 'vagabonds' and for 'idle and disorderly persons', who were not further defined.[56]

At the same time, however, the able-bodied poor were also being incorporated into statutes dealing with the impotent and deserving. The Acts of 1598 and 1601 authorizing payments in cash to the 'lame, impotent, old, [and] blind', also provided for the raising in each parish of stocks of wool, hemp, or other materials on which children and the unemployed could be set to work.[57] As we shall see, the statutes were not enforced as their authors intended. Parish authorities did not as a rule provide work for the labouring poor. Instead they gave them cash payments to supplement inadequate wages, thus vastly expanding the number of people on relief.[58] In practice they treated the labouring poor like the impotent poor.

Local authorities therefore used their discretion in order to fit the labouring poor into the dual strategy of punishment and relief erected by the poor law. They were left to discriminate between culpable idlers and genuinely overburdened householders and act accordingly. The result was a good deal of confusion both in the law and in its implementation, but from it there emerged an alternative strategy. It had a subsidiary place in the Elizabethan statutes relating both to the idle and to the impotent; it was to be applied to the poor who were not easily classified as either; and its widespread implementation and elaboration in the seventeenth century signalled a recognition that the simple moral judgements inherent in statutory images of the poor were inadequate, if not wholly unreal, bases for action. The alternative strategy rested on the twin pillars of labour and settlement.

The ideal of labour as a remedy for idleness was, of course, as old as the hills. It was proclaimed in fourteenth-century labour legislation, as we have seen; and employment for the able-bodied poor was one of the prescriptions of the Tudor poor law, suggested in the earliest projects and incorporated in a statute of 1576 which provided for houses of correction and work stocks in towns.[59] Vagrants whipped back to their parishes and the domestic unemployed poor of towns and villages were alike to be set to work. Compulsory employment was seen as a permanent cure for a large segment of poverty. It would remove some of the 'occasions and breeding' of beggars and vagabonds and guarantee that 'young children may be brought up and be instructed in honest arts'. Projects for setting the poor to work on wool, hemp, and flax therefore proliferated from the later sixteenth century, and so did houses of correction providing some kind of forced labour, and workhouses more positively designed to give training and employment in useful and profitable skills.[60]

As an attempt to obliterate the labouring poor, to make them self-sufficient and so give reality to the reassuringly marginal conception of poverty, the effort failed. The net result was rather to increase the number of people subjected to the machinery of the poor law. But the stress on labour did imply a shift away from simple condemnation of idleness to an examination of its causes. Lack of work or training was only one of them. The social and economic environment might be formative: in the early seventeenth century, plentiful commons and wastes were identified as nurseries of vagabonds and beggars, for example.[61] One or two commentators even acknowledged that Bridewells and houses of correction might spread the very habits of idleness and roguery they were designed to prevent.[62] More commonly there was a growing appreciation that the most hated of pauper vices might be consequences, not causes, of poverty. Peter Chamberlen made the point with unusual clarity in 1649: 'Cure them of poverty [and] you take away their unruly insolency'.[63]

The search for causes and cures had another incentive in the later seventeenth century, again neatly expounded by Chamberlen: 'The only riches of a commonwealth is by employing the poor and making such industrious as are not.'[64] This theme had been evident in social and economic projects from the middle of the sixteenth century;[65] but it undoubtedly gained in vigour and popularity from the middle of the seventeenth. The desire to increase the nation's wealth made economic theorists such as Josiah Child and Dudley North consider the state of the poor, and it informed the tracts and projects of their contemporaries. Much has been written about these authors, and it need not all be rehearsed here. As one of their first historians put it, in summary, they stressed the 'utility of poverty'.[66] Although they were divided over whether low or high wages best encouraged labour productivity, they agreed that England's 'national poverty',[67] particularly as compared with the Dutch, could only be remedied by full employment, and that that in turn depended on overcoming the lack of skills and leisure-preferences of the labouring classes.

Their answers to these problems were the old ones: compulsory training and employment. What seems to be new after 1640, however, is the general perception that the poor were not a threat, as they had been for a century, but an opportunity: a resource which only needed proper handling to be profitable. Although idleness and its associated vices still caused profound concern, there was little of the old feverish anxiety that the whole social and moral order might dissolve if poverty could not be held back beyond the margin. People still wished to prevent the labouring poor being dependent on public relief: they could not be profitable if they were. But concentration on the economic value of labour meant that there could be no doubt that they were a proper focus of the state's attention for as long as it took to make them produce a return. The concept of the labouring poor was now a useful and not a disturbing image, and their existence was a fact to be accepted and coolly examined, not denied.

The same transition emerges even more clearly from the history of settlement legislation. The principle of parish settlement, like that of compulsory labour, was explicit in Tudor statutes. Responsibility for the poor lay with the parishes where they were born or where they resided for a stated period (one year under the Vagrancy Act of 1598). People could move in certain circumstances, if they carried testimonials or were going to harvest work, for example; but if they ended up idle, without obvious livelihood or employment, the vagrancy laws prescribed their punishment and return to their birth- or dwelling-place. In short, lower-class mobility in general was frowned upon, and unsuccessful migrants were branded as culpable vagabonds. The law was never implemented so strictly. As we shall see, many wanderers were returned home without being whipped first. But it was not until the Act of Settlement of 1662 that a statutory procedure was provided for the return without punishment of any migrants who were 'likely to be chargeable'. The mobility of the poor was at last consciously separated from vagrancy. The 1662 Act even permitted some mobility, albeit hesitatingly and with careful safeguards, and amending legislation in 1697 positively encouraged migration to areas where there was a demand for labour – again in the interests of national wealth.[68]

One result was that the vagrancy laws could now be restricted to obvious rogues, those on the social periphery. There was no longer any need, and no longer any inclination, to apply them to all the wanderers and idle labourers theoretically covered by them. But the Settlement Act had also erected a new poor-law mechanism – a cumbersome machinery of certificates and parish registration – which applied to large numbers of the labouring poor. We shall look at that system again at the end of this book; but it is important for perceptions of poverty because, like attitudes towards employment, it presupposed that the poor who had to be managed were a large and integral part of the social order. In the later seventeenth century that proposition was accepted with few qualms. Sir Josiah Child's chapter on the poor, written around 1669, was representative in its rational tone of voice. There were some reflections of past attitudes. His projects for employment were to be undertaken by 'Fathers of the Poor' – an echo of old notions of charity. He referred still to the 'many loathsome diseases' of beggars. But he began his discussion with the words, 'This is a calm subject'.[69] No one would have said that fifty or a hundred years before 1669.

31

sum

Two gradual changes in perceptions of poverty in the sixteenth and seventeenth centuries have been described in this chapter. One was the hardening of an existing discriminatory distinction, culminating in two powerful images of impotent and idle, virtuous and vicious poor. The second was the identification of the labouring poor as a much larger, third category, who could not easily be subdivided between the deserving and the rogues, the respectable and the rough, although contemporaries never stopped trying. The first change represented an effort to define the problem of poverty as a marginal one and the poor as marginal men and women; and it placed many of them outside the bounds of charity. The second change in the end entailed a recognition that the poor for whom the rich had a public responsibility were a large and fundamental segment of society and a segment which should be neither punished, nor simply taken for granted and held in charity, but manipulated.

It is not easy to date these changes. It might be suggested that the first had begun in 1530, and was complete by 1600: it produced the Tudor poor law with its deliberate combination of repression and relief. The second was underway by the 1590s but it reached fruition only after 1640: it explains some of the confusions and inconsistencies in Elizabethan statutes and it produced the settlement legislation of 1662 and after. There were leads and lags, however, and one set of attitudes overlay another, as we have seen. What is certain is that perceptions changed. In the next chapter we must look at economic and social developments to see whether they provided any of the stimulus for new attitudes. We must also ask how serious the poverty which people perceived in such various ways actually was.

NOTES AND REFERENCES

1.   Exeter College, Oxford, MS. 195, pp. 138–9; **W. Whately,** *The Poore Mans Advocate* (1637), p. 4.
2.   **J. Thirsk** and **J. P. Cooper** (eds), *Seventeenth-Century Economic Documents* (Oxford UP, 1972), pp. 767, 769, 781, 785 (G. King); **P. Slack** (ed.), *Poverty in Early-Stuart Salisbury* (Wilts Record Soc., xxxi, 1975), pp. 80–2.
3.   **G. Himmelfarb,** *The Idea of Poverty. England in the Early Industrial Age* (Faber and Faber, 1984), pp. 77–8.
4.   **M. Sahlins,** *Stone Age Economics* (Tavistock, 1972), p. 37.
5.   E.g., **P. Jones,** *Certaine Sermons preached of late at Ciceter . . . wherein the two several states, of the riche and poore man are compared* (1588); **G. Phillips,** *The Life and death of the rich man and Lazarus* (1600). Cf. **J. Norden,** *A poore Man's rest* (1631), pp. 312–15.
6.   **W. K. Jordan,** *Philanthropy in England 1480–1660* (Allen and Unwin, 1959), pp. 169, 183. Cf. **T. Tymme,** *The Poore Mans Pater noster* (1598).

7. **Matthew,** 5 and 25: 34–45; **P. L. Hughes** and **J. F. Larkin** (eds), *Tudor Royal Proclamations* (Yale UP, New Haven, 1964–69), i. 401; **T. Lupset,** *A Treatise of Charite* (1539), ff. 4, 20; **W. Conway,** *An Exortacion to Charite* (?1552), sig. Aii. Cf. **F. Heal,** 'The Idea of Hospitality in Early Modern England', *Past and Present*, 102 (1984), 66–93; **S. Brigden,** 'Religion and Social Obligation in Early Sixteenth-Century London', *ibid.*, 103 (1984), 67–112.

8. *Ordinances made by Sir William Cecil . . . for the order and government of xiij poore men* (1597).

9. **Jordan,** *Philanthropy*, pp. 216–19; below, p. 106.

10. **Norden,** *Poore Man's rest*, p. 312; **C. Fitz-Geffrey,** *The Curse of Corne-horders* (1631), p. 21; **Jordan,** *Philanthropy*, p. 208; **H. Bedel,** *A Sermon exhorting to pitie the poore* (1573), sig. Dlv. Cf. **H. Smith,** *The Poore Mans Teares* (1592), p. 35.

11. **Jordan,** *Philanthropy*, pp. 191, 199, 230–1; **K. V. Thomas,** *The Perception of the Past in Early Modern England* (Creighton Lecture, London University, 1983), pp. 16–19.

12. **Heal,** 'Idea of Hospitality', *passim*.

13. **Fitz-Geffrey,** *Curse of Corne-horders*, pp. 51–2. Cf. **L. Lavater,** *Three Christian Sermons . . . of Famine and Dearth* (1596), pp. 128, 131; **H. Arthington,** *Provision for the poore, nowe in penurie* (1597), sigs. Clv–2, E2; [J. Fosbroke], *Solomons Charitie, or An Exhortation to . . . liberalitie towards the poore, groaning under the heavy burden of the famine* (Cambridge, 1633), p. 23 (the sermon was delivered in 1631).

14. **R. H. Tawney** and **E. Power** (eds), *Tudor Economic Documents* (Longmans, Green and Co., 1924), iii. 406; **Smith,** *Poore Mans Teares*, p. 8.

15. **R. Allen,** *A Treatise of Christian Beneficence* (1600), sig. Aiv, pp. 37, 41, 126–7.

16. **Galatians,** 6:10; **Allen,** *Treatise*, pp. 6–7; *Tudor Economic Documents*, iii. 445; **J. Downame,** *The Plea of the Poore, or A Treatise of Beneficence* (1616), p. 11; Anon., *Charity Enlarged* (1636), p. 49. Cf. **J. S. McGee,** *The Godly Man in Stuart England* (Yale UP, New Haven, 1976), pp. 211, 273–4.

17. *Seventeenth-Century Economic Documents*, p. 51; **R. Wakeman,** *The Poore-mans Preacher* (1607), p. 12; **Fosbroke,** *Solomons Charitie*, p. 9.

18. *Ibid.*, p. 10; **R. Baxter,** *An Apology for the Nonconformists Ministry* (1681), pp. 47–8.

19. **T. F.** [irmin], *Some Proposals For the imploying of the Poor* (1678), p. 15; **A. R. Fry,** *John Bellers 1654–1725* (Cassell, 1935), p. 133 (1714).

20. **G. Burnet,** *The Life and Death of Sir Matthew Hale* (1682), p. 150 (I owe this reference to Sarah Lloyd); **M. Hale,** *A Discourse Touching Provision for the Poor* (1683), sig. A2r.

21. **B. Tierney,** *Medieval Poor-Law* (California UP, Berkeley, 1959), pp. 59–65; **2 Thessalonians,** 3:10. Cf. **G. Ricci,** 'Naissance du pauvre honteux', *Annales*, xxxviii (1983), 158–77.

22. 23 Edward III, c. 7; 12 Richard II, c. 7.

23. **S. Wenzel,** *The Sin of Sloth: Acedia in Medieval Thought and Literature* (North Carolina UP, Chapel Hill, 1960), pp. 90–5.

24. **F. J. Sheeran** (ed.), *Dives and Pauper* (Scholars' Facsimiles and Reprints, New York, 1973), 9th precept, cap. xi, sigs. Gviii–Hii. This work was once attributed, probably wrongly, to Henry Parker. On the evolution of ideas

of voluntary poverty in the High Middle Ages, see **L. K. Little,** *Religious Poverty and the Profit Economy in Medieval Europe* (Paul Elek, 1978).

25. **S. Fish,** *A Supplication for the Beggars*, ed. **E. Arber** (1895), pp. 3, 13; **Whately,** *Poore Mans Advocate*, p. 111.

26. **F. R. Salter** (ed.), *Some Early Tracts on Poor Relief* (Methuen, 1926), pp. 6, 7, 37, 38.

27. *Tudor Royal Proclamations*, i. nos 63, 128, 250.

28. **J. Taylor,** *The Praise, Antiquity, and commodity of Beggery, Beggers and Begging* (1621), sig. B4r. Sir Dudley North was apparently abducted as a child by a beggar-woman who wanted his clothes: *D.N.B.*

29. **Brigden,** 'Religion and Social Obligation', p. 106.

30. *Tudor Economic Documents*, ii. 318; **Brigden,** 'Religion and Social Obligation', p. 108.

31. **F. Aydelotte,** *Elizabethan Rogues and Vagabonds* (Oxford UP, 1913), pp. 17–18, 68; below, pp. 124–5.

32. Cf, **J. Cheke,** *The Hurt of sedicion* (1549), sigs. Eiv–vii; **Heal,** 'Idea of Hospitality', pp. 87–8.

33. **W. Harrison,** *The Description of England*, ed. **G. Edelen** (Cornell UP, Ithaca, 1968), p. 185. Cf. the utopian prospect which Thomas Harman envisaged, once vagabonds were suppressed: **G. Salgado** (ed.), *Cony-Catchers and Bawdy Baskets* (Penguin Books, Harmondsworh, 1972), p. 83.

34. Cf. **B. Geremek,** 'Criminalité, vagabondage, paupérisme: La marginalité à l'aube des temps modernes', and **R. Chartier,** 'Les élites et les gueux', both in *Revue d'histoire moderne*, 21 (1974), 370–1, 388.

35. *Greevous Grones for the Poore* (1621), p. 7; **Allen,** *Treatise*, sig. Aiv; **Downame,** *Plea of the Poore*, p. 38; **J. Gore,** *The Poore Mans Hope* (1635), p. 22. Cf. **William Perkins** to the same effect, quoted in **C. Hill,** *Society and Puritanism in Pre-Revolutionary England* (Secker and Warburg, 1964), pp. 283–5; and on the analogy with beasts, see **K. Thomas,** *Man and the Natural World* (Allen Lane, 1983), p. 44.

36. **Salter,** *Early Tracts*, p. 43.

37. Cf. **P. Burke,** *Popular Culture in Early Modern Europe* (Temple Smith, 1978), pp. 185–91, 200–203.

38. See pp. 104–6. Much of the literature is printed in **Salgado,** *Cony-Catchers*, and in **A. V. Judges** (ed.), *The Elizabethan Underworld* (Routledge and Kegan Paul, 1930).

39. **R. Brome,** *A Joviall Crew* (1652), quoted in **C. Hill,** *The World Turned Upside Down* (Temple Smith, 1972), p. 39. Cf. **Harrison,** *Description*, p. 181; **C. Hill,** *Change and Continuity in Seventeenth-Century England* (Weidenfeld and Nicolson, 1974), p. 231.

40. For examples, see **P. M. Zall** (ed.), *A Hundred Merry Tales* (Nebraska UP, Lincoln, Nebraska, 1963), pp. 252, 305; **Salgado,** *Cony-Catchers*, pp. 97–101, 103–4; *The cunning Northerne Begger* (1634).

41. **R. Younge,** *The Poores Advocate* (1654), Ch. xiv, pp. 9–10.

42. **R. Allen,** *The Oderifferous Garden of Charitie* (1603), p. 127; **Wakeman,** *Poore-mans Preacher*, p. 12.

43. **Below,** 149–52.

44. **Hammond** quoted in **T. H. Breen,** 'The Non-Existent Controversy: Puritan and Anglican Attitudes on Work and Wealth 1600–40', *Church*

History, xxxv (1966), 281–2; **Gore,** *Poore Mans Hope*, pp. 20–1; **P. Chamberlen,** *The Poore Mans Advocate* (1649), p. 11.

45. Cf. **A. Gerardus,** *The Regiment of the pouertie* (1572), Ch. 6.
46. **J. Webb** (ed.), *Poor Relief in Elizabethan Ipswich* (Suffolk Records Soc., ix, 1966), pp. 23–31; **T. Kemp** (ed.), *The Book of John Fisher* (Henry T. Cooke and Son, Warwick, n.d.), pp. 3–7, 49, 51.
47. *An Ease for Overseers of the poore* (Cambridge, 1601), p. 29. For **Rowntree** and **Townsend,** see above, pp. 3–4, and **A. B. Atkinson,** *The Economics of Inequality* (Oxford UP, 1975), Ch. 10.
48. **C. Phythian-Adams,** *Desolation of a City. Coventry and the Urban Crisis of the Late Middle Ages* (Cambridge UP, 1979), p. 135; **L. Martz,** *Poverty and Welfare in Habsburg Spain* (Cambridge UP, 1983), pp. 5, 9.
49. *Tudor Economic Documents*, iii. 418. Cf. *ibid.*, 446; **Phythian-Adams,** *Desolation of a City*, p. 220; **G. R. Elton,** 'An Early Tudor Poor Law', in idem, *Studies in Tudor and Stuart Politics and Government* (Cambridge UP, 1974), ii. 145.
50. **S. and B. Webb,** *The Old Poor Law* (Longmans, Green and Co., 1927), p. 49; **Harrison,** *Description*, p. 180; **M. Dalton,** *The Country Justice* (1682 edn), p. 169; **Samuel Carter,** *Legal Provisions for the Poor* (1710), pp. 1–2.
51. *Three Sermons or Homilies* (1596), sigs. E3v–4r.
52. **E. Melling,** *Kentish Sources IV: The Poor* (Kent County Council, Maidstone, 1964), p. 13; Essex RO, D/DBa 08/2, 3; below, pp. 65–6.
53. **Jones,** *Certaine Sermons*, sig. E7; **Downame,** *Plea of the Poore*, p. 39; **Slack,** *Poverty in Early-Stuart Salisbury*, p. 83. Cf. Bodl., MS. Jones 17, f. 9r.
54. **Allen,** *Treatise*, sig. Aivr; **C. Webster** (ed.), *Samuel Hartlib and the Advancement of Learning* (Cambridge UP, 1970), p. 112; **J. Child,** *A New Discourse on Trade* (1693), p. 60. **Daniel Defoe** uses the term 'labouring poor' in *A Journal of the Plague Year* (1722): ed. **L. Landa** (Oxford UP, 1969), p. 198.
55. 39 Eliz. I, c. 4, sect. ii; *Tudor Royal Proclamations*, iii. no. 800; **T. G. Barnes** (ed.), *Somerset Assize Orders 1629–40* (Somerset Record Soc., lxv, 1959), p. 68.
56. Below, p. 128. On the continuing difficulty of defining a rogue, see **Carter,** *Legal Provisions for the Poor*, pp. 125–6; below, pp. 91–3.
57. 39 Eliz. I, c. 3, sect. i.
58. See below, pp. 82–3, 128, 179–80, 191–4.
59. **Elton,** *Studies*, ii. 142–4; below, p. 125.
60. **Jordan,** *Philanthropy*, pp. 174–6; below, Chs 6 and 7.
61. *Seventeenth-Century Economic Documents*, pp. 117, 122, 144–5.
62. *Tudor Economic Documents*, iii. 439; **Chamberlen,** *Poore Mans Advocate*, p. 47; **Dudley North,** 'Notes concerning the Laws for the Poor', B.L., Add. MS. 32,512, f. 125.
63. **Chamberlen,** *Poore Mans Advocate*, p. 13.
64. *Ibid.*, p. 14.
65. See **J. Thirsk,** *Economic Policy and Projects* (Oxford UP, 1978), *passim*, and for an example, *Tudor Economic Documents*, ii. 308–9.
66. **E. S. Furniss,** *The Position of the Laborer in a System of Nationalism* (Houghton Miffin, Boston, 1920), Ch. VI. For later discussions, see **C. Wilson,** 'The Other Face of Mercantilism', in **D. C. Coleman** (ed.), *Revisions in Mercantilism* (Methuen, 1969), pp. 118–39; **J. O. Appleby,** *Economic Thought and Ideology in Seventeenth-Century England* (Princeton

UP, 1978), Ch. 6; **J. C. Davis,** *Utopia and the Ideal Society* (Cambridge UP, 1981), Ch. 11.

67. *Seventeenth-Century Economic Documents*, p. 89.
68. Below, pp. 194–5.
69. **Child,** *New Discourse*, pp. 65, 56, 55. For the date of composition, see **W. Letwin,** *The Origins of Scientific Economics* (Doubleday, New York, 1964), pp. 251–2.

Chapter 3

THE ECONOMIC CONTEXT

People reached poverty, and different degrees and kinds of poverty, by a variety of routes. For many it was a permanent condition, a result of those gross inequalities in the distribution of wealth which are evident in any collection of Tudor and Stuart inventories. At the bottom were people with property valued at less than £2: odd sticks of furniture, some bedding, a few clothes and utensils, and little else. Farm labourers in Oxfordshire sometimes owned a cow or a pig. A Norwich labourer possessed simple carpenter's tools, and the widow of 'a poor man' in Hertfordshire had a few pounds of linen yarn and a spinning wheel. A Plymouth sailor, and a Somerset parish clerk, literate though he was, owned next to nothing. A petty chapman in Staffordshire had only the clothes he stood up in and 14s. in his purse, although there were goods worth £12 – his working stock – in a pack on his back.[1] By comparison with husbandmen and master craftsmen whose inventory totals were often £50 or more, these people were plainly very poor; and there were men and women poorer still who left no inventory because their property was not worth appraising.

Whether such people were also paupers, relying on charity or public relief, depended on a multitude of factors which influenced income and expenditure. General economic conditions determined the level of prices and wages and hence employment opportunities and rewards in the various sectors of the economy. Standards of living also fluctuated with demographic circumstances. Although fertility and mortality rates were not as high in England as in some other countries, they were high enough to guarantee that family budgets were often strained by an extra baby or by the death of a working parent. Something like a fifth of all children living at home in the seventeenth century were probably orphans.[2] Accidents and sudden illnesses also cut into income, and the meagre possessions of the poor were as vulnerable as their persons. One Elizabethan projector saw the need to provide for

> any poor widow, poor cottager or labourer that hath had a cow, horse or
> any other cattle or else any other thing needful or necessary towards their

living that hath been lost, stolen, died or miscarried, and are not able to buy the like again without the selling of some other thing to their great hindrance.[3]

Livestock and working tools, even old clothes and bedding drying on hedges, were valuables worth stealing. Fire could consume the whole property of a family in a night, and often did so. It left three hundred inhabitants of Tiverton impoverished in 1598 and destroyed almost the whole of Nantwich in 1583.[4] Fears of illness, fire, debt and loss of livestock were among the worries which brought anxious and disturbed patients to the Buckinghamshire astrologer, Richard Napier, in the early seventeenth century; and it must have been the reality of some of them which made one 'poor sick man ready to make away with himself' by throwing himself into the Thames in 1624.[5]

The risks of personal misfortune in an insecure economic environment were greatest in old age. Then downward social mobility was accelerated. Those who became dependent on public relief late in life included a former minister of All Saints, Dorchester, who ended his days 'very poor' in an almshouse; an alderman of Ipswich on the dole because of age and illness; and the widow of a deputy alderman of London who had been left without property although 'always of good name and fame and esteemed with the better sort'.[6] If individuals such as these became paupers, it was the almost inevitable end of the labouring poor. John Pearce, a Somerset thatcher too old to work, died a parish pensioner in 1628: his inventory showed property worth 23s. The cost of his funeral and his arrears of rent amounted to 23s. 2d.[7] It does not require a Mr Micawber to measure his misery.

Poverty was therefore an individual, personal, contingent, infinitely variable phenomenon. In this chapter, however, we must distance ourselves from individuals and look at them in the aggregate, in order to see whether their misfortunes were likely to have increased over our period because of broad economic and social changes, and if so, in what ways. Did poverty increase or decrease over time?

LEVELS OF POVERTY

In order to approach an answer to that question, we need first to return to some of the problems of measurement touched on in Chapter 1. We saw there that the relative nature of poverty makes it impossible to define a poverty line which has universal validity. Let us suppose, however, that we have drawn a line which Tudor and Stuart Englishmen would have accepted. (We shall see some of the empirical difficulties involved in this later.) We can now measure the extent of poverty by the number of people falling below that line. The number will normally alter little from year to year, but there will be sudden jumps in it, caused by temporary crises such as bad harvests, epidemic diseases and commercial slumps. It will therefore be useful to distinguish between long-term levels of poverty and the levels reached during crises, which might be four or five times as high. The two have been called 'structural' and 'conjunctural' poverty by some historians of France.[8] It seems more accurate and more descriptive, however, to borrow terms from the study of mortality and to call them the *background level* and the *crisis level* of poverty.

The background level will be affected by such broad economic variables as the proportion of the population unemployed and the real incomes of those in employment. The crisis level will be influenced by the same phenomena in so far as they determine the number of people close to the poverty line, who then topple over when prices rise or sickness reigns or employment slumps. Background and crisis levels may be expected to be associated to some degree. But the periodicity and severity of the crises themselves will also act independently, determining the frequency with which crisis levels are reached and their height. Crisis levels therefore fluctuate much more than the background level, which alters only in the medium to longer term. We shall see that there is good reason to think that the latter rose up to the middle of the seventeenth century and stabilized thereafter.

There is one major difficulty here, however. Both levels measure only the number of people below a given poverty line. They tell us nothing about the distance which people fell below the line. They do not measure the intensity of poverty.[9] We need to distinguish here, not between background and crisis, but between *shallow* and *deep poverty*. Some people in poverty may be much more deprived than others; they may be starving while others simply lack fuel or clothes. And the intensity of poverty can vary independently of the number in poverty. The number of people in shallow poverty may increase while the number of people in deep poverty declines. If the former rises more than the latter falls, then the total number of people below the poverty line will increase although the intensity of poverty overall diminishes. We shall find evidence to suggest that both the intensity of poverty and the number below the line increased in the sixteenth century; but we shall also see that intensity declined after about 1620, while the number of poor was first rising slightly and then levelling off. Over the seventeenth century as a whole, it seems probable that the number of people in deep poverty – those in danger of starvation – markedly declined, while the number in shallow poverty – those who might be described as 'poor' – increased by at least as much. The background level did not fall, therefore, and it may even have risen. In terms of intensity, poverty was ameliorated in the seventeenth century; in terms of numbers, it was not.

If the evidence were good enough, it might be possible to incorporate both intensity and numbers, depth and background level, into a single calculus. The evidence is not good enough, however. As far as background levels are concerned, we can draw some conclusions from the distribution of wealth and from the likely effects of demographic and economic change. It is much more difficult to measure the depth of poverty. The deepest poverty necessarily means starvation; and that is not easily investigated. Ideally we should like to know how many people died because of lack of food throughout the period. The best the sources will allow is an examination of the relationship between food prices and mortality, particularly in moments of crisis, when the harvest failed. In what follows, we shall look in turn at inequalities of wealth and economic changes which throw light on background levels of poverty; and then at crisis years which tell us something both about crisis levels and about the depth of poverty.

DISTRIBUTIONS OF WEALTH AND POVERTY

The most promising sources of information on the distribution of wealth and poverty in early modern England are two sets of tax assessments, conveniently situated towards the beginning and end of our period: those for the subsidy of 1523–25, and for the hearth taxes of the 1660s and 1670s. The two sources record different things, chiefly the value of property in the first case, and the number of hearths in each household in the second. The first therefore tells us more about wealth at the apex of the social pyramid, the second more about the breadth of its base. They are not strictly comparable, although in each case it was intended that only the genuinely poor should escape taxation altogether.

The extreme concentration of wealth in a few hands emerges clearly from the early Tudor subsidies, and it is unlikely to have changed very much by the 1660s. Five per cent of the population of London owned 80 per cent of its taxable wealth in the 1520s, for example. In part of Suffolk less than 2 per cent of the population owned more than half the land, while 60 per cent owned no land or house of their own.[10] For the number who were too poor to be taxed in 1523–25, however, we have only scattered information drawn from surveys of 1522 which happen to survive. It seems probable that one third of adult males on average escaped the taxation net. That seems to have been the proportion in the towns of Worcester, Leicester and Exeter, although it rose to 50 per cent in Coventry; and while 58 per cent were exempt in Staincross Wapentake in the West Riding of Yorkshire, little more than 25 per cent escaped in one hundred of Norfolk.[11]

It is not easy to say how poor the exempt third were. In theory they earned less than £1 a year in wages and did not have goods worth that amount. It is clear in practice, however, that this was a wholly artificial criterion and that everything depended on local judgement. In Coventry some of those exempted were householders with servants. In Great Yarmouth men rated at less than £1 in 1522 were nevertheless taxed in 1524. £1 a year was in any case hardly a living wage in the 1520s: it is impossible to believe that a third of the population fell below that level.[12] In short, it seems probable that the assessors simply ignored the people they regarded as poor. The level of exemption is therefore not an objective test of economic status but a record of contemporary perceptions.

The later Stuart hearth-tax records present similar, though perhaps less severe, problems of interpretation. The proportion of householders exempted seems again to have averaged between 30 and 40 per cent. There were local variations which we shall comment on in a moment, but roughly one third of all households in Kent, Essex, Leicestershire and Devon were not taxed.[13] This time there were two criteria for exemption. First, those who inhabited houses worth £1 a year or less, who had no real property worth more than that, and whose personal estates were worth less than £10, could claim exemption. Secondly, exemption was automatically granted to householders who did not pay either church or poor rates. The second group, that automatically exempt, was the larger, and again its members were people who were locally regarded, and often listed, simply as 'the poor'.[14]

The taxation records do not provide us with an exact measure of the economic condition of the poor, therefore; and they probably include quite a range of wealth within their exempt categories. It seems plausible to argue, however, that the range was narrower in the 1660s than it was in the 1520s. Men with servants cannot often have escaped the hearth tax. The issue of precise exemption certificates and the low but realistic rent and rate qualifications ought to have made it more difficult to evade taxation in the later seventeenth century than in the early sixteenth. If this were the case, the third exempt in the 1660s and 1670s would be poorer than the third exempt in the 1520s; and it would follow that the background level of poverty increased between the reign of Henry VIII and that of Charles II. The hypothesis is open to argument, however. In order to establish it more firmly, we shall need to consider whether it is consistent with the course of economic development between the two dates.

Taxation records indicate geographical variations in the distribution of wealth more effectively than alterations over time. The 1520s subsidies show that wealth was concentrated in the south-eastern half of England, south of a line from the Wash to Plymouth; and that distribution was little altered at the end of the seventeenth century, although the Home Counties had grown richer and the south-west and East Anglia had declined relative to the rest.[15] The geographical distribution of wealth is usually measured in terms of the amount of tax paid per square mile, however, and a high score on this count may conceal large numbers of paupers. Impoverished wage-labourers certainly existed in quantity in south-eastern England, as they did in the richest towns. By the same token, low scores for tax paid per square mile may only show an absence of the very rich: behind them may lie a relatively egalitarian social structure in which not many people were very poor either. The geographical distribution of wealth certainly tells us which areas of the country were best able to cope with poverty, especially in crises, by means of charity and poor rates. It does not necessarily tell us where the highest background levels or the deepest poverty were to be found.

The distinctions which agrarian historians make between different farming regions are relevant here. The line between the Wash and Plymouth is close to the divide between arable lowland and pastoral upland England. Some further insight into the distribution of wealth may therefore be found in the social contrasts which have been observed between the lowland zone of mixed farming on the one hand, and pasture farming regions, whether in the highlands or in forests and fens, on the other. In the first, farms were large; primogeniture, concentrated settlement and social control prevented a rapid increase in resident population and encouraged out-migration; and many labourers were dependent on wages and had little or no property of their own. In pasture and forest areas, on the other hand, ample land, the absence of resident lords, and sometimes partible inheritance produced a flatter social pyramid and a less stratified society of cottagers. They also allowed populations to grow, however, and that encouraged further subdivision of holdings and greater impoverishment in the sixteenth and seventeenth centuries.[16] Any economic advantage which the cottagers and squatters of woodland and open pasture might conceivably have had over landless labourers in fielden regions was gradually eroded.

This simplified model receives some support from local studies, which confirm that poverty might mean different things in different agrarian economies. In the corn-growing fielden parishes of south Cambridgeshire, for example, it was to be seen among wage-labourers, who were already numerous at the beginning of our period; while in the Cambridgeshire fens it was typified by the small, relatively independent cottager with common rights or a patch of land of his own. Pressure on land in the fens, as in forest and upland areas, intensified with population growth in the later sixteenth and seventeenth centuries, however. In the Cambridgeshire fens, the Northamptonshire forest and in pastoral Cumbria the number of subtenants and cottagers with marginal holdings increased, and so did visible poverty.[17]

The distribution of industry was a further variable introducing complexities. When an industry prospered and expanded, as the new draperies did in East Anglia after 1570, it boosted taxable wealth but also the proportion of the population dependent in one way or another on the vicissitudes of the market. Temporary slumps in demand hit the whole labour force, whether it consisted of small independent masters, urban wage-labourers, or cottager families kept from destitution by women and children spinning and weaving under the putting-out system. Industrial development thus raised the potential crisis level of poverty. It also raised the background level, and imposed economic blight on a whole town or region, once an industry went into long-term decline, the chief but by no means the only example in our period being the depression in the old textile centres of western England, including Salisbury, Winchester and Gloucester, in the later sixteenth and early seventeenth centuries.[18] Once again poverty was local, and variable in quality as well as in quantity.

There were thus many different social and economic histories behind the regional variations which are to be found in rates of exemption from the later Stuart hearth taxes. Industrial towns produced some of the highest proportions of exempt householders, especially small places like Bocking (81 per cent) and Braintree (67 per cent), but also centres with as large and prosperous a mercantile elite as Norwich (62 per cent). The proportion was also high in parts of rural Cumbria (66 per cent) where there was open pasture and cottage industry. In general, rather more people were exempt in forest areas than in those of mixed farming: 40 per cent in the Forest of Arden, Warwickshire, and 44 per cent in the forest villages of Northamptonshire as compared with 35 per cent in non-forest villages.[19] The proportion was markedly below average only in towns which had adjusted to the decline of staple industries and diversified their economies, such as York (20 per cent) and Bristol (20 per cent); in areas of fresh industrial growth, as with the metal-working area around Sheffield (10–13 per cent); and above all in farming regions close to and benefiting from the demand of London. In Kent exemption rates varied from 38 per cent of householders in the east, where there was a large number of landless labourers, through 36 per cent in the Weald, an area of smallholdings and a decaying textile industry, to 26 per cent in the north-west, near the capital. In Essex 53 per cent were exempt in the rural textile region of the north but only 23 per cent in the south, in the neighbourhood of London.[20]

We need to bear these local diversities in mind when considering economic and social change in broader terms. It operated on a patchwork economic landscape, in which there were areas of growth and prosperity as well as many points of particular stress.

ECONOMIC AND SOCIAL CHANGE

There were two powerful forces making for change over most of the period: population growth and inflation. The population of England rose from about 2.3 million in 1524 to a peak of 5.3 million in 1656. It more than doubled in a little over a century, the rate of increase being greatest between 1561 and 1586 and probably also from the 1520s to the 1540s. In the early seventeenth century the pace of growth slackened, and it stopped altogether after 1656 when the population fell until a period of recovery at the very end of the century. In 1701 the population was 5.1 million, still not back to its 1656 level.[21] Prices moved in a similar way, since they were in part determined by demand. According to the index compiled by Phelps Brown and Hopkins, the cost of a basketful of consumer goods in southern England rose sixfold between 1500 and the 1640s and then stabilized, even falling slightly until the 1690s.[22] Together, these movements of population and prices largely shaped the curve described by background levels of poverty.

One link between population change and poverty was the impact of the former on the age-structure. Demographic growth meant a younger population and more dependent mouths to be fed. When growth was rapid, around 1581, 35 per cent of the population were aged under 15 and 8 per cent over 60. By contrast, when growth had stopped in 1676, only 30 per cent were under 15 and 10 per cent were now over 60. Comparatively speaking, therefore, the young were a greater burden in the later sixteenth century and the old in the later seventeenth: hence the perception of poverty among householders with too many children in Tudor records, and the number of old pensioners in poor-relief accounts of the later Stuart period. Most of the latter were widows whose chances of remarriage were reduced by a further demographic feature of the seventeenth century, a declining sex-ratio which meant a shortage of men. Taking the two age-groups together, however, the problem of unproductive hands was much greater in the sixteenth century than in the seventeenth. The dependency ratio – that is, the number of people over 60 and under 15 per thousand adults between those ages – fell from 780 in the mid-Tudor period to 624 in 1671.[23]

Demographic changes also affected population mobility. Population growth produced vagrancy. The number of vagabonds on the roads in Tudor England has often been attributed to the dissolution of the monasteries and to enclosure. The first probably had little or no effect on mobility, although serious pockets of poverty were left wherever monasteries had attracted the poor to their gates. Enclosure was more influential. It undoubtedly led to depopulation in some parts of England, in Leicestershire, for example; but in other areas, like the north-west, enclosure was not a cause of demographic decline but a symptom of growing populations carving new holdings out of plentiful commons and wastes.[24] The real motor behind the escalating problem of vagrancy was surplus population, particularly in regions of mixed farming. People were pushed onto the roads, probably moving first to areas of waste, forest and pasture and then, from the later sixteenth century, to towns. What Peter Clark has called subsistence migration was superimposed on normal patterns of betterment migration, and for the less fortunate it meant movement over long distances, months or even years on the road, and the life of a vagabond.[25]

After the middle of the seventeenth century, this phenomenon appears to have declined. Long-distance mobility was less common and so, it is reasonable to deduce, was pauper migration.[26] One reason for this was the end of demographic growth. Another, however, was the expansion of employment opportunities in later Stuart England, many of them close to home. People did not have to wander so far or so long in search of work. In other words, surplus population was no longer quite so surplus. By the later seventeenth century a million or so extra hands were being employed and three million extra mouths fed, as compared with 1500; and we must now turn to the difficult question of how this was accomplished and what the consequences for poverty might have been. We have seen part of the background to the problems of the impotent and vagrant poor, the old, the young and the mobile. When did the idle poor become the labouring poor and what changes were there in their condition?

There is no doubt, to begin with, that the English economy succeeded in pulling itself up by its own bootstraps. It was halted on a downward spiral towards the ultimate Malthusian checks of famine and disease in the early seventeenth century, and that was a remarkable and distinctive English achievement.[27] As far as food supplies for the extra mouths are concerned, the country was successfully feeding itself by 1650 and it was about to enter a period when corn would be exported – an unthinkable prospect in 1600. That came partly from improved agricultural techniques and new crops, beginning in the later sixteenth century; but it probably owed more to an extension of land under cultivation and to regional specialization. As for extra employment, some of it was provided by expanding agriculture, but more by the growth of rural and urban industries, catering both for export markets and for that domestic consumer demand for a whole range of commodities from pins to stockings and hats which Joan Thirsk has described.[28] This development also began in the later sixteenth century, although again the pay-off was probably delayed until the middle of the seventeenth. In the end, therefore, rising demand was translated into increased production and employment.

It did not happen quickly, however, and it naturally benefited the lowest ranks of society last. Something of the process of redistribution is reflected in relative price movements. Until the middle of the seventeenth century the price of cereals rose faster than that of livestock and industrial products. Arable farmers profited more than pastoral farmers or industrial producers, and the terms of trade did not turn decisively in favour of the latter until after 1650.[29] Evidence of earlier redistribution between sectors may be found in the towns, where yeomen and gentry spent their incomes on goods and services. There is no sign of general urban growth and much evidence of urban decay before 1570. But most of the larger English towns grew from the 1570s onwards, and many of them grew rapidly after 1600. To begin with, that may have been due to push rather than pull factors, as the many municipal complaints about impoverished immigrants and disorderly inmates in the years around 1600 suggest. Urban growth would not have continued, however, if the attractions of urban employment had not been real. London grew most of all, from around 100,000 in 1580 to 575,000 in 1700. Other towns were far behind in size though not in their rate of growth in the seventeenth century. Between 1600 and 1700 the proportion of the English population living in towns of 5,000 people or more almost doubled, from roughly 8 per cent to slightly over 15 per cent.[30] There was substantial urbanization, and that signified an increase in the labouring and also in the landless population.

The same consequence followed from economic developments in rural England. We have already touched on changes in woodland and pasture, where cottage patches got smaller, pressure on commons greater, and people became more dependent on domestic industries and less on agrarian occupations. Social change may have been still more radical in mixed and arable farming regions, where inflation spelt the beginning of the end for the middling peasant and widened the gap between prosperous yeoman farmers on the one hand and labourers on the other.[31] The fortunes of the latter depended to some degree on whether they were living-in servants or employed by the day. Before 1650, when labour was plentiful, they were more likely to be living out than living in, and therefore all the more precariously situated in an inflationary age.[32] But whatever their precise position, their numbers increased through the period. Demographic growth here did not lead to a general reduction in the size of holdings, as it sometimes had in the thirteenth century; it produced a dichotomy between rich farmers and landless labourers.[33]

The term 'social polarization' has often been applied to these changes, both in rural and in urban society.[34] It has its limitations as a descriptive tool, and it is in some danger of replacing the rise of the middle class as a phenomenon which can be identified in any and every period of history.[35] But it usefully suggests the price which had to be paid for economic development in the later sixteenth and seventeenth centuries. In the short term there were painful processes of adjustment, involving migration and dislocation, downward social mobility for many of the children of the middling sort, and obvious deprivation in urban tenements and rural cottages, wherever population pressure was finally concentrated. Over the longer term a landless, market-dependent labour force grew in size. By 1700 'labouring people, outservants, cottagers and paupers' made up most of that half of the population which Gregory King disparagingly described as 'decreasing the wealth of the kingdom'.[36]

The wealth of the labouring poor themselves depended on what they could earn, and some flickering, if controversial, light is thrown on that by the behaviour of wages. Two wage series are available, one for agricultural labourers, the other for building craftsmen.[37] Wages rose between 1500 and 1650, from 4d. to 1s. a day for agricultural labourers, and from 6d. to 1s. 5d. a day for building craftsmen; but they did not keep pace with the six-fold rise in prices. Their real value fell by more than half, and the lowest point came in the years around 1620. Expanding employment clearly did nothing to mop up surplus labour before then. Unfortunately, the timing of the subsequent recovery is obscured by deficiencies in the building workers' series between 1630 and 1650. Tangible improvements in real wages were probably delayed until the 1650s, however, thanks to the high prices of the later 1640s. There were some further gains in the 1670s and 1680s, but they were temporarily eroded by high prices once more in the 1690s, and they were not great. At the end of the seventeenth century wages were still worth no more than they had been in the third quarter of the sixteenth century, that is 30 per cent less than in 1500.

There seems no reason to dispute the conclusion that economic conditions for wage-earners – a growing fraction of the population – deteriorated down to 1620 and improved slightly after 1650. There would be general agreement also that this mirrored the movement of living standards for the poorer sections of society as a whole. The difficulty is to determine the meaning of the drop in real terms. The limitations of the wage series as indicators of real income are well known.[38] They relate only to southern England. They tell us nothing about variations in the number of days worked or in the expenses which wages had to cover. Many workers were fed or housed by their employers, and so to some degree insulated against inflation. Once employment picked up, many families certainly cushioned themselves against falling real wages by setting more hands to work.

In the present state of our knowledge it seems safe to make only two broad generalisations. First, real living standards for wage-earners certainly did not fall by as much as 50 per cent. If they had, positive Malthusian checks would surely have come into operation and they did not. It has been well said that England was further away from a Malthusian trap in the early seventeenth century than it had been in the early fourteenth.[39] Moreover, if living standards had sunk so low, it is difficult to believe that a small improvement in real wages in the later seventeenth century, even with rising numbers in employment, would have been sufficient to produce the growth in aggregate consumer demand which seems to have occurred.

Secondly, however, there is no doubt that there was a fall down to 1620. Contemporaries saw it and reacted to it, most eloquently in their demographic behaviour. For although population growth was not halted by the stark positive checks of famine and disease, it was ended by a prudential check which reduced fertility. From the later sixteenth century onwards, people delayed marriage as they saw living standards fall and opportunities for successful household formation contract.[40] We can point also to evidence for a deterioration in popular diets over the sixteenth century: the movement towards cheaper grains and the decline of meat consumption which are suggested by relative prices.[41] Neither is there any lack of contemporary reference to the real hunger of the poor between 1580 and 1650.[42] For how serious and how widespread hunger was, however, we need to look at years of dearth; and we must look at crisis years more generally before we can attempt any conclusions about the depth of poverty in the early seventeenth century, or about what was happening to the background level over the period as a whole.

CRISIS YEARS

The clearest indication of deep poverty, of large numbers of people hovering just above subsistence level and falling below it when harvests were deficient, would be a long-term correlation between the price of food and the level of mortality. There is some evidence for such an association, and it seems to have been weakening at the end of our period, as one might expect from the economic trends outlined above. But it was never a strong association because other factors besides malnutrition influenced the mortality variable, particularly autonomous epidemic diseases such as plague.[43] Rather than look for long-term correlations, therefore, it is preferable to concentrate on obvious years of dearth, when grain prices rose and contemporaries complained that poverty and hunger were mounting in quantity and intensity. What happened to mortality then?

The short answer is that mortality rose significantly after every bad harvest between 1500 and 1622, and that it rose only modestly by comparison after the bad harvests which occurred between 1630 and the end of the seventeenth century.[44] This is not to say that every one of the early coincidences of high mortality and high food prices was necessarily more than mere coincidence. Grain was certainly scarce in some localities in 1520–21 and 1527–28, for example, but we do not know whether it was starvation, malnutrition or some independent epidemic disease which caused mortality crises like that which killed a fifth of Coventry's population at the beginning of the decade.[45] It was certainly plague which raised mortality in many areas of England after the bad harvests of 1545 and 1550; and it was notoriously influenza which overtook 'famine' and possibly typhus in some parts of the country in 1557, and produced the greatest mortality crisis of the whole period between 1557 and 1559, when 11 per cent of the population of England may have died.[46] Hunger added to the general misery on these occasions, but it may not have contributed substantially to mortality. For evidence of purer crises of subsistence we must turn to the months following the next three harvest failures, in 1586, 1596–97 and 1622.

In 1586–87 and 1622–23 high mortality was largely confined to northern, highland England. Odd instances of exceptional mortality in the south-east, in 1623–24 for example, were probably due to fevers unrelated to malnutrition. It is from the north that firm evidence of famine diseases such as typhus and dysentery and references to the burial of 'hunger-starved beggars' and children who died 'for want of food' come. These circumstances were more general in the later 1590s, when prices rose much higher. The north still suffered most. In the north-east people were 'starving and dying in our streets and in the fields for lack of bread', and the number of burials was four times higher than usual over much of Cumbria. But mortality also came close to quadrupling in so central and well-placed a town as Reading, which could be supplied by the grain trade along the Thames. Twice the usual number of burials in a year was common elsewhere: in the pastoral highlands of Devon, in some of the textile-producing parishes of northern Essex where villagers were 'chiefly relying on the clothiers' for work, and in the poorer suburban parishes of Exeter and Bristol. Over the country as a whole, the death rate in the two harvest-years 1596–98 may have reached 6 per cent.[47]

This was the closest England came to famine in our period, and it needs to be seen in proportion. The crude national death rate was not as high as in the influenza epidemic of 1557 to 1559. It was probably nothing like as great as in the famine of the early fourteenth century; and it did not match the level reached in France a century later, in 1693–94, when more than 10 per cent of the population is estimated to have died.[48] It is unlikely that conditions were as bad in England in the 1590s as in other parts of northern Europe where malnutrition and starvation reigned. If deep poverty was less widespread in England, however, the location of high mortality shows us where it was concentrated and what some of its roots were. Charity obviously dried up in the poorer regions of England, which is why marginal people, beggars, died in the streets. But the labouring poor in rural and urban industries and in pastoral areas were also hit hard, because their incomes were savagely cut when rising grain prices depressed demand for all other commodities. Their desperate condition sprang not so much from a shortage of food as from a drop in what one economist, writing of modern famines, has termed their 'exchange entitlements'.[49]

These circumstances clearly had implications for shallow as well as for deep poverty. The universal consequence of high food prices in the later 1590s, and to a lesser degree in 1587 and 1622–23, was not starvation but general impoverishment. The number of vagrants and beggars on the roads increased; so did the number of people claiming poor relief. There were food riots and an increase in petty theft, both of them symptoms of perceived deprivation. As we shall see in the next chapters, background poverty rose to critical levels.[50] Moreover, some of these consequences of high food prices continued after 1623, when the threat of famine itself receded; for there was no decline but rather an increase in the number of people employed outside agriculture, at the mercy of market forces when demand for everything except foodstuffs collapsed. An increasingly complex economy based on division of labour and regional specialization magnified the effects of temporary disturbance in any one sector of it.

It is not entirely clear why the crisis of 1630–31 did not produce famine. The price of grain, and especially of barley, the bread-corn of the poor, was higher in 1630 than in 1622, in the south of England at least. Yet there is no sign of malnutrition-related diseases: plague was responsible for the local mortalities which did occur. Living standards in the south may already have been improving at the margin of subsistence, while in the north the vulnerable sections of the population may already have succumbed in 1623. Alternatively, it is possible that the price rise was the result of panic, rather than of real shortage, or that public-relief measures such as special purchases of corn and increases in poor rates alleviated the situation: there was much talk of famine in 1630 and there was a co-ordinated government response to the threat in 1631. Whatever the reason for the absence of starvation, however, the reactions of local authorities show that there was no decline in the critical level of poverty. It seemed overwhelming.[51]

It seemed so again in the later 1640s. The bad harvests of 1647 and 1648 produced complaints of destitution as vociferous, especially in the north, as those of the 1590s, although there was no great jump in mortality, any more than there was in 1661 when prices rose once more. John Graunt's observation that few were 'starved' in London between 1629 and 1662 although there was a 'vast number of beggars', might have been extended to the rest of the kingdom. Even in 1693–94, when the impact of high grain prices alone had been muted by gradually rising standards of living since 1650, and when England was far from the disaster which simultaneously hit France, there was a sufficient increase in shallow poverty and in the cost of poor relief to provoke the Board of Trade into an inquiry into ways of reducing them.[52]

Bad harvests were never the only cause of critical levels of poverty, however, and by the 1690s they were not the most important. We have noticed already some of the exogenous determinants of mortality crises: epidemic diseases which always incapacitated at least as many people as they killed, thus reducing incomes as well as leaving orphans and widows in their wake. On a national scale, the fevers of 1557 to 1559 were the worst; but locally, and particularly in towns, outbreaks of plague were more serious and more common. From 1500 until the last epidemics of the 1660s, they occurred every 15 or 16 years in the largest English towns, often killing between 10 and 20 per cent of urban populations.[53] As with crises of subsistence, their incidence tells us something about the location of the worst deprivation. Plague was most fatal in overcrowded unhygienic tenements in the suburbs of towns: in St Sidwell's parish, Exeter, for example, or St Mary Redcliffe, Bristol, and in Aldgate and Bishopsgate just outside the walls of London. To an extent, therefore, plague epidemics were a symptom of poverty. But they were also one of its prime causes since they totally disrupted employment and marketing. Like dearth, plague forced people to spend their savings and to pawn their goods and even their clothes, in order to make ends meet. A relatively minor epidemic in Salisbury in 1627 left half the population of the town in need of relief and many of them close to famine, looking 'as green and pale as death'.[54]

War was as damaging as famine and pestilence, especially when at home: destroying men and property, leaving suburbs burned and houses looted in the 1640s.[55] Wars abroad also had serious repercussions, hitting export markets and depressing domestic demand when taxes were raised for English fleets and armies. The country was unfortunate in that foreign wars often coincided with high prices, as in the 1590s and 1690s. In 1587 a chronicler in Barnstaple noted that 'the dearth of corn yet remains ... and yet this country is daily further charged with ammunitions and harness, expecting and providing for invasions and wars, which maketh the common sort to fall into poverty for want of trade, so that divers fall to robbing and stealing'.[56] The cumulative effect of different sorts of crisis was most obvious in the 1620s. War in northern and then in southern Europe hit foreign demand first for old and then for new draperies, bringing depression and unemployment successively to the West Country and East Anglia. Bad harvests at the beginning and end of the decade and plague in London and other towns between 1625 and 1627 added their own momentum.[57] It is not only the last genuine example of famine conditions and the low point in the indices of real wages which lead us to conclude that the years around 1620 were the nadir for the poor of early modern England.

The 1620s also form a turning point because the complex inter-relationships and insecurities of a slowly developing economy then became conspicuous. They had been visible much earlier, in the problems of an industrial town like Coventry in the 1520s and in the need for higher wages for labourers in Essex in the 1590s, for example.[58] But it had been possible for people in authority to see sixteenth-century crises largely in terms of subsistence, and to respond by managing grain supplies and corn markets. In the 1620s the debates in government circles about the deadness of trade and the extent of poverty showed that things were not so simple. In 1630 the government was still thinking in terms of dearth, of a population unable to feed itself and for which corn must be provided; but justices of the peace in the provinces reported that what the poor needed was not grain, which was available, but cash in their pockets with which to buy it.[59]

The problem of fluctuations in employment and earnings in industry, especially rural industry, therefore came to the forefront of attention. When disinvestment was easy, and when, as one contemporary remarked, 'all clothiers in general do set more or less on work according to the quickness and deadness of the market', the introduction of new manufactures could both be welcomed and be opposed. Textiles in Lancashire gave people 'employment for their children in spinning and other necessary labour', but employing children on bonelacemaking in Honiton, Devon, meant that the town was 'like to come into great poverty'.[60] The different degrees of poverty involved here are well revealed in a surveyor's report on Glastonbury, where the dissolution of the abbey had meant misery in the 1540s: in 1628 there were still

> very many poor people in the said town and yet by reason of their large
> commons and benefit of turves, they make good shift to live, employing
> themselves in spinning and knitting of worsted stockings, by means
> whereof they keep themselves from begging.

'For the moment', he might have added. Instability was such that in the space of less than a year, in 1633–34, it could be reported from part of Hampshire, first that trade was 'very dead' and unemployment great, and then that 'clothing is now very quick . . . and the poor are well set to work'.[61]

This profound sensitivity to economic fluctuations lay behind critical levels of poverty in years of dearth and plague in the early seventeenth century; and it remained a source of fragility in the later seventeenth century, when food supplies improved and plague finally disappeared. There were other infectious diseases, wars, slumps in overseas markets, and sudden switches in fashion to throw people out of work. Some of the causes of temporary impoverishment had altered, but not the result. One symptom of changed circumstances was the way in which the weather affected the economy. In the 1580s and 1590s its main impact was through the harvest: town corporations rushed to purchase grain when prices rose. In the 1680s and 1690s they were still concerned about high food prices, but there were more references in urban records to sickly, cold winters which depressed trade and employment and raised the price of fuel.[62] In effect, industry replaced deep poverty with oscillating, shallow poverty, and it did so, according to a pamphlet of 1677, because

> though it sets the poor on work where it find them, yet it draws still more
> to the place; and their masters allow wages so mean that they are only
> preserved from starving while they can work; when age, sickness or death
> comes, themselves, their wives or their children are most commonly left
> upon the parish.[63]

PERIODS OF STRESS

Partial and uncertain as much of it is, the evidence employed in this chapter permits some broad generalizations both about the depth and about the background level of poverty. As far as depth is concerned, it should be emphasized that early modern England suffered less intense poverty than many other societies. When it occurred, famine was much less severe that it had been in the early fourteenth century and than it is today in some African and Asian countries. Comparative demographic regimes suggest that French peasants lived closer to subsistence level in the later seventeenth century than English labourers and cottagers at any time in our period.[64] Poverty in England certainly deepened down to about 1620, and abject misery was particularly notable in the crisis of the later 1590s; but conditions could have grown much worse. They did not, because the tide turned: after 1620 there was gradual improvement, as employment opportunities expanded and population growth slowed down. From then on we are increasingly dealing with shallow rather than with deep poverty.

When we turn to the background level, therefore, to the number of people in poverty, much depends on where we set the poverty line. If we set it at subsistence level, the number will fluctuate with deep poverty and be almost negligible outside crisis years. But no contemporary would have drawn it as low as that. If we include among the poor those people who had few economic resources besides their labour, as the hearth-tax assessors seem to have done, we would find no improvement after 1620 but rather continuing deterioration, probably for the rest of the century: the number of landless wage-labourers continued to grow, and gains in real wages after 1650 offered few opportunities for saving and no security. That seems too broad a definition of poverty, however, embracing perhaps 30 per cent or even, according to Gregory King, 50 per cent of the population in 1688. More realistic in contemporary terms would be a poverty line drawn just above those who were thought to require alms and poor relief at any single point in time: people who were given charity or the dole, not because they were already starving, but because they could not, for the moment, buy clothes or food for themselves or their children or fuel for their fires. We shall see that they might amount to 5 per cent of local populations in the early seventeenth century, rising to 20 per cent or so in years of crisis.[65]

On this definition, the background level of poverty obviously deteriorated down to 1620; and there seems no reason to assume any improvement before 1650 or more than stability thereafter. Although employment was picking up after 1620, it remained irregular and precarious for many wage-earners. Slumps, illness, the death of a breadwinner, an extra child or a particularly cold winter would throw them onto the dole or send them out begging. As long as population was still growing and real wages not rising, their demand for supplementary poor relief would continue to increase. Modest improvements in real wages after 1650 may have given some of these people greater room for manoeuvre, and have worked to reduce the proportion of wage-earners seeking relief; but the total number may still have declined little, if at all, given continuing urbanization and the higher mortality and risks of disease that involved. In short, the nature of poverty changed after 1620 without reducing the background level, which probably rose up to 1650 and then levelled off. The proportion of the population who were almost permanently destitute, the unemployed who required alms or poor relief for years at a time, declined; the proportion liable to claim relief for a few months or a year or two when family incomes failed to meet expenditure increased.

We might therefore conclude that there was a period of decline down to 1620 followed by recovery, or a period of decline down to 1650 followed by stability – depending on which kind of poverty is thought to be the more important, deep or shallow. There is another variable, however, which is particularly relevant to contemporary views of poverty: the state of the English economy generally and the way in which that was perceived. If we incorporate this perspective, a division of the period into three may be more accurate and more suggestive as a summary of the economic background: 1500 to 1570; 1570 to 1650; and 1650 to 1700.

The first period, from 1500 to 1570, might be characterized as one of depression. Economic demand generally was still low after the late medieval slump; rural depopulation and enclosure were still widely regarded as serious social problems; many towns were in decay. Inflation was obvious after the 1520s, but it was attributed to currency manipulations, to covetousness and usury, or to a general dearth – rather than to rising demand. Population growth was less obvious, but one of its manifestations – an increase in begging and vagrancy – was conspicuous; and it elicited a clear and hostile response. Apart from that, however, the social consequences of inflation and population growth seemed part of a general poverty which threatened the whole common weal, because decay was common to all.[66]

The second period, from 1570 to 1650, was one of polarization. Demand was now plainly reviving, towns were growing, and despite periodic crises and depressions, many people were getting rich relatively quickly, building new houses, buying extra furniture, living more comfortably.[67] At the same time, however, population continued to grow, and background and crisis levels of poverty continued to rise. There was some amelioration of deep poverty after 1620 and some decline in under-employment, but disruptive processes of adjustment *via* migration, urban growth and the decline of small landowners were involved. One result, it may be suggested, was a heightened perception by the rich of the relative deprivation of the poor. Another was a

54

growing appreciation of the particular characteristics of poverty. Much of it was still marginal, and indeed in a literal sense it grew ever more conspicuously so: it was concentrated outside the mainstream of economic activity, in woodlands and on commons, in the back alleys and on the fringes of towns. Yet there were also the labouring poor, either working in new rural and urban industries, or failing to find sufficient employment in those wholly depressed industrial areas which were the victims of economic change, particularly some of the old textile towns. For a time poverty was visibly and confusingly the product of ✳ economic growth and economic depression simultaneously.

The third period, from 1650 to 1700, was one of redistribution. Economic growth continued and more of the profit went to the lower orders, to towns and to areas of pasture farming, the last of which now began to display some of the domestic comforts to be found earlier in grain-growing regions.[68] As population growth stopped and prices levelled off, employers began to worry about labour costs and landlords to complain of declining rents. Underpopulation and labour shortage seemed to be the problems rather than overpopulation and labour surplus. Labour discipline was advocated as a remedy for the new diseases of excessive luxury and leisure preference among the labouring classes.[69] This is not to say that labour resources were in fact now fully employed. If they had been there would have been no room for the further growth in output which came in the early eighteenth century. Like modest real wages, underemployment was still a reality. But the economic atmosphere had changed and with it had come an acceptance of high background levels of poverty.

This periodization is undoubtedly too schematic, but it serves to set the scene for the chapters which follow. It suggests that the stresses imposed by poverty were greatest in the first two periods, and these will occupy most of our attention in this book. It also suggests that the stresses were most evident between 1570 and 1650, and the most revealing sources for poverty come from that period, in particular the listings and surveys which will be used in the next two chapters. They can be employed to give some real quantities, albeit only for certain localities, to the levels and trends discussed above. The third period also has a special interest, however, since despite the stabilization of poverty indicated by the economic background, the costs of poor relief continued to rise between 1650 and 1700. We must return to explore that paradox in Chapter 9.

NOTES AND REFERENCES

1.   M. A. Havinden (ed.), *Household and Farm Inventories in Oxfordshire, 1550–1590* (Oxfords Record Soc., xliv, 1965), pp. 202, 258; J. Pound,

Poverty and Vagrancy in Tudor England (Longman, 1971), pp. 102–3; **L. M. Munby** (ed.), *Life and Death in Kings Langley: Wills and Inventories 1498–1659* (Kings Langley Local History and Museum Society, 1981), p. 63; **M. Cash** (ed.), *Devon Inventories of the Sixteenth and Seventeenth Centuries* (Devon and Cornwall Record Soc., n.s., xi, 1966), p. 46; **J. S. Moore** (ed.), *Clifton and Westbury Probate Inventories 1609–1761* (Avon Local History Assoc., 1981), p. 61; **D. G. Vaisey** (ed.), *Probate Inventories of Lichfield and District* (Staffs Record Soc., 4 ser., v, 1969), p. 238.

2.   P. Laslett, *Family Life and Illicit Love in Earlier Generations* (Cambridge UP, 1977), pp. 164, 166.

3.   Bodl., MS. Jones 17, ff. 14v–15r.

4.   Devon RO, Q.S. Order Book 1592–1600, pp. 210, 285; **C. J. Kitching**, 'Fire Disasters and Fire Relief in Sixteenth-Century England: The Nantwich Fire of 1583', *Bull. Inst. Hist. Res.*, liv (1981), 178.

5.   M. MacDonald, *Mystical Bedlam* (Cambridge UP, 1981), pp. 67–8, 74; Guildhall Library, London, MS. 942A, f. 14r.

6.   Dorset RO, Dorchester Records, B2/16/3, f. 28v; **J. Webb** (ed.), *Poor Relief in Elizabethan Ipswich* (Suffolk Records Soc., ix, 1966), p. 31; Guildhall Library, MS. 12828/1, letter of 25 Nov. 1582.

7.   *Clifton and Westbury Probate Inventories*, pp. 74–5.

8.   J. -P. Gutton, *La société et les pauvres: L'exemple de la généralité de Lyon* ('Les Belles Lettres', Paris, 1971), p. 53; **C. C. Fairchilds**, *Poverty and Charity in Aix-en-Provence 1640–1789* (Johns Hopkins UP, Baltimore and London, 1976), p. 73.

9.   There is an excellent analysis of these problems of measurement in **A. Sen**, *Poverty and Famines* (Oxford UP, 1981), espec. pp. 32–4, 156–7.

10.   W. G. Hoskins, *The Age of Plunder* (Longman, 1976), pp. 38, 32.

11.   A. D. Dyer, *The City of Worcester in the Sixteenth Century* (Leicester UP, 1973), pp. 175–6; **W. G. Hoskins**, *Provincial England* (Macmillan, 1964), p. 83; **Hoskins**, *Age of Plunger*, pp. 40, 43, 44. Cf. **J. Cornwall**, 'Sussex Wealth and Society in the Reign of Henry VIII', *Sussex Arch. Coll.*, 114 (1976), 9; **P. A. J. Pettit**, *The Royal Forests of Northamptonshire* (Northants Record Soc., xxiii, 1968), p. 143.

12.   C. Phythian-Adams, *Desolation of a City. Coventry and the Urban Crisis of the Late Middle Ages* (Cambridge UP, 1979), pp. 132–4; **Hoskins**, *Age of Plunder*, p. 41; **C. Phythian-Adams**, 'The Economic and Social Structure' in *The Fabric of the Traditional Community* (Open University, Milton Keynes, 1977), pp. 34–5. Mr. Phythian-Adams' work strongly suggests that some conventional estimates of the extent of poverty in the 1520s based on the subsidies have been grossly exaggerated.

13.   L. A. Clarkson, *The Pre-Industrial Economy in England 1500–1750* (Batsford, 1971), p. 233; **K. Wrightson** and **D. Levine**, *Poverty and Piety in an English Village: Terling 1525–1700* (Academic Press, 1979), p. 34.

14.   E.g., **W. G. Hoskins** (ed.), *Exeter in the Seventeenth Century: Tax and Rate Assessments 1602–99* (Devon and Cornwall Record Soc., n.s., ii, 1957), pp. 65–86. Criteria for exemption and fluctuations from year to year are discussed in **M. M. B. Weinstock** (ed.), *Hearth Tax Returns for Oxfordshire 1665* (Oxfordshire Record Soc., xxi, 1940), pp. vi, xii–xiii; **J. Patten**, 'The Hearth Taxes, 1662–1689', *Local Population Studies*, 7 (1971), 18–19.

15.   Hoskins, *Age of Plunder*, p. 28; **Clarkson**, *Pre-Industrial Economy*, p. 216.

Cf. **A. Browning** (ed.), *English Historical Documents 1660–1714* (Eyre and Spottiswoode, 1953), pp. 458–9.

16. **J. Thirsk** (ed.), *The Agrarian History of England and Wales, IV: 1500–1640* (Cambridge UP, 1967), pp. 1–15, 36–40, 93–8.

17. **M. Spufford**, *Contrasting Communities* (Cambridge UP, 1974), pp. 33, 36–7, 44, 143–4, 148; **Pettit**, *Forests of Northants*, p. 143; **A. B. Appleby**, *Famine in Tudor and Stuart England* (Liverpool UP, 1978), pp. 63–4.

18. For general discussions of rural and urban industry, see **D. C. Coleman**, *Industry in Tudor and Stuart England* (Macmillan, 1975), Ch. 3; **G. D. Ramsay**, *The English Woollen Industry 1500–1750* (Macmillan, 1982), Ch. 3; **J. Thirsk**, 'Industries in the Countryside', in **F. J. Fisher** (ed.), *Essays in the Economic and Social History of Tudor and Stuart England in honour of R. H. Tawney* (Cambridge UP, 1961), pp. 70–88; **P. Clark** and **P. Slack**, *English Towns in Transition 1500–1700* (Oxford UP, 1976), Ch. 7.

19. *Ibid.*, pp. 113–14; **Appleby**, *Famine*, pp. 167–8; **V. Skipp**, *Crisis and Development. An Ecological Case Study of the Forest of Arden, 1570–1674* (Cambridge UP, 1978), p. 78; **Pettit**, *Forests of Northants*, p. 145.

20. **J. Patten**, *English Towns 1500–1700* (Dawson, 1978), p. 34; **Clarkson**, *Pre-Industrial Economy*, p. 233; **Wrightson** and **Levine**, *Poverty and Piety*, p. 34.

21. **E. A. Wrigley** and **R. S. Schofield**, *The Population History of England 1541–1871: A Reconstruction* (Arnold, 1981), pp. 568, 208–9, 212.

22. **D. C. Coleman**, *The Economy of England 1450–1750* (Oxford UP, 1977), pp. 21–2, 100–101.

23. **Wrigley** and **Schofield**, *Population History*, pp. 217–19, 443, 449, 528. On the problems faced by widows in the seventeenth century, see **B. J. Todd**, 'The remarrying widow: a stereotype reconsidered' in **M. Prior** (ed.), *Women in English Society 1500–1800* (Methuen, 1985), pp. 54–92.

24. **J. Hadwin**, 'The Problem of Poverty in Early Modern England', in **T. Riis** (ed.), *Aspects of Poverty in Early Modern Europe* (European University Publications, 10, Florence, 1981), pp. 222–3; **Thirsk**, *Agrarian History*, IV, pp. 242–6. On poverty around old monastic sites, see **M. Prior**, *Fisher Row* (Oxford UP, 1982), pp. 34, 51–2; **B. H. Cunnington** (ed.), *Records of the County of Wiltshire* (George Simpson and Co., Devizes, 1932), pp. 118–19.

25. **P. Clark**, 'The Migrant in Kentish Towns 1580–1640', in **P. Clark** and **P. Slack** (eds), *Crisis and Order in English Towns 1500–1700* (Routledge and Kegan Paul, 1972), pp. 117–63.

26. **P. Clark**, 'Migration in England during the late Seventeenth and early Eighteenth Centuries', *Past and Present*, 83 (1979), 73, 81–2; **D. Souden**, 'Migrants and the population structure', in **P. Clark** (ed.), *The Transformation of English Provincial Towns 1600–1800* (Hutchinson, 1984), pp. 135, 147–8.

27. **Coleman**, *Economy of England*, Ch. 6 provides the best brief account, and **K. Wrightson**, *English Society 1580–1680* (Hutchinson, 1982), Ch. 5 the best account of the social consequences. See also **Wrigley** and **Schofield**, *Population History*, Ch. 10; **R. B. Outhwaite**, 'Progress and Backwardness in English Agriculture', *Econ. Hist. Rev.*, 2 ser., xxxix (1986), 1–18.

28. **J. Thirsk**, *Economic Policy and Projects* (Oxford UP, 1978), *passim*.

29. **Coleman**, *Economy of England*, pp. 23, 101–103; **A. Kussmaul**, *Servants in*

Husbandry in Early Modern England (Cambridge UP, 1981), p. 104, fig. 6.4.

30. **Clark** and **Slack,** *English Towns in Transition*, pp. 11–12, 83–4; **R. Finlay,** *Population and Metropolis. The Demography of London 1580–1650* (Cambridge UP, 1981), pp. 6–7. Cf. below, pp. 67–8.

31. **Spufford,** *Contrasting Communities*, pp. 47–53, 90–1, 118, 165–6. Cf. C. **Howell,** *Land, Family and Inheritance in Transition: Kibworth Harcourt* (Cambridge UP, 1983), pp. 118, 134–5, 190, 195; **Wrightson** and **Levine,** *Poverty and Piety*, pp. 34–42, 108; **A. Macfarlane,** *The Origins of English Individualism* (Blackwell, Oxford, 1978), pp. 69–70, 76–7.

32. **Kussmaul,** *Servants in Husbandry*, pp. 97–101.

33. **Howell,** *Land, Family and Inheritance*, pp. 269–70. For other discussions of the rising number of cottagers and labourers, see **Thirsk,** *Agrarian History IV*, pp. 399–400, 417–18; **Skipp,** *Crisis and Development*, pp. 79–80; **Appleby,** *Famine*, pp. 45, 63–4; **D. G. Hey,** *An English Rural Community: Myddle under the Tudors and Stuarts* (Leicester UP, 1974), pp. 53–4.

34. E.g. **Wrightson,** *English Society*, p. 140; **Clark** and **Slack,** *English Towns in Transition*, p. 114.

35. For evidence of it in the later Middle Ages, see **Z. Razi,** *Life, Marriage and Death in a Medieval Parish* (Cambridge UP, 1980), pp. 147, 150.

36. **J. Thirsk** and **J. P. Cooper** (eds), *Seventeenth-Century Economic Documents* (Oxford UP, 1972), p. 781.

37. **E. H. Phelps-Brown** and **S. V. Hopkins,** 'Seven Centuries of the Prices of Consumables Compared with Builders' Wage-Rates', in **E. M. Carus-Wilson** (ed.), *Essays in Economic History*, II (Arnold, 1962), pp. 179–96; **Thirsk,** *Agrarian History IV*, pp. 598–600, 865; **J. Thirsk** (ed.), *The Agrarian History of England and Wales V. ii. 1640–1750* (Cambridge UP, 1985), pp. 3–5, 879.

38. See **D. M. Woodward,** 'Wage rates and living standards in pre-industrial England', *Past and Present*, 91 (1981), 28–45.

39. **D. M. Palliser,** 'Tawney's Century. Brave New World or Malthusian Trap?', *Econ. Hist. Rev.*, 2 ser., xxxv (1982), 342–7. Cf. **D. Loschky,** 'Seven Centuries of Real Income per Wage Earner Reconsidered', *Economica*, xlvii (1980), 463.

40. **Wrigley** and **Schofield,** *Population History*, pp. 416–22, 435, 440, 450–3, 469–71.

41. **A. B. Appleby,** 'Diet in Sixteenth-Century England', in **C. Webster** (ed.), *Health, Medicine and Mortality in the Sixteenth Century* (Cambridge UP, 1979), pp. 107–16.

42. For Essex examples, see **Wrightson** and **Levine,** *Poverty and Piety*, pp. 39, 42.

43. **Wrigley** and **Schofield,** *Population History*, pp. 328, 331, 399.

44. For years of bad harvest, see **W. G. Hoskins,** 'Harvest Fluctuations and English Economic History 1480–1619', *Agricultural Hist. Rev.*, xii (1964), 28–46, and '1620–1759', *ibid.*, xvi (1968), 15–31; **C. J. Harrison,** 'Grain Price Analysis and Harvest Qualities, 1465–1634', *ibid.*, xix (1971), 135–55; and for mortality, **Wrigley** and **Schofield,** *Population History*, pp. 319, 321, 333, App. 10; **P. Slack,** 'Mortality Crises and Epidemic Disease in England 1485–1610', in **Webster,** *Health, Medicine and Mortality*, pp. 10–59; **R. B. Outhwaite,** 'Dearth and Government Intervention in English Grain Markets 1590–1700', *Econ. Hist. Rev.*, 2 ser., xxxiv (1981), 401–2.

45. **Slack** 'Mortality Crises', p. 54; **D. Dymond,** 'The famine of 1527 in Essex', *Local Population Studies*, 26 (1981), 29–40; **Phythian-Adams,** *Desolation of a City*, pp. 59, 64–7, 196–7.

46. **Wrigley** and **Schofield,** *Population History*, p. 333; **Slack,** 'Mortality Crises', pp. 27–32.

47. *Ibid.*, pp. 33–40; **Appleby,** *Famine,* Chs 7–9; **Wrigley** and **Schofield,** *Population History*, p. 333; **P. Clark** (ed.), *The European Crisis of the 1590s* (Allen and Unwin, 1985), Chs 2, 3; **P. Laslett,** *The World We Have Lost* (3rd edn, Methuen, 1983), Ch. 6. For a local crisis, perhaps of a similar kind, in 1613–19, see **Skipp,** *Crisis and Development, passim.*

48. **I. Kershaw,** 'The Great Famine and Agrarian Crisis in England 1315–1322', *Past and Present*, 59 (1973), 11–13; **F. Lebrun,** 'Les crises démographiques en France au XVIIe et XVIIIe siècles', *Annales*, 35 (1980), 219–20. The evidence for French mortality before 1670 is slight, but see **P. Goubert,** 'Recent Theories and Research in French Population between 1500 and 1700', in **D. V. Glass** and **D. E. C. Eversley,** *Population in History* (Arnold, 1965), pp. 457–73.

49. Sen, *Poverty and Famines, passim.* Cf. **Appleby,** *Famine*, pp. 146–8.

50. Below, pp. 71–3, 95, 101. For the importance of the wider social consequences of 'famine' as against brute starvation, see **D. J. Oddy,** 'Urban Famine in Nineteenth-Century Britain', *Econ. Hist. Rev.*, 2 ser., xxxvi (1983), 68–72.

51. **Appleby,** *Famine*, p. 185; below, pp. 140, 147. For a particularly good example, see **W. L. Sachse** (ed.), *Minutes of the Norwich Court of Mayoralty 1630–1* (Norfolk Record Soc., xv, 1942), *passim.*

52. *Seventeenth-Century Economic Documents*, pp. 48–52; **Appleby,** *Famine*, pp. 155–6; **C. H. Hull** (ed.), *The Economic Writings of Sir William Petty* (Cambridge UP, 1899), ii. 352–3; below, pp. 170–1, 196.

53. **Slack,** 'Mortality Crises', pp. 40–9; **P. Slack,** *The Impact of Plague in Tudor and Stuart England* (Routledge and Kegan Paul, 1985), Chs 3, 7.

54. *Ibid.*, pp. 190, 192. On pawning, see **W. Muggins,** *London's Mourning Garment or Funerall Teares* (1603), sigs. C4v, D1r; **P. Clark,** *English Provincial Society from the Reformation to the Revolution* (Harvester, Hassocks, 1977), p. 233.

55. See, for example, **I. Roy,** 'England Turned Germany? The Aftermath of the Civil War in its European Context', *Trans. Roy. Hist. Soc.*, 5 ser., 28 (1978), 127–44; **E. B. Saxton,** 'Losses of the Inhabitants of Liverpool in the taking of the town in 1644'. *Trans. Hist. Soc. Lancs. and Cheshire*, 91 (1939), 181–91; **Cunnington,** *Records of Wiltshire*, p. 182.

56. **J. B. Gribble,** *Memorials of Barnstaple* (Barnstaple, 1830), p. 436.

57. **B. E. Supple,** *Commercial Crisis and Change in England 1600–1642* (Cambridge UP, 1964), Chs 3, 4, 5.

58. **Phythian-Adams,** *Desolation of a City, passim*; Essex RO, Q/SR 145/58, 136/82.

59. **P. Slack,** 'Books of Orders: The Making of English Social Policy, 1577–1631', *Trans. Roy. Hist. Soc.*, 5 ser., 30 (1980), 12–13. Cf. below, pp. 140–2, 145–7.

60. PRO, SP 16/243/23; 16/364/122; Asz 24/20, f. 170.

61. **Thirsk,** *Economic Policy and Projects*, p. 157; PRO, SP 16/250/11 (iv), 16/268/23.

62. On the winters of 1673–74, 1683–84 and 1694–95, for example, see Norfolk and Norwich RO, Mayor's Court Book 24, f. 270r; Court Book 25, ff. 149v, 332v; Colchester Borough Records, Assembly Book 1663–92, f. 213v; Bristol Archives Office, Common Council Proceedings 1687–1702, f. 117v; Q.S. Minutes 1681–1705, ff. 28v–29r. For corn provision, see below, pp. 146–7.
63. Quoted in **C. Hill**, *Change and Continuity in Seventeenth-Century England* (Weidenfeld and Nicolson, 1974), p. 220.
64. **Wrigley** and **Schofield**, *Population History*, pp. 450–2.
65. Below, pp. 71–5, 175–9.
66. There is an account of mid-Tudor literature on economic matters in **A. B. Ferguson**, *The Articulate Citizen and the English Renaissance* (Duke UP, Durham, N.C., 1965), Ch. x.
67. Cf. **D. M. Palliser**, *The Age of Elizabeth* (Longman, 1983), Ch. 4.
68. **R. Machin**, 'The Great Rebuilding: A Reassessment', *Past and Present*, 77 (1977), 33–56; **M. Spufford**, *The Great Reclothing of Rural England* (Hambledon Press, 1984), pp. 1–3.
69. **Coleman**, *Economy of England*, pp. 103–5. Cf. **P. Mathias**, *The Transformation of England* (Methuen, 1979), pp. 148–56. In many respects this was a return to attitudes common in conditions of labour shortage in the late fourteenth century.

Chapter 4

THE RESPECTABLE POOR

The poverty line employed in the generalizations which were advanced at the end of the last chapter had to be drawn in sixteenth- and seventeenth-century terms. It was the line below which Tudor and Stuart Englishmen recognized deprivation and need. When we come to view the hard reality which lay behind the trends suggested there, we are even more dependent on contemporary perceptions. The quantity and quality of poverty can only be seen through documents which were created by the social and political elite. The subject necessarily divides itself, therefore, according to the basic contemporary distinction between the deserving and the undeserving poor, between the respectable pauper and the dangerous vagabond. This chapter will consider the people who were thought to merit charity and relief; the next chapter will concentrate on those who were suitable cases for other kinds of treatment.

Rich as the sources are, they leave two areas of the subject cloudy. The first is the situation in the early sixteenth century, before the surveys of poverty which were stimulated by the poor law became fashionable. The likely trends indicated in the last chapter suggest that a larger proportion of the population was poor in 1570 than in 1500, and the growth in contemporary comment on the problem over that period supports the hypothesis; but it cannot be conclusively established. Secondly, the sources tell us more about the number of people below the poverty line than about the depth of their poverty. We saw that comparatively few of the poor starved, even at the nadir of their fortunes between 1580 and 1620; but we do not know how close most of them came to it. Unfortunately, we cannot *see* beggars and cottagers, the labouring householders and widows of late Tudor England, in order to judge just how emaciated and unhealthy, how ragged and miserable they were. The sources are in every sense partial.

They do not impose wholly opaque blinkers, however. Listings and surveys revealed unexpected facets of poverty, and they can be used to show the limitations of contemporary perceptions and contemporary prescriptions. Neither the deserving poor in this section nor the undeserving poor in the next were quite as people expected them to be.

THE RURAL POOR

The deserving poor remained closest to contemporary stereotypes in the countryside. In small villages and hamlets those who needed alms, a small sum from the parish poor box, or a weekly dole after the introduction of poor rates, were usually few and conspicuous. They were the impotent poor. The earliest poor relief accounts, dating from the 1560s, show that widows were the commonest subjects of relief, and that the number on relief was usually very small.[1] In many parts of the country this continued to be the case in normal times. In Wheatley, Oxfordshire, for example, ten people were regularly given weekly alms in the 1630s: five of them were permanent pensioners and all five were widows.[2] It was only in the very smallest places that the impotent poor occasionally imposed insupportable burdens: in Hastenleigh in Kent in the early seventeenth century, for example, where as few as eight householders had to relieve five poor widows.[3] The list of recipients of outdoor relief might lengthen at certain times of the year. Landless labourers often found themselves unemployed and dependent on alms in the winter. In many parishes payments to the poor were lowest at harvest time and highest in December. But these variations were predictable and they were mitigated to some degree by the customary charitable gifts to respectable poor householders at Christmas. The number of the poor was for long kept within manageable bounds.

One reason for this was the sort of neighbourly pressure and mutual help possible in the small face-to-face society of the rural community. Local opinion could force people to recognize their obligations to relations and friends. Informal sanctions were not always successful, of course, and it is the failures which occur most commonly in the records. Thus Ralph Josselin, Vicar of Earls Colne in Essex, noted the case of Samuel Burton in his diary in the 1650s: Burton had refused to help his widowed sister and her many children, and let them fall a charge on the parish. This was probably an exceptional case, however. A few years later, when a foundling was left in Josselin's barn, it took only a week for the father to be identified and persuaded to come and collect it. Credit might also be available in villages to tide small folk over difficult times, even when there was little hope of repayment. One year after the death of her husband, Widow Reyner was lent £10 by Josselin so that she could pay her rent – although he had his qualms: 'It was a hard venture, but I hoped God would show me kindness, and I could not withhold my bowels from a widow.'[4]

Above all, in small communities the deserving poor were well known, outsiders could easily be denied relief, and the odd rogue might be cheerfully accepted, provided he was a native and an exception. Parishes often had a single problem family or even dynasty. There were several

Wilds listed among the poor of Crompton, Lancashire in the 1590s, for example, and there were the Peanes, all of them beggars, in Eccleshall, Staffordshire, a century later. The Davies's in the Shropshire village of Myddle in the 1660s included Sina Davies, 'a crafty, idle, dissembling woman', who 'did counterfeit herself to be lame, and went hopping with a staff when men saw her, but at other times could go with it under her arm . . . and she had maintenance from the parish many years before she died'.[5] Such characters could be tolerated because their behaviour contrasted so sharply with the standards set for and generally maintained by their neighbours.

When the poor were thus an easily recognized and normally small minority, traditional attitudes could persist longer than in the more transient and less easily monitored society of the towns. The impotent poor could be allowed to beg from door to door, even if, in theory, only under licence. In Norfolk in the 1590s, those licensed to seek 'alms, charities [and] devotions at the house or houses of the inhabitants' included one couple, aged 86 and 84, whose house had burnt down; a 'very poor man' who had 'many poor young children depending upon him'; and a man who had 'very honestly lived in his vocation, taking great pains for his living, until by reason of his age and sore diseases, which are fallen to his legs and other parts of his body, he was enforced to leave his former labour and painstaking, which have been the only cause of his extreme poverty'.[6] No deserving pauper could hope for a better testimonial than that.

Yet even in rural society circumstances were changing by the end of the sixteenth century, as the pressures caused by population growth mounted. These formal and discriminatory beggars' licences are one indication that customary mechanisms for dealing with poverty could not function smoothly when the number of potential paupers rose. New strains can also be detected in legislation passed in 1589 against the building of new cottages on commons and wastes and the housing of lodgers or inmates. In the first decades of the seventeenth century justices of the peace all over the country were both trying to enforce the statute and confessing defeat by authorizing infringements of it. Cottages, and flimsy lean-tos erected against them, were often pulled down, and their occupants turned out to 'lodge under hedges'. A drive against strangers and inmates led to a poor couple living in a hollow tree in Wiltshire, and to a whole family living in a shed 'that they used to make tile in, where hogs and others lie also' in Essex.[7] At the same time, however, cottages were built on the waste of Lacock, Wiltshire, for 60 people who were said to be living in the streets, while in parts of Norfolk householders were 'pressed' by the authorities to take in poor inmates who could not be provided for otherwise.[8]

The new squatter and labouring populations, scraping a living on commons and from domestic industries, threatened to impoverish whole areas of the country, especially in years of crisis of one kind or another. Between the 1580s and the 1620s many Essex parishes were complaining that they were 'very sore charged with poor', and the clothing villages in the north of the county were overwhelmed by 'poor artisans' in the 1590s. 'Poor handicraftsmen' and their children were a burden when epidemic sickness hit Worcestershire in 1617.[9] In the later 1640s when harvests were bad and the demand for textiles depressed, a village like Earls Colne was 'full of poor', and its spinners especially 'in a sad condition'.[10] In Oxfordshire likewise, the dearth of 1647 forced the overseers of Wheatley to provide bread for poor people in general, besides their usual doles to a few named individuals.

It is not surprising therefore that the authorities were most often impelled to measure the extent of deprivation in rural England in years of dearth. From the 1520s to the 1620s the government's grain policy, which we shall consider in a later chapter, ordered local surveys of corn supplies in crisis years. The earliest of the surviving returns reveal severe local shortages, like that in Hinckford hundred, Essex, in 1527, where there was only 22 per cent of the breadcorn needed to feed the population.[11] But later surveys more often indicate an unequal distribution of scarce resources than a large aggregate deficiency. While some households in a region were well provided for, there were also large proportions of the population which had no grain at all. In Clacklose hundred, Norfolk, on the edge of the fens, for example, just over a third of the population had no grain in March 1557 and were dependent on the market for their food; while another third probably had more than enough to last them until the next harvest. When the same hundred was surveyed again in the great dearth of 1596, the surveyors did not bother to record the households with no grain. They listed only the corn-holding households, whose stocks were needed to furnish local markets. Some of the smaller arable farmers were probably omitted from the record in 1596; but it may nevertheless be significant that whereas 529 corn-holding householders had been enumerated in 1557, only 243 were listed in 1596.[12] The proportion of the population dependent on markets had probably increased.

The labouring populations of small towns were naturally still less well supplied than those of the fens. In the three Kent parishes of Chatham, Gillingham and the Isle of Grain, in 1596, 71 per cent of the population had no corn, and there were more people with than without only in the Isle.[13] Similarly in Sandwich, in the next dearth of 1622, 73 per cent of the population was without corn.[14] By then, however, many mixed farming regions had similar problems. In Odiham In hundred, Hampshire, 19 people with corn had to support 186 who were without, and if one adds the households of the 19 to the total, that meant at least half the population dependent on the market.[15] In short, the problem of dearth was increasingly a problem of distribution. In many regions in 1622, and probably in some even earlier, there was enough grain to go round if it was properly managed. In Sandwich, for example, the calculations in the survey show that the corn-holders had enough to feed the whole town, provided that they brought it to the local market. The same was probably the case in Odiham. Hence the government's policy of trying to ensure that markets were in fact regularly supplied.

Since the problems were increasingly those of a market – and not a subsistence – economy, local surveys in years of dearth gradually focused attention, not on corn supplies, but on the number and condition of poor consumers. Thus in the crisis of 1622–3 some parishes of northern Hampshire described how high prices and the consequent recession had thrown many besides the impotent into poverty. The inhabitants of Silchester reported that they had to support very few people permanently; but 'many others in our parish we are fain to relieve daily and we have many poor men . . . which would work and we have it not for them'. These were the labouring poor. The overseers of Heckfield and two neighbouring villages listed the two groups by name: there were only thirty impotent and aged poor, including two orphans and one lunatic; but no less than 203 people, nearly seven times as many, 'do work and yet have collection when need is nevertheless'.[16]

The ratio of impotent poor to labouring poor was roughly the same in parts of northern Kent in the earlier harvest crisis of 1596–98. Lists of the poor were drawn up in 1598 in the three parishes whose corn stocks had been surveyed in 1596. While only three people received the parish dole in the Isle of Grain, there were 21 'other poor', made up of six families whose fathers 'so long as it shall please God to send them their health . . . make shift to live well and keep their poor wives and children, which be a great many in so small a parish'. In Gillingham there were 11 impotent poor, including two backward 'innocents' and a blind woman, but 12 families which could not afford to support their 17 children. A few miles away, in the growing settlement of Chatham, the situation was worse still: the parish had only 8 pensioners, but 63 people in the category of 'able poor that labour towards their relief'.[17]

In quantitative terms alone these numbers were disturbing, since they represented a substantial slice of the total rural population. We can calculate some proportions for the three Kent parishes. The impotent poor formed 7 per cent of all households and the labouring poor no less than 21 per cent. In terms of population, the proportions were lower, however. The households of the poor were small, with no servants and often fewer children than their social superiors; and the impotent poor were often solitary individuals. Even so, a comparison of the 1596 and 1598 listings suggests that while only 1.5 per cent of the population of these parishes normally received poor relief, almost 10 per cent lived in the households of the labouring poor. In other villages the proportions were even greater. In Harlow hundred, Essex, in 1598–99, a survey of three parishes showed that while just under 4 per cent of the population were among the impotent, 20 per cent 'do work for their living' but 'being not able to maintain themselves and their charge by their labour do many times receive relief of the parish'. Some of the latter were 'greatly charged with young children'.[18]

It was not only the quantitative aspect of the problem which was threatening, however. The quality of poverty also changed when the safe criterion of impotency had to be abandoned. If the impotent were often solitary individuals and always marginal people, the labouring poor formed whole families indistinguishable in many of their characteristics from the majority of the population. When the poor were listed in Crompton, Lancashire, in 1597, for example, there were found to be 17 or 18 beggars, most of them women and children, some of them lame. But in addition there were 99 resident labouring poor, of whom only 12 were single or solitary men or women. The rest were grouped into complete nuclear families: father, mother and children. Some of the fathers were colliers who were not earning enough to pay their rent and maintain their families. None of them were said to be impotent.[19]

The nature of the problem can be seen still more clearly in another north Kent parish, Strood, where the overseers made a comprehensive list of householders in 1598.[20] At the top of the social scale were 80 householders who were rate-payers, none of them in any danger of destitution. At the bottom were those receiving relief, 9 impotent poor from 8 families, one of them a boy of twelve with 'his toes rotted off'. But in-between was a vaguely defined group of 61 families: 'the poorer sort of people which as yet are able to work and doth neither give nor take, but if the husband should die are likely to be a parish charge'. Some were worse off than others. There were four widows, and 19 families which had 'children unable to be at service'. But most were ordinary families with respectable, middle-aged men at their head, like 'Matthew Spepping, butcher, of 50 years, his wife 45' and five children, or 'Thomas Suedall, sailor, of 35 years, his wife 30,' and their three children. In this parish 40 per cent of the households, at least a quarter of the inhabitants (we do not have complete totals), were close to poverty.

The threat of an escalating number of paupers was thus sharply perceived in the countryside by 1600, and it did not come from a gang of idle wastrels but from the respectable labouring classes. Most parishes might manage for most of the time by supporting the two, three or four per cent of the population who were impotent, as they had always done. But they could not ignore the ten or twenty per cent of the population who hovered around the poverty line and who might fall below it when the harvest failed, when sickness hit the chief breadwinner, when employment opportunities for wives and children in rural industries contracted, or simply when there was a particularly bad winter. How soon and how widely this problem manifested itself it is impossible to say with any confidence. The conditions which created it, such as squatter settlements and domestic rural industries, came earlier and in sharper form to some communities than to others.[21] As the listings referred to above show, the problem was also most obvious in years of demonstrable crisis, when the threat of a large number of undeniable claimants on relief became a reality. By the end of the crisis of the 1590s, however, the new situation had plainly forced itself on the attention of parish officials in many parts of the country.[22]

THE URBAN POOR

The same pressures were felt to a much greater degree, and from an earlier date, in towns. They did not come only with a rapidly increasing population, as was sometimes the case in villages; neither did economic growth banish them. From the 1520s onwards towns found themselves overburdened with poor. To begin with, the problem was largely one of downward social mobility. In those 'grievously decayed' towns, whose delapidated and empty houses evoked the concern of social commentators and legislators from the 1520s to the 1540s, craftsmen and labourers were thrown out of work and into beggary. At the same time, as rural populations grew, there may have been some inflow of poor migrants from the countryside: readily available lodging was a potent attraction for newcomers to 'places decayed, as Lincoln, Stamford, Coventry, Leicester and Nottingham', or so it was thought rather later in the century, in 1573.[23] There were certainly complaints of vagrants in several towns, including Coventry, between 1517 and 1521. There were also the special stresses brought by epidemic diseases in 1517–18 and by harvest crises in 1520 and 1527. The evidence suggests that poverty emerged as a major problem for towns in the second and third decades of the sixteenth century.[24]

The revival in the economic fortunes of towns in the later sixteenth century did little to improve matters, however. The growing wealth and philanthropic inclinations of the mercantile elite could be tapped for the relief of the poor, but the poor did not disappear. Rather their numbers grew, partly through natural increase, but chiefly through an even greater influx of migrants, many of them with little hope of finding permanent employment or adequate housing for themselves and their families. In 1562 restrictions were imposed on the immigration of apprentices to Bristol because 'the poverty within the city daily increases and the number great of idle boys born in the city which wander and range abroad and about the city for want of masters and are not placed into service to some trade'. Concern about high fertility and the number of young immigrants was general by the early seventeenth century. There were efforts to deter early marriage by maintaining long apprenticeships; and in Great Yarmouth poor people were not to be married at all unless they had certificates testifying that they were inhabitants of the town.[25]

Above all, the poor inmate now became for the town what the poor cottager on the waste was for the village – a public nuisance, a potential threat to public order, and in time of crisis a burden on the community. Local authorities tried in vain to prevent 'the pestering of houses with divers families, harbouring of inmates, and converting great houses into several tenements or dwellings'; and if they did not act, they were reminded of their responsibilities by juries of local worthies in courts leet, horrified by 'the intolerable number of inmates and undertenants overmuch increasing ... to the great annoyance of all the honest inhabitants'.[26] In the 1560s and 1570s there was still little sign of overcrowding in towns, even in the poor suburbs of Canterbury or, as we shall see, in the poorer parts of Norwich.[27] Between 1580 and 1640, however, it is impossible to find a single town where there was not some complaint about strangers living in congested tenements.

Naturally there were local enquiries into the problem. In Nottingham in 1612 one profiteering landlord was found renting rooms to 'strangers out of the country that have great charges of children', some of whom 'do now go abegging'. An enterprising minister in Worcester similarly built small cottages along Foregate Street in 1609 and filled them with paupers, and in Chester the constables tried to remove fifteen tenants from one small house in 1604. Further north, a survey of strangers in Manchester in 1613 revealed a much worse case of overcrowding: one roof sheltered a strange assortment of families – a couple, the wife's daughter by a previous marriage and four or five children; a widow, her sister and two or three children; a woman and two children deserted by their father; another abandoned wife and her two children, together with her sister and another child; and 'divers men of loose behaviour' besides.[28] Similar conditions were uncovered by local surveys in Southwark and Cambridge, and in Oxford where there was an eloquent lament about the consequences: 'a great multitude of poor people ... in this city and suburbs, wandering, walking and going idly up and down the streets and other places, begging and oftentimes pilfering, filching and breaking of shops and houses'.[29]

This description tells us more about the fears of the richer sort than about the real activities of the poor, but it refers in passing to one of the reasons for contemporary paranoia: the suburban concentration of poverty. There was no rigid social zoning in early modern towns. Behind every main street there were alleys and yards where the labouring poor lived within a few feet of the mansions of the social elite. But in every large town mansions were fewer and poor tenements much more common on the periphery, just inside the walls, or outside the main gates where ribbon development was beginning in the later sixteenth century. In Oxford, for example, the poorest area lay on the western edge of the city, in the parish of St Peter in the Bailey, and especially in St Thomas's outside the walls, which was almost a ready-made slum. Run down since the dissolution of its two rich abbeys, on unhealthy marshy land by the

Thames where river trades provided employment for casual labour, it was also marginal territory, between rival jurisdictions, on the edge of the city and the county, so that it was easy for vagrants and petty criminals to evade the arm of the law.[30] Oxford was not singular in this respect. All major towns had at least one suburb where mortality rates were always high, where plague and harvest crises had their worst effects, where alehouses and drunkenness were common, where immigrants found lodging and from which beggars came to pester the more prosperous parts of town. In Redcliffe ward Bristol, on the southern edge of Norwich, along Foregate Street Worcester, outside the walls of Canterbury and in St Giles parish, Cambridge, there was a vicious circle of poverty, high death rates, immigration and instability.[31]

In such circumstances the poor were more easily seen as an undifferentiated and dangerous mass than as individuals to whom the community had a collective responsibility. Their anonymity should not be exaggerated. In the parish, if not in the town, many of the poor were familiar figures and there were problem characters as notorious as those in villages. There was Sarah Biby in Salisbury, for example, a widow who turns up again and again in lists of paupers and recipients of Christmas and Easter doles, whose children were pauper apprentices, and who herself took in poor lodgers. Not surprisingly perhaps, in the 1660s the mayor could still remember her as the woman who burned the pesthouse down in 1627.[32] But she was one among hundreds of paupers in this cathedral city, not one among a score in a village.

The problem of numbers was greatest and most threatening, of course, in London. In the 1540s it brought a host of afflictions on the city, including 'beggary, vagabuncy, unthriftiness, theft, pox, pestilence, infections, diseases and infirmities'. Forty years later John Howes, the chronicler of the London hospitals, was driven to the famous conclusion that 'It is not the poor of London that pestereth the city, but the poor of England'.[33] The activities of the institutions whose achievements Howes was describing throw light on some aspects of the metropolitan problem. Founded or refounded between 1544 and 1557 to cater largely for traditional categories of pauper, the hospitals were all stretched to the limit by 1600. St Bartholomew's and St Thomas's were soon under pressure. St Bartholomew's complained of increasing numbers of incurable patients occupying its beds; St Thomas's was pestered with beggars claiming a night's lodging and with old paupers who, once safely in the hospital, refused to leave.[34]

Christ's Hospital never satisfied the demand for its services as a refuge for orphan and foundling children, despite the high death rates which kept the admission rate high. Between 1552 and 1564 1,916 children and infants were taken in, of whom 38 per cent died before they were old enough to go out into service. In the next eleven years, 850 children were admitted and the death rate rose to 52 per cent.[35] Yet there was never any shortage of candidates for vacant places. Foundlings like 'John Stairs' and 'Elizabeth Window' were still being left on the doorstep or other bits of the building in the 1650s, when Christ's was already well on the way to becoming a public school rather than a hospital. Bridewell also had to fulfil too many, though rather different, functions. Its role as workhouse and industrial school for poor children was increasingly overshadowed by its punitive function: the whipping of vagrants and the temporary incarceration of the petty criminal fraternity of the capital. Those brought in included prostitutes, gamblers and pickpockets like the Jewish boy who 'says that there is no God, besides which he was found ... playing with false dice'.[36] We shall see in the next chapter that the number of vagrants admitted rose more quickly than that of other offenders; but none of the inmates were promising material for industrial training, and they taught more than they learnt. Bridewell's officers were notorious for their corruption.

Inadequate as these institutions were, however, their records show something of the scale of poverty in the capital. In the 1560s there were roughly 750 people supported by or housed in the hospitals (excluding Bedlam) at any one time, of whom half were in Christ's. By 1600 the figure was nearly 1,200 and by 1656 it had doubled to 1,615. Many more people were dealt with in the course of a year, however, especially in Bridewell. Table 1 gives some indication of the annual numbers passing through the four institutions in selected years. No great claims can be made for their accuracy. Before 1610 the figures are based on fragmentary original records, and where no records exist, guesses (given in parentheses) have had to be made.[37] From 1610 onwards, the figures are taken from printed summaries intended for public consumption, which may have been inclined to inflate the totals, particularly in the cases of St Thomas's and St Bartholomew's.[38] Nevertheless, there can be little doubt that the general impression given is a realistic one. The problems of the capital, as crudely measured by these institutions, were growing rapidly between 1560 and 1610; and they seem even to have been growing relative to the total population. The aggregate figures in Table 1 amount to rather less than 2 per cent of the City's population in

TABLE 1. Annual admissions to the London hospitals, *c.* 1560–1656

Date	Christ's	Bridewell	St Thomas's	St Barth.'s	Total
*c.*1560	386	445	243	346	1420
*c.*1580	564	586	737	(580)	2467
*c.*1600	716	899	(700)	(600)	2915
1610	684	1827	998	855	4364
1634	1032	1380	1143	1181	4736
1645	763	941	1172	1158	4034
1656	958	783	1295	1740	4776

1560 and 2.5 per cent in 1610.[39] After 1610 the numbers stabilized, not because the problems lessened necessarily, but more probably because the hospitals no longer tried to keep pace with them.

These figures relate, however, only to special categories of the poor, and probably only to a minority of them. The municipal and parish authorities were left to deal with the rest. Bridewell clearly could not stem the flow of beggars who wandered into the city from the outparishes, despite the mayor's attempts to have them kept outside the walls, or stop the vagrants who came across London Bridge from Southwark, about whom the governors of Christ's Hospital themselves complained. And behind them lay the more fundamental problem of the inner suburbs of the city, stretching in a circle from Southwark round through Aldgate, Bishopsgate and Cripplegate to the Fleet ditch and Bridewell. Here, and not least in the properties owned by the hospitals, were blocks of tenements and disorderly inmates. By 1638 there were said to be between 700 and 800 families of 'miserable poor' in St Bride's, just north of Bridewell, and a 'multitude of poor people' in St Giles Cripplegate.[40] At the same time, some of the inner parishes of the City had only a handful of resident paupers to support.

These gross differentials between parishes make any estimate of the total number of poor people in London both difficult to arrive at and potentially misleading. Some tentative calculations can, however, be made for three different dates. In 1552, when the hospitals were being organized, a rounded and obviously rough count of the number of poor in the city recorded 2,100 people in various categories. If we subtract the 200 vagrants in the list, because they were non-resident, and add another 2,000 to cover the families of the 650 'decayed householders' and the 350 'poor men overburdened with children', we reach a total of nearly 4,000: probably around 5 per cent of the inhabitants of the City at that time.[41] A century later, in the 1650s, between 3 and 4 per cent of the population of sample parishes in the centre of the City were receiving poor relief.[42] If we made some allowance for the greater burdens of fringe parishes, the result would probably be a proportion similar to that of 1552. That does not mean that the problem had not increased in magnitude in the interim, however. The people counted in 1552 were those thought to require public relief; the total recorded in the 1650s represents those who actually received it, a very different thing.

Surveys of the poor taken between these two dates, in the crisis of the 1590s, show that the level of poverty was in fact no more stable in London than in the countryside, and no easier to measure. There were at least three listings of the poor between 1596 and 1598, and the last of them produced the smallest total. In 1598 2,196 poor people were counted in 102 parishes. They seem to have been the recipients of parish poor relief, the majority of them probably the impotent poor. Their families would therefore have been small. If we double the number to take account of wives and children where they existed, that gives us roughly 3 per cent of the population, and a total of about 5 per cent if we add the inmates of the hospitals.[43] This was undoubtedly an absolute minimum, however; for the survey was only made because another inquiry into poverty earlier in the same year had certified 'a far greater number of poor in every parish than need to be relieved'.[44] The aldermen ordered a recount because they were determined to keep the number down. Two years before, in 1596, a third listing had produced the much larger figure of 4,015 poor households in the city. Many of the labouring poor were clearly included, and they probably comprised around 9 per cent of the inhabitants if there were three people in every poor household.[45] We might conclude that roughly 5 per cent of Londoners were dependent paupers at any one time, while at least 9 per cent could be counted as poor and might make demands on social welfare in crisis years.

These very speculative calculations receive powerful support from the records of other towns. We shall see in a later chapter that 4 or 5 per cent was commonly the proportion of urban populations granted poor relief in the later sixteenth and early seventeenth centuries.[46] In years of crisis, however, or in towns with particular problems, the number of people obviously in poverty was very much higher. A census of Stafford in the dearth year of 1622 described 25 per cent of the population as poor; 23 per cent of the population of Worcester were 'unprovided and poor' in 1646, after the destruction wrought by civil war; and 20 per cent of the population of Coventry has been estimated to be in serious poverty in the early 1520s.[47] The crisis level could go higher still. A listing taken in Sheffield in 1616 counted at least 20 per cent and perhaps as many as 33 per cent of the population as 'begging poor', and there were other householders who '(though they beg not) ... are not able to abide the storm of one fortnight's sickness but would be thereby driven to beggary'. When sickness in the form of plague hit Cambridge in 1630, 2,858 people – 36 per cent of the population – were thought to require relief.[48]

The weight of the evidence therefore suggests that 5 per cent was the normal background level of poverty in urban societies, and around 20 per cent the potential crisis level. These figures are consistent with estimates of the numbers of poor in continental towns at this time,[49] and (given the different kinds of community involved) with the proportions calculated for villages earlier in this chapter. One final point must be made about them, however. Although relatively constant, the line between the 5 per cent and the other 15 per cent was clearly maintained only with difficulty. We shall see in Chapter 8 that in some towns the proportion of the population on relief rose slightly after 1650, to 6 or 7 per cent, as institutional constraints were relaxed and as income from poor rates increased.[50] When we turn to the most detailed surviving censuses of the urban poor, we can see that the pressure to raise the 5 per cent threshold existed long before 1650.

CENSUSES OF THE POOR

Taking a census of the poor was a common practice in the late sixteenth and early seventeenth centuries. By 1601 there was even a printed guide on how the job should be done, describing the number of columns which should be used in the documents, and the information, from ages to occupations and earnings, they should contain.[51] Unfortunately, the results of only a few of the surveys which were ordered now survive. Some of them we have already referred to; others amount to little more than a list of paupers in small communities.[52] But there are six listings of the poor in towns which can usefully be compared with one another. Not all are as detailed as the model recommended in 1601, although each records the members of poor households throughout a town or a large part of it. They come from different places and were taken at different dates. Those who compiled them also had different definitions of poverty in mind, and found what they were looking for. Hence the documents describe overlapping but not identical segments of society. Taken together, however, they allow us to see urban poverty in more than one of its several dimensions.

The six censuses are listed in chronological order in Table 2. It is no accident that four of them were compiled in the major years of dearth and high prices between 1550 and 1640: 1557, 1587, 1597 and 1622. One of the exceptions, the Norwich census of 1570, was taken at the end of a long period of decline in the town's staple worsted industry. The Salisbury census of 1635 similarly came during a prolonged depression, this time in the broadcloth-weaving industry. All the listings were made in unusually harsh economic circumstances. Yet they defined very different proportions of the population as poor, from 5 per cent to more than 20 per cent. For purposes of discussion, they can best be ranked, not in chronological order, but according to the proportion of the population listed.

TABLE 2. Urban censuses of the poor, 1557–1635

Date	Place	No. of Poor	Poor households	Poor as proportion of total population
1557	Worcester	777	321	18%
1570	Norwich	2359	790	22%
1587	Warwick (St Mary's parish)	236	85	12%
1597	Ipswich (9 parishes)	410	120	13%
1622	Huddersfield	700	155	20–25%
1635	Salisbury (2 parishes)	250	109	5%

The narrowest in focus was that taken in two of the three parishes of Salisbury in 1635.[53] It described only the people receiving parish relief, but it recorded their ages, those of other members of their families, and some information about their earnings and occupations. Here, as in other towns at this time, 5 per cent of the population was receiving relief – the inescapable residuum of the urban poor. Above it, however, was a much larger group of labouring poor, as we can see from another document of the same year. A less detailed but more inclusive list of 'the poor' in the third parish in Salisbury contained no less than one third of its inhabitants.[54]

The Warwick survey of 1587, which recorded the names of roughly 12 per cent of the inhabitants of St. Mary's parish (much the larger of the two parishes in the town), was provoked by 'complaints ... touching the disorder of beggars'.[55] It concentrated on mendicants, therefore, but also noted other members of their families and something of their circumstances. Although only a little more than half of the poor in the census were given poor relief in 1587, there was clearly a general recognition of the much greater potential extent of poverty in Warwick at this time. Five years earlier, 11 per cent of the householders in the same parish were on relief, but many others, making the total up to almost 30 per cent, were described as 'ready to decay'.[56]

The Ipswich survey of 1597 covered nine of the twelve parishes in the town, and those compiling it were asked to list not only 'all impotent and lame persons not able to work' but also 'all other poor people'.[57] Like the Warwick census, it therefore included many who were not receiving poor relief as well as those who were: the latter group made up 4 per cent of the population of these parishes; the two groups together comprised 13 per cent of the population.

The proportion of the population contained in the Worcester census of 1557 was even larger, but it was not surveyed in similar detail. Only the names of heads of households, their wives and the number of their children were generally given, and even wives were sometimes omitted.[58] Again, however, the poverty line was broadly defined to take in the 'blind, lame, impotent, sick and those that are not able to get their livings without the charitable alms of the people'.

The most famous of these documents and the most valuable is the Norwich census of the poor of 1570.[59] It refers only to the English population of the town, and ignores the large community of foreign refugees – probably 5,000 of them in all – many of whom were also poor. But it lists 22 per cent of the English population and describes their households in some detail. Only a quarter of the families were receiving parish relief at the time of the census, although some of the rest were added to the list of pensioners later. Thus the Norwich census fully confirms what the other listings suggest: that while 5 per cent of the population of a town were on the dole at any moment, another 20 per cent or so might have a legitimate claim to relief in difficult times (even if they were not granted it) and would probably need public support at some point in their lives.

All these were well-established urban centres, old county towns, three of them cathedral cities. Salisbury, Norwich and Worcester were also ancient industrial centres, although only the last was still prospering. The woollen industry was equally important in Huddersfield, but in every other respect this was a very different kind of community. Scarcely a proper town at all yet, but certainly no longer a mere village, it was expanding rapidly in the early seventeenth century. The four 'townships' in the parish (all of them surveyed in 1622) were growing together to form one of those early industrial agglomerations like Halifax and Bradford which by the end of the century characterized the West Riding. Huddersfield in fact bridges the gap between the villages considered earlier and the mature towns like Norwich, and thus forms an important link in our chain of evidence. For in the dearth and depression of 1622 poverty was no less severe here than in Norwich. A list of the 'names of all the poor' included more than 20 per cent of the population.[60]

We can learn much more from the listings than simply the numbers of the poor, revealing though the numbers are. The unique value of the censuses lies in the light they throw on their social characteristics. The marital and family status of those listed is shown in outline in Table 3. We can see that many of the poor in each town were children. But there was not an excessive number of them. With one exception, the proportion ranged from 42 to 53 per cent, only a little higher than the proportion of children to be found in the population as a whole.[61] The exception was Huddersfield, where rapid demographic growth meant that 60 per cent of the poor were children still living at home. Elsewhere the proportion of children was kept down by the large number in another vulnerable group: single women, who were almost always widows or wives abandoned by their husbands. In this case, however, the proportion varied more between different censuses. When attention was restricted to the absolutely dependent poor, as it was in Salisbury, single women were twice as common as married women. As the

TABLE 3. The status of the poor

	Husbands + Wives	Spinsters/ Widows*	Bachelors/ Widowers	Children	Total
Salisbury 1635	58	68	9	115	250
Warwick 1587	64	49	11	112	236
Ipswich 1597	124	59	10	217	410
Worcester 1557	222	146	77	332	777
Norwich 1570	990	362	17	990	2359
Huddersfield 1622	228	38	15	419	700

*Includes deserted wives.

definition of poverty broadened, it encompassed more married couples, more 'normal' families, just as it did in the countryside.

This important point can be shown more clearly if we put the households and families in the censuses alongside those to be found in the whole population of a comparable community at this time. We can then see how in various respects poor households differed from households in society at large. A convenient control group for purposes of comparison is provided by the inhabitants of Ealing, who were listed in a census in 1599, and whose household structure seems to have been similar to that of other small towns at this time.[62] There are some difficulties involved in this procedure, not least because the 'households' of the poor have to be identified from the divisions made by the men taking the censuses. The precise nature of these blocks of people is not always clear, and in the less detailed listings cases where two unrelated individuals or even two nuclear families lived together may be concealed. Nevertheless, it seems unlikely that the basic characteristics of poor households shown in Table 4 were far from the reality; and they can be compared with the data for Ealing provided at the foot of each column.

The most interesting feature of the table is the way in which the averages and percentages gradually approach those of Ealing as one descends from the narrow to the more comprehensive censuses. Among the dependent and impotent poor, as in Salisbury, households were very small and rarely made up of complete nuclear families with a married couple at their head. Death and old age had already taken their toll. More than half the households consisted of single persons, usually widows, and some of the rest were also headed by women. Few had resident children. Where the definition of poverty was broader, however, as in Norwich, households were larger and solitary individuals less common, there were more than twice as many households headed by married couples, and more families had children living with them. Here

TABLE 4. Poor households

	Mean Household Size	Percentage of Households				Children per household where present
		with married heads	with female heads	consisting of solitary persons	with children	
Salisbury	2.3	26.6	62.4	55.0	37.6	2.8
Warwick	2.8	37.6	50.6	30.6	55.6	2.4
Ipswich	3.4	50.8	43.3	15.8	71.7	2.5
Worcester	2.4	34.3	41.4	50.2	38.6	2.7
Norwich	3.0	62.0	36.1	21.5	56.3	2.2
Huddersfield	4.5	73.5	18.1	1.9	85.2	3.2
(Ealing 1599)	(4.75)	(71.0)	(18.0)	(12.0)	(71.8)	(2.4)

the broken families, which were a major cause of pauperization, were vastly outnumbered by the households of the labouring poor.

There are two exceptions to this tidy and revealing progression, to warn us that local variations could be important. The poor of Huddersfield were in many ways unlike those in other towns. In some respects indeed their households were even less 'abnormal' than those in Ealing. Thus there were even fewer solitaries in Huddersfield than in Ealing and far more families with children. This was another sign of the booming population of the West Riding town, which must have contained many immigrants with growing families and very few old people. Worcester is the other town whose poor seem from the table to have been somewhat unusual. Although relatively few households were headed by women, fewer still were headed by married couples and there were, as Table 3 shows, many single men in the listing. Whether this was because wives were simply omitted from the document more often than appears at first sight, or whether there were in fact large numbers of unmarried labourers in this industrial town, it is impossible to say. What is clear is that while the precise character of poverty might vary to some degree with the economy of the community concerned, it was determined much more by the definition of poverty employed. Once the peculiar territory of the impotent had been left behind, the labouring poor shaded imperceptibly into the whole population.

The range of characters and circumstances revealed in these documents is therefore wide. At base were the old and the sick, often living alone. There was Dorothy Bird in Salisbury, 'her husband gone from her and she very sick', or the 'impotent and foolish' woman in Warwick, also deserted by her husband, who now lived with her brother. In some families misfortunes came thick and fast. In Warwick again there was Dorothy Story, aged 80, 'blind and lame', with her daughter Margaret, also lame, whose husband had left town. But there were also ordinary families, like that of Rowland Broune, an Ipswich labourer, who needed fuel and clothing from the parish because his wife could not supplement their earnings: 'she doth nothing but tend to her children'. There was William Tyner of Warwick, aged 50, whose wife and three children all had to go out begging. Commonplace families such as these, and there were many like them in Norwich and Huddersfield, were classed among the dependent poor in English towns by 1600.

That is not to say, however, that they were permanently poor. Five years before the Warwick census, William Tyner, to whom we have just referred, had been classed not as poor but as 'ready to decay'. So had twelve other householders who were among the begging poor by 1587. There were even 11 families well able to maintain themselves in 1582 who were impoverished by 1587.[63] Some of them may have been able to scramble their way back to self-sufficiency again when prices fell. People were also more or less liable to be dependent at different stages in their lives, as Seebohm Rowntree showed in the case of York in 1899;[64] and the life-cycle was no less important in early modern England. Table 5 shows the proportions in various age groups in the listings which contain this information, and alongside them comparable figures from Ealing, so that we can see where the ages of the poor differ from the age distribution of a more normal population.

The heavy incidence of poverty among the very old and the very young emerges most clearly. The ages up to 10 and over 59 included between them more than 40 per cent of the poor, compared with less than 30 per cent of the population of Ealing. The elderly were much more common than in Ealing, and the proportions under 10 would also be considerably larger if they included the several 'young children' whose ages were unspecified. People aged between 10 and 30 were under-represented among the poor, as we should expect in a society where children left home early to go into service and where marriage was relatively late.

More surprising are the relatively large proportions of the poor in their forties – an age at which Rowntree found the inhabitants of nineteenth-century York improving their condition as children left home. In part this is a result of distortion in the documents, for they tend to report people of middle age, perhaps including some in their late thirties, as '40'. But it also reflects the length of the child-rearing period in some of these families, where children were still being borne by mothers in their mid thirties. There were also cases of step-parents and grand-parents bringing up young children who were not their own. The responsibility for children did not disappear as quickly in the sixteenth century as Rowntree assumed it did in 1899. It seems that the only ages at which ordinary people could count on being economically secure, and at which those brought up in poverty might hope to escape it, came between 10 and 30 or 35.[65]

It will be clear by now that there can be no simple or generally valid summary of the main causes of poverty in early modern towns. Even the

TABLE 5. Ages of the poor (percentage distribution)

Age Group	Salisbury (n. 250)	Warwick (n. 236)	Ipswich (n. 410)	Norwich (n. 2,359)	(Ealing) (n. 427)
0–9	17.6	25.0	28.5	24.8	(20.6)
10–19	14.8	17.4	19.3	10.0	(28.8)
20–9	2.0	2.1	3.7	7.2	(13.4)
30–9	5.2	3.4	7.6	11.5	(12.7)
40–9	10.4	8.9	10.0	14.6	(7.0)
50–9	5.6	8.1	10.0	8.4	(10.5)
60 and over	30.8	23.3	14.6	14.0	(7.0)
unspecified	13.6	11.9	6.3	9.6	—
Total	100.0	100.1	100.0	100.1	100.0

censuses provide insufficient information, since they describe a state rather than a process. We cannot investigate in any depth, as Rowntree did, the role of such variables as low wages, large families and unemployment, in putting the poor where they were. The best we can do is to take two of the more detailed of the surveys, those compiled in Norwich and Salisbury, and to pick out the most obvious cause of impoverishment in the case of each family. The result is an oversimplification of a complex situation: families often had more than one disadvantage to contend with. But the chief misfortunes and the proportion of families affected by them (shown in Fig. 1) tell us something about the origins of poverty in two concrete instances.[66]

As one might expect from the nature of the two censuses, the relative importance of different causes of poverty varied between the two towns. Salisbury's is the simplest case. The concentration on the impotent poor is evident from the fact that 80 per cent of households were on relief either because of old age (over 65) or illness, or because of the death of a wage-earner or the absence of a father. Even in Norwich, however,

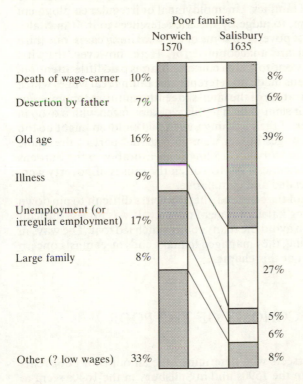

FIGURE 1. The causes of Poverty in Norwich (1570) and Salisbury (1635)

79

where the poverty line in the census was set much higher, age, illness or accident played a major part in determining who fell below it.

The absence of a father was the critical circumstance in those cases, one sixth of the total, where a mother and young children were alone. Either the father had died, or run away, or – in a few cases – he was in gaol. As a result, as many as one fifth of the children in the Norwich census (compared with one third in Salisbury) were in effect orphans; and an unknown number of others were no doubt living with step-parents. In another quarter of families poverty was apparently the result either of the illness or the old age of a breadwinner. Thus a surprisingly high proportion of the Norwich families, 42 per cent in all, could be described as in one way or another 'impotent', although less than half of them were actually receiving poor relief.

The other 58 per cent were the victims of economic circumstances rather than of accident or personal misfortune. Obviously large families were rarely responsible for poverty, despite what one might expect from demographic trends.[67] The situation may have been different in Huddersfield, but in Norwich very few parents had more than three children living with them, and this was apparently the crucial factor in less than one tenth of families. Unemployment or irregular employment was twice as common, to judge by specific references to it. It may also have been the cause of poverty in some of the remaining cases, one third of the whole, which are unaccounted for. Here, however, the vital element was probably one to which contemporaries paid little attention, and to which the census made no reference: the falling real wages which were a fundamental feature of the later-sixteenth-century economy. For unskilled labourers or semi-skilled textile workers, faced with a drop in the purchasing power of their earnings, even two children might be too large a family. Low wages in fact were an essential part of the whole structure of poverty in Norwich, adding immeasurably to the burdens caused by death and sickness. All too often the causes of poverty were not single but interrelated and cumulative.

Even with the help of the censuses, therefore, it is difficult to pin down and isolate the shifting kaleidoscope of poverty. It was no less difficult for contemporaries to avoid the many roads which led to it. The ways in which, notwithstanding, they managed to make ends meet must concern us in the final section of this chapter.

THE FAMILY ECONOMY OF THE POOR

The justices and overseers who determined the amounts of poor relief paid out in Ipswich in the 1590s and in Salisbury in the 1630s seem to have had a rough rule of thumb in mind. At both dates, despite the rate of inflation between them, they appear to have assumed that 8d. to 1s. a week was the cost of subsistence for an adult, and 4d. to 6d. a week for a child; and they used the dole to bring family incomes up to at least that level. Since they were often more generous to particularly deserving cases, it would not be extravagant to conclude that the minimum necessary income for an average poor family in one of the censuses was 2s. a week. Earned incomes certainly fell below this level. Poor families in Salisbury in 1635 earned on average only 9d.; and in Ipswich, where the definition of poverty was broader, the average was 1s. 10d. Their penury was certain and apparently measurable. Yet these averages obscure the necessarily elastic domestic economy of the poor. They lived in a world of changing circumstances and desperate makeshifts, not one of fixed predictable quantities.

On the expenditure side, the basic variable was the cost of food and drink. Since this might rise by as much as fifty per cent in a single year when the harvest failed, it could totally exhaust family incomes. There was some room for manoeuvre, especially for workers who were fed by their employers, like William Hall of Salisbury, who earned 20d. a week 'and his diet'. This did not apply, however, to the unemployed, or to the large numbers who were self-employed, working in their own homes as weavers or spinners or carpenters. They could switch to cheaper qualities of bread and beer when prices rose, but the opportunities for saving here were strictly limited, and the limits must often have been reached. The poor in Gloucestershire in 1586 who were 'driven to feed their children with cats, dogs and the roots of nettles' may have been exceptional; but there must have been many like the pauper in Eccleshall, Staffordshire in the 1690s whose 'common dinner is only bread and water'.[68] The cost of subsistence must often have pre-empted any other form of expenditure in years of dearth.

Chief among these other costs was housing. Here again aspirations and commitments varied widely. Even in the poorest parishes there were gradations of comfort. Simplest of all were opportunities for squatters, in sheds at the back of tenements, or, as in Norwich, in towers in the town walls. Many of the poor, a quarter of those listed in Warwick in 1587, were lodgers or inmates, renting rooms in the houses of others. Some managed to rent whole houses and the more ambitious sought to buy their own property. Eight per cent of the poor families in Norwich in 1570 were owner-occupiers. In hard times, however, it was inevitable that savings would be made first in housing. Rent fell into arrears, and tenants were evicted.[69] Owner-occupiers were unable to complete their purchase or were forced to mortgage property they had bought or inherited in better times. Some of the Norwich poor still owed £5 or £6 for their houses and others had mortgage debts. John Harrison, for example, had abandoned his wife, leaving her with six children, two servants and her bed-ridden mother to support: the house was 'in mortgage' and its inmates 'very poor'.

The Norwich census shows that it would be inaccurate to paint a uniformly dismal picture of housing conditions in the poor neighbourhoods of sixteenth-century towns.[70] Overcrowding was less common than might have been supposed, partly because the population of the town had grown little in the fifty years before 1570. On average there were only five people to a house, and rather fewer where the poor were owner-occupiers. The omens for the future were not favourable, however. In the next sixty years the population of Norwich expanded without any considerable new building, and at the time of the census there was already evidence of the exploitation to come. One third of the houses of the poor were owned by aldermen and councillors, and tenants had been packed tight in some of them. One councillor had eleven families, comprising 34 people, in one building. Another, Henry Shipdam, had a house in which there were, amongst others, two old women, one of them a 'scold', a deserted wife, a one-legged hatter and his children, and an unemployed brewer, who was in bed with a whore when the surveyor called. We do not know how much councillors pocketed privately in rents, while they complained vociferously in public about exactly this sort of inmate; but it is difficult to believe that they were not aware of their own interests when poor relief was paid out. By the 1630s, £1 a year was the common rent for one room in parts of East Anglia, and some inmates took in pauper children in order to get parish funds with which to pay it.[71]

Adequate housing was not the only requirement of the respectable poor. If their children were to have any future, they needed education in some trade or skill. A few children in Ipswich, Norwich and Salisbury were at school, sometimes specified as a 'knitting school', which could cost as much as 6d. a week per child. For the larger number who taught their own children at home, capital was needed for tools, such as a spinning wheel, and for materials to work with. Again, however, a food crisis or depression prevented even rudimentary capital accumulation and made future recovery impossible, as tools and other household goods were pawned. In 1597 many of the poor in Ipswich were said to be in need of 'wheels', 'cards' or 'teaching', as well as other basic essentials such as 'firing', 'clothing' and 'bedding'. When opportunities for saving were so slight, it is not surprising that some of the poor resorted in good times to the alehouse, and drank while the sun shone.

In order to pay their way, poor families needed as many sources of income as there were items of expenditure. By definition very few of the poor in the listings could survive solely on the wages of the head of the family. The most affluent workers in the Salisbury and Ipswich surveys were weavers earning 3s. a week, but they were few and far between. Average wages for poor men were only 2s. in Ipswich and 1s. 2d. in Salisbury. Women and children therefore worked whenever they could, women in textile trades, spinning or birling or at housework, 'drudging' as it was described in one case. Children from the ages of seven or eight helped their mothers or fathers. A woman or a child earned on average 8d. or 9d. a week in Ipswich and Salisbury, and two of them together could thus double the family income if the father was employed. More often, of course, they replaced his earnings when he was sick, or absent, or dead.

Where employment was not available for women and children, other shifts were necessary. Some women were prostitutes, but not, it would appear, very many, unless the more successful of them escaped detection. The Norwich census uncovered only eleven harlots: four of them were literally spinsters, taking to the streets to supplement their meagre earnings; one had a lame old father to support. More women probably went out begging, though again the shame involved helped to guarantee that they were a minority.[72] The hostile reaction of those in authority, exemplified in the Warwick census of 1587, may also have had an impact on adult mendicity, at any rate in small, well-policed towns: only one of the Salisbury poor was said to be a beggar. The sanctions of shame and punishment did not apply to children, however, and they were a common sight in the streets throughout the period. In Ipswich two children aged six and three were sent out begging in 1597 in order to add to the 6d. a week which their mother earned by spinning. Since the father was unemployed, the family could not have survived without the alms the children got from passers-by.

The approved alternative to beggary was the weekly dole, financed by the poor rate. From the beginning it provided supplementation for inadequate wages, and by the middle of the seventeenth century outdoor relief made an important contribution to family incomes. It was a gradual process, however. In Norwich the average weekly amount given to families on relief in 1570 was only 3d. although it had reached 8½d. in Ipswich by 1597 and attained the same level in Salisbury by 1635. There was always heavy discrimination in favour of the impotent poor, for whom the dole was sometimes the major, though rarely the only, source of income.[73] For the labouring poor, if they were lucky enough to receive it, poor relief seldom amounted to a third of their total income.

At least as important was mutual aid, the reciprocal exchange of services and support. Some families took in lodgers who may have contributed something to the domestic labour force as well as paying rent. They were present in twenty households in Norwich; and while a few were unmarried labourers, others were undoubted paupers themselves, like 'Alice Live-by-Love', a widow who wove lace. Five families looked after orphan children, and probably received extra poor relief in return. One family of four, in which the mother was sick, had taken in a woman deserted by her husband; she probably helped with the children. Another couple found room for a pregnant girl, fresh from service in the country, who helped the wife to spin. Neighbours also helped one another. The daughters of the one-legged hatter in Henry Shipdam's house were taught spinning by a widow living next door.

Money changed hands no doubt, but there was more than economic calculation in such transactions, just as there was more than a monetary reward for those several women in Norwich (one or two of them perhaps midwives) who were said to 'help other women in need' or to 'help neighbours at need'. Neighbourhood meant something more than mere proximity in the poorer quarters of sixteenth-century towns.

Special interest attaches to the way in which the poor treated their kin, and particularly their elderly parents. It might be thought that they had little incentive to undertake responsibility for relatives outside the nuclear family, once there was the safety net of poor relief; and little opportunity in the mobile society of early modern England. In fact, the evidence points both ways, suggesting that poverty sometimes strengthened kinship ties and sometimes ruptured them. The poor law was itself notably ambivalent on the subject. According to the Poor-Relief Act of 1601, grandparents, parents and children were obliged to support one another.[74] Consequently, there are cases of grandparents being compelled to take in grandchildren; and of children being forced to contribute weekly pensions to their aged parents.[75] At the same time, however, the poor law authorities were equally concerned to avoid new burdens on the parish, and that set them against people who housed impoverished relations coming from elsewhere. In Norwich John Hollins and his wife had given lodging to John's mother shortly before the census was taken; and Edward Thornton and his wife had taken in their daughter and son-in-law when they came to town. Both households were identified so that the newcomers could be expelled. Similarly, a poor husbandman in Wiltshire who lodged his father- and mother-in-law 'out of his charity' was persuaded to 'quietly put them away'.[76] For what it is worth, overseers and justices seem as often to have found it necessary to prevent the fulfilment of family obligations as to insist upon them.

Yet as far as the old were concerned, obligations did not normally extend very far. Children were not expected to *house* their parents, if they had already established separate households. Indeed, they could rarely afford to do so, since at the time their parents needed support they very often had dependent children of their own.[77] The division of households was accepted, and parents were assumed to have made their own arrangements for their old age. When their dispositions failed, the parish stepped in. They got alms from the parish collection, a dole from the poor rate, or, if they were lucky, a place in an almshouse. In the later seventeenth century, the old were sometimes encouraged to make over their own houses to the parish, in return for a weekly allowance. As a result, poor relief was very often given to people who had adult children still alive; and expectations and norms may not have been very different from those in the modern world of pensions and old-people's homes. Generally speaking, it was the community not the family which supported the elderly in early modern England, and, despite the letter of the 1601 Act, the machinery of poor relief reinforced the pattern.[78]

A lonely old age was therefore the lot of most of the labouring poor. Of the households in the Norwich census, 22 per cent comprised solitary individuals, many of them over 60. Only 2 per cent spanned three generations, and another seven families had grandparents living separately, in their own 'house room', under the same roof. It is notable also that several of the small minority of unusually composed households in Norwich were the product of necessity as much as sentiment. They were the result of a determined attempt to patch together viable economic units. When John Tittle was very sick and unable to work, his mother lived with him, adding her income as a spinster to that of his wife, and helping to look after the children. In three-generation households the grandparents seem often to have taken care of young children, while the mother made the most of her earning power. If the ages given in the censuses are to be believed, viable households were also created by marriages between people of very disparate ages. In Norwich there were at least four women with young children who were married to men more than forty years their senior, replacements no doubt for dead spouses. Conversely, two young men in Ipswich were married to women twenty years older than they were, and again there were young children to support.[79]

It would be absurdly patronizing to assume that only economic ties held such families together, of course, but it would be equally absurd to romanticize the virtues of the poor. The records simply show ordinary people struggling to do what they could in difficult circumstances and within the limits set by contemporary norms of behaviour. Both sides of the coin are exemplified in the case of Widow Manning. When her daughter and grandchildren were deserted by her son-in-law in Salisbury in 1634, she offered to take them in. She knew enough about the machinery of poor relief to ask for some financial help from the Salisbury overseers in return; but there is no reason to disbelieve her when she claimed that 'motherly love' prompted her to 'suffer in her old age and bear some part of her daughter's misery and poverty, though she suffer herself'.[80] Even through the dry annals of the poor there appears a sensibility and a hard sense, which alike command respect.

The records used in this chapter contradict some of the facile assumptions which contemporaries made about the poor of their own towns. The picture which the instigators of the Norwich census drew – of idle, filthy beggars, wasting their income on drink, sleeping in doorways, and producing bastards – bore little relation to the facts revealed by the census itself.[81] There was another side to the problem: the beggars and vagrants in the streets of London and Warwick, of whom we shall see more in a moment. But what the listings of the resident poor show are people desperately striving to maintain respectability. When the economic cards were so heavily stacked against them, it is remarkable not that so many, but that so few gave up the struggle altogether.

NOTES AND REFERENCES

1. **F. G. Emmison,** 'The Care of the Poor in Elizabethan Essex', *Essex Review*, lxii (1953), 10; *idem*, 'Poor-relief Accounts of two rural parishes in Bedfordshire 1563–98', *Econ. Hist. Rev.*, iii (1931), 106.
2. Bodl., MS. D.D.Par. Wheatley, b.5.
3. *Records of Maidstone* (Maidstone, 1926), p. 256.
4. **A. Macfarlane** (ed.), *The Diary of Ralph Josselin 1616–1683* (British Academy, Records of Social and Economic History, new series, iii, 1976), pp. 332, 590, 375, 411.
5. Lancs. RO, UDCr 18; Lichfield RO, B/A/21; **D. G. Hey,** *An English Rural Community. Myddle under the Tudors and Stuarts* (Leicester UP, 1974), p. 177.
6. **B. Clarke,** 'Norfolk Licences to Beg: an unpublished collection', *Norfolk Archaeology*, xxxv (1970–73), 331–2.
7. 31 Eliz. I, c.7; PRO, Asz 24/20, f. 108r; **B. H. Cunnington** (ed.), *Records of the County of Wiltshire* (Devizes, 1932), p. 178; Essex RO, Q/SBa 2/105, Epiph. 1665/6. Cf. **W. Hunt,** *The Puritan Moment. The Coming of Revolution in an English County* (Harvard UP, Cambridge, Mass., 1983), p. 71.
8. *Records of Wiltshire*, p. 31; PRO, SP 16/329/10. Cf. Essex RO, Q/SR 111/51; *Records of Wiltshire*, p. 102; Wilts RO, Q.S. Minute Book 1598–1604, p. 41; PRO, SP 16/310/104; 39 Eliz. I, c.3, sect. v.
9. **Hunt,** *Puritan Moment*, pp. 42–3; Essex RO, Q/SR 136/82; **J. W. Willis Bund** (ed.), *Worcester County Records. Quarter Sessions Rolls 1591–1643*, pt. 1 (Worcs Hist. Soc., 1899), p. 229.
10. *Diary of Josselin*, pp. 135, 237.
11. **D. Dymond,** 'The famine of 1527 in Essex', *Local Population Studies*, 26 (1981), 32. Cf. **C. Phythian-Adams,** *Desolation of a City. Coventry and the Urban Crisis of the Late Middle Ages* (Cambridge UP, 1979), p. 59; below, pp. 117, 139–48.
12. Norfolk and Norwich RO, PRA 652, 653 (382 x 8).
13. Staffs RO, Sutherland MSS., D593/S/4/14/12, 13.
14. BL, Add. MS. 33511, ff. 299–300 (I owe this reference to Peter Clark).
15. Hants RO, J. L. Jervoise, Herriard Coll., 44M69/012.
16. *Ibid.*
17. Staffs RO, D593/S/4/55/1. Cf. **P. Clark,** *English Provincial Society from the Reformation to the Revolution* (Harvester, Hassocks, 1977), pp. 230–41.
18. **Hunt,** *Puritan Moment*, p. 68; Essex RO, D/DBa 08/1–5.
19. Lancs RO, UDCr 18.
20. Staffs RO, D593/S/4/55/1.
21. They appear not to have affected Myddle, for example, until well into the 17th century: **Hey,** *English Rural Community*, pp. 7–10, 42, 48, 177–8.
22. Cf. **Emmison,** 'Poor-relief Accounts', pp. 110–12.
23. London Corporation RO, Repertory 18, ff. 148v–149.
24. **M. D. Harris** (ed.), *The Coventry Leet Book*, pt. iii (Early English Text Soc., o.s., 138, 1909), pp. 652, 658. Cf. **Phythian-Adams,** *Desolation of a City*, p. 64 and *passim*; below, pp. 116–17.

25. F. F. Fox (ed.), *Some Account of the Guild of Weavers in Bristol* (Bristol, 1889), p. 51; HMC, *Various*, i. 75; HMC, *9th Report*, App., p. 319.

26. 35 Eliz. I, c. 6; F. J. C. Hearnshaw (ed.), *Southampton Court Leet Records* (Southampton Record Soc., 1905–8), ii. 386. For earlier examples, see *ibid.*, iii. 236, 298; J. P. Earwaker (ed.), *Court Leet Records of the Manor of Manchester* (Manchester, 1884–8), i. 197; W. H. Stevenson (ed.), *Records of the Borough of Nottingham* (Nottingham, 1882–1914), iv. 191; R. Savage (ed.), *Minutes and Accounts of the Corporation of Stratford-upon-Avon,* vol. i (Dugdale Soc., i, 1921), p. 80.

27. P. and J. Clark, 'The Social Economy of the Canterbury Suburbs: the Evidence of the Census of 1563', in A. Detsicas and N. Yates (eds), *Studies in Modern Kentish History presented to F. Hull and E. Melling* (Kent Arch. Soc., Maidstone, 1983), p. 74; below, p. 82.

28. *Records of Nottingham*, iv. 305–7, 311–15, 381; S. Bond (ed), *The Chamber Order Book of Worcester 1602–50* (Worcs Hist. Soc., viii, 1974), p. 103; Chester Corporation Records, QSF/S2/30–4; *Court Leet Records of Manchester*, ii. 288–9.

29. H. Raine, 'Christopher Fawsett against the Inmates', *Surrey Arch. Coll.*, lxvi (1969), 79–85; N. Goose, 'Household size and structure in early-Stuart Cambridge', *Social History*, 5 (1980), 349–57, 379–80; Oxford Corporation Records, 0.5.9, pp. 76, 78, 279, 201–2; *Acts of the Privy Council 1625–6*, pp. 303–4.

30. Oxford Corporation Records, 0.5.9, p. 88; 0.5.11, f. 3v; M. Prior, *Fisher Row* (Oxford UP, 1982), Ch. 1.

31. P. Slack, *The Impact of Plague in Tudor and Stuart England* (Routledge and Kegan Paul, 1985), Ch. 5; I. Roy and S. Porter, 'The social and economic structure of an early modern suburb: the Tything at Worcester', *Bull. Inst. Hist. Res.*, liii (1980), 203–17; Goose, 'Household size', *passim;* Clark, 'Social Economy of the Canterbury Suburbs', *passim.*

32. P. Slack (ed.), *Poverty in Early-Stuart Salisbury* (Wilts Record Soc., xxxi, 1975), pp. 75, 105, 107, 125.

33. London Corporation RO, Journal 15, f. 203; R. H. Tawney and E. Power (eds), *Tudor Economic Documents* (Longmans, Green and Co., 1924), iii. 426.

34. St Bartholomew's Hospital, Minutes of the Board of Governors, 1549–61, ff. 6r, 93r, 120, 1567–86, f. 78v; Greater London Council RO, H1/ST/A1/1, f. 77r, A1/4, f. 178r. For the origins of the hospitals, see below, pp. 119–21.

35. Calculated from the annual totals in Guildhall Library, London, MS. 12818/2, f. 22r and *passim*. The numbers dying were not separately given in the annual summaries after 1575. On infant mortality in the hospital, see C. Cunningham, 'Christ's Hospital: Infant and Child Mortality in the Sixteenth Century', *Local Population Studies*, 18 (1977), 37–40.

36. These instances come from the extracts from Bridewell Court Books printed in *Under the Dome*, vols xi and xii (London, 1902–3).

37. Guildhall Library, MS. 12818/2, ff. 22r *et seq.* (Christ's Hospital); St Bartholomew's Hospital, Ledger of the Treasurers 1547–61, 1549–50 account, and Minutes of Board of Governors, 1586–1607, f. 27r; Greater London Council RO, H1/ST/A1/1, A1/3, Governors Minute Books (St Thomas's); A. L. Beier, 'Social Problems in Elizabethan London', *J. Interdisciplinary Hist.*, ix (1978), 204 n. 3.

38. The 1610 figures are in **T.S.**, *A Psalme of thanksgiving, to be sung by the children of Christ's Hospitall* (1610); the others have been taken from **E. S. De Beer**, 'The London Hospitals in the Seventeenth Century', *Notes and Queries*, 177(1939), 362.

39. For the population of the City and Liberties, see **R. Finlay**, *Population and Metropolis* (Cambridge UP, 1981), pp. 9, 155.

40. London Corporation RO, Journal 35, f. 269r; Guildhall Library, MS. 12806/2, 18 Oct. 1563; St Bartholomew's Hospital, Minutes of the Board of Governors, 1586–1607, ff. 118r, 113r, 82v; **E. G. O'Donoghue**, *Bridewell Hospital, Palace, Prison, Schools* (Bodley Head, 1929), ii. 18; **T. C. Dale**, *The Inhabitants of London in 1638* (Society of Genealogists, 1931), pp. 201, 238.

41. *Tudor Economic Documents*, iii. 418. I assume the population of the City to have been 75,000.

42. **R. W. Herlan**, 'Poor Relief in London during the English Revolution', *J. British Studies*, xviii (1979), p. 41 and note 27.

43. London Corporation RO, Journal 24, ff. 322–3. For the doubling of the total to include families, see below, pp. 76, 173–4. I have assumed the population of the City to be 140,000 at this date (**Finlay**, *Population and Metropolis*, p. 155).

44. London Corporation RO, Journal 24, f. 306r. The results of this inquiry do not survive.

45. **M. J. Power**, 'London and the Control of the 'Crisis' of the 1590s', *History*, 70(1985), 375. Cf. Journal 24, f. 139r. For the size of the households of the labouring poor, see Table 4 below, p. 76.

46. Below, pp. 176–9.

47. **K. R. Adey**, 'Seventeenth-Century Stafford: A County Town in Decline', *Midland History*, ii (1974), 154, and *idem*, 'Aspects of the History of the Town of Stafford 1590–1710', Keele Univ., M.A. thesis, 1971, p. 8; **I. Roy** and **S. Porter**, 'The Population of Worcester in 1646', *Local Population Studies*, 28 (1982), 39; **Phythian-Adams**, *Desolation of a City*, p. 134.

48. **S. and B. Webb**, *The Old Poor Law* (Longman, Green and Co., 1927), pp. 82–3; **Goose**, 'Household size', pp. 353, 355. In the case of Sheffield, the proportion depends on whether the wives of householders were included in the original totals: if they were, the begging poor were 33 per cent of the population.

49. **P. Benedict**, *Rouen during the Wars of Religion* (Cambridge UP, 1981), pp. 10–11; **L. Martz**, *Poverty and Welfare in Habsburg Spain* (Cambridge UP, 1983), pp. 118–19; **Herlan**, 'Poor Relief in London', p. 42, note 33.

50. Below, pp. 176–7.

51. *An Ease for Overseers of the poore* (Cambridge, 1601), p. 4.

52. In addition to the six listings of the poor discussed below, the following may be noted: Crompton, Lancs, 1597 (above, note 19); Cawston, Norfolk, 1601 (discussed in **T. Wales**, 'Poverty, poor relief and the life-cycle: some evidence from seventeenth-century Norfolk', in **R. M. Smith** (ed.), *Land, Kinship and Life-Cycle* (Cambridge UP, 1984), pp. 351–404; part of Southwark, 1618 (Greater London Council RO, P92/SAV/1465); Thirsk 1630 (North Yorkshire RO, ZAG 282, f. 25r); and parts of Cambridge c. 1630 (Cambridge University Library, CUR 37.5, docs. 37–39, discussed in **Goose**, 'Household size'.) For surveys ordered for

which no returns survive, see **Clark**, 'Social Economy of the Canterbury Suburbs', p. 67; **Phythian-Adams**, *Desolation of a City*, p. 220.

53. Printed in **Slack**, *Poverty in Early-Stuart Salisbury*, pp. 75–80.

54. **Slack**, 'Poverty and Politics in Salisbury 1597–1666', in **P. Clark** and **P. Slack** (eds), *Crisis and Order in English Towns 1500–1700* (Routledge and Kegan Paul, 1972), p. 176.

55. Printed in **T. Kemp** (ed.), *The Book of John Fisher 1580–1588* (Warwick, n.d.), pp. 165–72. The census is dated May 1586 there, but it properly belongs to March 1587 according to A. L. Beier: 'The Social Problems of an Elizabethan Country Town: Warwick 1580–90', in **P. Clark** (ed.), *Country Towns in Pre-Industrial England* (Leicester UP, 1981), pp. 46–85. Dr. Beier discusses the census and its background in some detail. My figures in the tables below differ slightly from his, largely because I have excluded strangers and inmates who were subsequently sent away from the town.

56. **Beier**, 'Social Problems of ... Warwick', pp. 58–9, 77.

57. Printed in **J. Webb** (ed.), *Poor Relief in Elizabethan Ipswich* (Suffolk Records Soc., ix, 1966), pp. 122–40. The population of the nine parishes has been estimated from the total for 1603 and the proportions in 1664 given in **M. Reed**, 'Economic Structure and Change in Seventeenth-Century Ipswich', in **Clark** (ed.), *Country Towns*, pp. 92, 131.

58. The listing is in Worcester Corporation Archives, View of Frankpledge, vol. I, ff. 50–54v. It is clear that wives were not included by the surveyors in the parish of St Andrew. I have supplied them in my figures where they are obviously absent, but I may not have caught all of them. This accounts in part for the different totals given in **A. D. Dyer**, *Worcester in the Sixteenth Century* (Leicester UP, 1973), pp. 166–7. For the total population of Worcester, see *ibid.*, p. 26.

59. Printed in **J. F. Pound** (ed.), *The Norwich Census of the Poor 1570* (Norfolk Record Soc., xl, 1971). The English population of the city is estimated *ibid.*, p. 10.

60. The listing, dated 22 December 1622, is in Huddersfield Public Library. The population of the parish is uncertain, but the parish register (film in Huddersfield Public Library) suggests that it cannot have been more than 3,500 and it may have been much lower.

61. **P. Laslett** and **R. Wall** (eds), *Household and Family in Past Time* (Cambridge UP, 1972), p. 148.

62. Figures for Ealing have been taken from *ibid.*, pp. 74–85 and chapter 4, *passim*.

63. **Beier**, 'Social Problems of ... Warwick', p. 60.

64. **B. S. Rowntree**, *Poverty* (Macmillan, 1901), p. 137.

65. For a similar age-specific analysis of the censuses, see **R. M. Smith**, 'Some Issues Concerning Families and their Property', in **Smith**, *Land, Kinship and Life-Cycle*, pp. 73–8.

66. The categories in Figure 1 have been adapted from those used by **B. S. Rowntree**, *Poverty. A Study of Town Life* (Macmillan, 1901), pp. 120–1.

67. Cf. **C. Lis** and **H. Soly**, *Poverty and Capitalism in Pre-Industrial Europe* (Harvester, Hassocks, 1979), p. 91.

68. **W. B. Willcox**, *Gloucestershire. A Study in Local Government 1590–1640* (Yale UP, New Haven, 1940), p. 135; Lichfield RO, B/A/21.

69. For examples, see *Book of John Fisher*, pp. 15–20, 64–5.
70. For a full discussion, see **Pound,** *Norwich Census*, pp. 13–15.
71. Cambridge University Library, CUR 37.5, doc. 37; PRO, SP 16/310/104.
72. Cf. above, pp. 27–8, below, p. 192.
73. **Slack,** 'Poverty and Politics', p. 175. Cf. below, p. 179.
74. 43 Eliz. I, c. 2, sect. vii.
75. E.g. **D. H. Allen** (ed.), *Essex Quarter Sessions Order Book 1652–1661* (Essex County Council, Chelmsford, 1974), p. 24; Dorset RO, Dorchester Borough Records, B2/8/1, ff. 3r, 18v.
76. Wilts RO, Q.S. Roll, Easter 1636, petition on behalf of Richard Huntenford, Cf. *Essex Quarter Sessions Order Book 1652–61*, pp. 85, 94.
77. **R. M. Smith,** 'The Structured Dependence of the Elderly as a Recent Development: Some Sceptical Historical Thoughts', *Ageing and Society*, iv (1984).
78. Cf. **D. Thomson,** 'Welfare and the Historians', in **L. Bonfield, R. Smith** and **K. Wrightson** (eds), *The World We Have Gained* (Blackwell, Oxford, 1986), pp. 355–78, and for other comments on family ties among the poor, **Wales,** 'Poverty, poor relief and the life-cycle', *passim*; **M. Chaytor,** 'Household and Kinship: Ryton in the late 16th and early 17th centuries', *History Workshop*, x (1980), 38.
79. Cf. **K. Thomas,** 'Age and Authority in Early Modern England', *Proc. British Academy*, lxii (1976), 42 note.
80. *Poverty in Early-Stuart Salisbury*, p. 100.
81. *Tudor Economic Documents*, ii. 316–18.

Chapter 5

THE DANGEROUS POOR

Some of the poor did give up the struggle for respectability, either voluntarily or through necessity. They became vagabonds, took to a life of crime, and abused the conventions of polite society. The dangerous poor existed. Whether they were as dangerous as contemporaries supposed is another question, however. According to the sixteenth-century stereotype, the undeserving pauper was typically rootless, masterless and homeless – a vagrant. His behaviour was disorderly and criminal, that of a rogue. He might even be seen as a member of a deviant sub-culture, with a social hierarchy and norms of behaviour of its own. In order to complete our view of the poor, we must try to test the validity of this multiple indictment.

VAGRANTS AND VAGABONDS

'Vagrancy, at one time swelling, at another shrinking in volume, merges into a shifting and shiftless fringe of the population in such a way as to elude definition.' So concluded the Poor Law Commissioners of 1909, echoing both the Tudor theme of marginality, and the perennial problem of determining who the marginal poor were.[1] From the beginning there was gross imprecision in the law, which defined vagrancy as 'wandering' or 'loitering' and designated houses of correction for people who were 'idle' or 'disorderly'.[2] The result was confusion at the time, and it has left ample room for historical controversy and misconception since. Interpretations of vagrancy have ranged between two poles. On the one hand, vagrants have been seen as innocent hapless victims, culpable only because the law made mobility and unemployment criminal. On the other hand, they have been branded as a segment of society readily indulging in crimes of other kinds, especially petty theft.[3]

Neither of these approaches can be sustained without qualification, and the only way of identifying a sure path between them is to look more closely at the legal and administrative complexities which lie behind them. The important fact is that vagrancy legislation was discretionary. It cast a broad net which quite intentionally left opportunity for selective enforcement. It compelled justices and constables to discriminate when confronted by the large mass who might be caught by it, and they did so.[4] They certainly did not punish all poor wanderers as vagrants. Neither, on the other hand, did they punish as vagrants people who could be convicted of some other crime.

Only a small minority of migrants, and only a minority even of poor migrants, were whipped and sent back to their parish of birth or last residence with a vagrant's passport. Other kinds of settlement regulation were invoked against obviously respectable travellers. Sometimes they were allowed to remain in a town after giving sureties, or were expelled without punishment. Their names often occur in the same records as vagrants, but they were clearly thought to be distinct.[5] Other strangers were legally distinguishable from vagrants because they had obtained employment, or recently rented accommodation in a town, or had certificates to travel in search of work.[6] Less reputable wanderers were also allowed on their way without punishment, however. Constables' accounts show that less than one in ten of the migrants passing through a parish were usually whipped. The rest were given alms, 3d. or 4d., and even a night's lodging, provided they continued on their way. Some of them were vagrants carrying passes who had been punished elsewhere; but many were paupers who might in one way or another be regarded as deserving: licensed beggars, victims of fire, theft or the Irish rebellion, disabled children, maimed soldiers, or women looking for their husbands or with some other excuse for their mobility. Out of 321 'poor distressed travellers' dealt with by the constables of Coventry in the 1640s, only 12 were described as vagrants.[7]

At the same time, however, vagrants were not in any other respect proven criminals at the time of their punishment. If they had been, they would have been indicted and convicted for the more serious offence. They were often suspected, of course. In many cases that was why they were apprehended in the first place. More than half the poor strangers arrested and examined by magistrates in Warwick in the 1580s were alleged to have committed other criminal offences, although some of them were simply whipped as vagrants in the end.[8] It should be stressed also that poor strangers and wanderers, known vagabonds, were in actuality very often involved in crime. This fact can be underestimated because of the legal rule which prevented the description 'vagrant' being attached to people who were accused of other forms of crime before quarter sessions or assizes: they were termed 'labourers' or given no status designation at all. Recent research shows beyond doubt, however, that poor wanderers made a large contribution to criminality in early modern England.[9] It might seem reasonable to call such offenders vagrants. Yet there is much to be said for reserving the term for people who were convicted and punished for vagrancy alone, and not for any other crime. For these were the people for whom the offence was invented: suspicious persons in the middle ground between the deserving poor and the criminal fraternity. They were a sub-group among migrants; they were not – or not yet or not for certain – serious criminals. Theirs was a socially defined offence; and their characteristics and numbers tell us a good deal about contemporary attitudes to poverty and crime and about the realities.

Simple vagrancy, as we might call it, was thus as elastic in its way as deserving poverty. It lay equally in the eye of the beholder, the constable, overseer or justice of the peace. Its quantity is consequently no easier to measure, and no easier to interpret once measured; and different records show different facets of it. Contemporary estimates like that of William Harrison, who put the number of vagrants at over 10,000 in the 1570s, are probably worthless.[10] His view that the number of beggars and wandering rogues had been increasing over the past half-century has more to recommend it, given the economic and social trends described earlier. It is likely also that the number of people whose characteristics were such that they could be labelled as vagrants continued to increase into the early seventeenth century, and then declined in the later seventeenth century, as long-distance migration within England declined. But it is difficult to substantiate the suggestion. We do not have anything like complete figures of the total numbers punished, and in any case the numbers apprehended may tell us more about trends in enforcement of the law than about the phenomenon which was being attacked. There were certainly thousands rather than hundreds of vagrants to be found, however. In 1571–72, when special searches were organized in the aftermath of the Rising in the North, 742 of them were caught in 18 counties, most of them in the Midlands and the south-east.[11] Sixty years later, reports of local arrests made to the Privy Council recorded the punishment of nearly 25,000 vagrants in 32 English counties between 1631 and 1639.[12] That perhaps suggests some increase over the period.

The clearest evidence for a real growth in vagrancy – for an increase both in the number of people who were, and in the number who might be, thrust into that category – comes from London, from the records of Bridewell. The number of vagrants punished there rose from 69 a year in 1560–61, to 209 in 1578–79, 555 in 1600–01 and 815 in 1624–25: a growth-rate three times greater than that of the City's population as a whole. Still more persuasive is the fact that vagrancy came to overshadow other categories of offences punished at Bridewell. Intended as it was to 'punish sin', Bridewell dealt with all kinds of petty crime, and especially with sexual misdemeanours. In the early 1560s, therefore, only 16 per cent of all offenders were vagrants. After that, however, the proportion grew rapidly, reaching 62 per cent of the total in 1600–01 and then levelling off: it was 50 per cent in 1624–25.[13] It would be difficult to argue that this change was caused by an autonomous shift in attitude on the part of magistrates or constables. The proportion of sexual offenders declined, not because of any increase in official tolerance, but because of the crowds of rogues and wandering beggars left little time for anything else. Moreover, Bridewell dealt with only a small part of the problem in the capital. Large numbers of simple vagrants were summarily expelled by the parish authorities. In the 1630s 6,000 printed passports were being issued every year to constables in the City for this purpose.[14] Unfortunately, we do not know how many of them were used, or what the number had been earlier.

Quantitative estimates of vagrancy in the provinces are similarly bedevilled by the variety of ways in which vagrants could be punished. Until 1572 punishment was generally summary, at least for first offenders: often a stocking before 1531 but a whipping after the statute of that year.[15] It was undertaken by local authorities and is badly documented. After 1572 and until 1593 the law provided that vagrants were to be committed to gaol for indictment at sessions or assizes, where they could be sentenced to be whipped and bored through the ear. Although summary local punishment continued in some places, most vagrants are therefore to be found in the fragmentary surviving records for these courts: in gaol calendars, for example, and in the assize indictments for Essex, Hertfordshire and Sussex, where there were 324 of them between 1572 and 1603.[16] After 1593, however, a summary whipping by lesser authorities again became the general rule, and it was clearly enunciated in the 1598 Vagrancy Act. Only 'dangerous and incorrigible rogues' had to be presented before quarter sessions.[17] There were efforts to tighten up the machinery in some counties by employing special paid officials, called provost marshals, of whose activity little record survives.[18] But for the most part, the execution of the law was left to parish constables, under the more or less watchful eye of magistrates, whether in towns or in their county divisions.

The best records of simple vagrancy after 1598 are therefore to be found at the level of local summary jurisdiction, in the town, parish or county-divisional lists of people punished and sent home with a passport. They start too late to document the probable rise in the number of potentially suspicious wanderers before 1598; and they end too soon – generally in or before the 1660s – to tell us anything about its likely decline. But a sample of 3,000 vagrants drawn from these sources shows something of the nature of the problem as it was seen in the early seventeenth century, when it may well have been at its worst.[19]

The vagrant's most obvious characteristic was his long-term and often long-distance mobility. He was certainly homeless, though not necessarily rootless. He often knew the roads of England like the back of his hand, and sometimes he had a regular itinerary between temporary bases. Edward Yovell, for example, a vagrant taken in Salisbury, had been born in London and begun wandering after ending an apprenticeship in Worcester. Twice in two years he took up casual work back in London, where he had friends, then helped with the harvest at his uncle's in Surrey, next worked at various inns in Chichester, and finally returned to Worcester via Salisbury, Bristol and Gloucester, where he might hope for casual work or charity.[20] Other vagrants had a single destination in view. Yovell's companion suggested they might break their circuit through the rich southern counties and go to 'Andover and from Andover to Newbury and from Newbury to Oxon and from Oxford directly to York', to pastures new.

In the case of most vagrants, however, we can determine only two points in their journey: their place of punishment and the birth- or dwelling-place to which they were returned. The distance between these two points, measured in a straight line, is clearly only the crudest indicator of distance actually moved; but it does show that vagrants were more mobile than other migrants. Studies of apprentices and of deponents in ecclesiastical courts suggest that a large majority of them moved less than 40 miles.[21] By contrast, of the vagrants in our sample whose place of origin can be determined, 50 per cent had travelled more than 40 miles and 22 per cent had gone more than 100 miles. Although the majority had moved less than 50 miles and the median distance was rather less than 45 miles, substantial numbers of them had wider geographical horizons than other mobile groups in the population.

Some of the reasons for their mobility appear from chronological and geographical variations in the incidence of vagrancy. Numbers fluctuated from month to month and year to year in predictable ways. There were peaks in March and October, because vagrants began to move in the spring, found agricultural work in the summer, and were then on the move again, looking for a berth for the winter, usually in a town. The rhythms of the agricultural year dictated seasonal unemployment and mobility. The harvest was also instrumental when it failed. Local distress sent labourers and their families off to the nearest town, to beg and join long-distance vagabonds on constables' lists. Everywhere the number of poor wanderers arrested was greatest in years of dearth: in 1598 and 1630 in Salisbury, in 1631 and 1648 in Colchester, in 1623, 1631 and 1661 in Exeter.[22]

Some local economies produced more vagrants than others. Many of those found in Salisbury, for example, came from the wood-pasture area on the Wiltshire-Somerset border, where there were rural industries, burgeoning populations and sporadic unemployment. For the long-distance vagabond, however, experience of urban life seems to have been crucial. The further a vagrant had moved, the more likely he was to have come from an urban environment, although he might not have been born there. The typical background to vagrancy seems to have been short-distance movement to a town, temporary employment there, and then further movement to other towns, generally in the direction of London.

The rich Home Counties exercised an understandable attraction. Overall, despite the regular circuits of some wanderers, there was a dominant stream of migration from the highlands to the lowlands, and towards the south-east. If we look only at vagrants who had moved some distance, more of those found in Salisbury had come from the west than from the east, a majority of those taken in Lancashire were from places further north, and there was a southward flow through Colchester. Not all of them were intending to move as far as London itself, of course, and some who arrived there soon returned. There was a contrary movement away from the south-east. But provincial records plainly show why places round London, like Southwark, St Giles in the Fields, Blackheath and Stepney, and the main roads south through Hertfordshire and north-east through Hampshire and Surrey, were pestered with them. A fictitious sermon in praise of rogues was delivered, appropriately, at Hartley Row, alongside the main highway from Salisbury to London.[23]

The origins of the vagrant's exceptional mobility in the 'push' and 'pull' factors built into the economic fabric of early modern England are intelligible enough, therefore; and the consequence for individuals was often weeks, months or even years on the road and the acquisition, in the end, of some of the other characteristics which marked the vagabond. Humphrey Reade and his wife, taken in Salisbury in 1610, had no 'certain place of dwelling and have wandered many years'. Anne Standley had been wandering for a year and 'hath received punishment three times before this time'. Others had been following the progress of the Court or moving from fair to fair for months. It is not surprising that a few had turned to the traditional wayfaring skills of popular entertainers. Among the Salisbury vagrants were a fortune-teller, a minstrel, a morris-dancer and two conjurors. An old harper was found in Maldon, Essex, in 1634: once employed in a noble household, he now wandered from fair to fair with his apprentice, and got 'money at divers men's houses of worth ... by the use of his harping'.[24]

There were also a few who fitted the categories of professional beggar described by Thomas Harman and other Tudor pamphleteers. There were 'counterfeit Bedlams' and a counterfeit cripple in Hertfordshire. One of the Salisbury vagrants was a 'Dummerer', pretending 'he hath no tongue'. One or two vagrants were unintelligible because they used Pedlar's French, the canting slang which Harman described, although it must be said that references to it outside literary contexts are extremely rare.[25] By the early seventeenth century gipsies were also uncommon in the records, though they must have existed in some numbers. There were fewer assize indictments of real and counterfeit gipsies than there had been in the later sixteenth century; and it may well be that the distinction between them and other more or less permanent wanderers was becoming blurred, as the number of the latter increased.[26]

We can find examples of large, apparently well organized, vagrant bands too. But there were not many of them, and their members were not threatening adult rogues but children, who were no doubt trained to be beggars, pickpockets and thieves as circumstances permitted. A group of 30 vagrants in Essex, led by a Wakefield shoemaker, included 26 children who had been picked up on the road in Yorkshire, Lincolnshire and Cambridge.[27] Habitual criminality is suggested also by the common use of *aliases*, and by the organized evasion and manipulation of settlement regulations. There was a wholesale trade in counterfeit passports of the sort prescribed by the Statute of Artificers for people travelling in search of work. One Salisbury vagrant had a certificate made 'by a stranger under a hedge'; another paid 3s. for one in London, while the price was 2s. in Dorset. Forged certificates claiming losses by fire or allowing travel as maimed soldiers were even more useful. Two rogues claiming to have been wounded in Ostend were given money by a string of county treasurers in 1602, before they admitted that their passports had been forged by a man in Shoreditch.

Yet this sort of information is provided in only a small proportion of cases. The picturesque or professional rogue appears to have been the exception not the rule. As one might expect, the majority of vagrants were less willing and less comfortable occupants of the shifting no man's land between criminality and respectability. Of the 651 taken in Salisbury between 1598 and 1638, 70 were credited with or claimed reputable trades. There was a joiner, a shoemaker, a wiredrawer and two weavers, obviously descending the social scale; and there were two dozen petty chapmen or pedlars, more firmly fixed in an ambiguous social position. Petty chapmen were condemned as vagrants in the statute of 1598, but they were also subjected to occasional licensing schemes by Stuart governments who saw their utility and wished to make money out of it. Some of them were certainly on the fringes of the criminal fraternity, doubling as receivers of stolen goods, like Margaret Legg *alias* Jackson *alias* Smith, found in possession of a stolen cloak, who claimed that a beating from her husband had prevented her practising her trade. Others, however, were productive and necessary cogs in the local economy, distributing a wide range of consumer goods. One sold ballads, another rapiers and daggers, while a third was found 'selling of small books, seeming to be distracted'. A tinker found dead in Leicestershire had only 'one blanket to cover him and his wife in the night time as they chanced to lodge in barns or such places', but he kept a working stock of £4 with a friend who acted as his banker.[28]

There were three other notable sub-groups, still more precariously situated, among the sample of vagrants. There were allegedly runaway apprentices and servants, some of them maltreated by their masters, others suspiciously pregnant: the casualties of an unstable and overpopulated labour market, like Margaret Lamphy of Dengie, Essex, dismissed by her master when she became lame and whipped out of town as a vagrant.[29] Then there were soldiers, straggling back from military campaigns, sometimes in groups of four or five, with little hope of finding steady work: provost marshals were intended primarily to deal with them.[30] Finally there were the Irish. Nineteen of them were punished as vagrants in Salisbury, twelve of them between 1629 and 1633 when Irish famine pushed hundreds of emigrants into the western counties of England. They were more conspicuous than their numbers suggest, since they often moved in gangs of a dozen or more. In Colchester in October 1631 one Irishman, five women and four children were apprehended together; in the Colyton division of Devon a few years later, fifteen Irish adults and fourteen children were taken in a band. Sometimes, naked and begging, they were given alms by local authorities, but in the early seventeenth century these groups of foreigners, moving towards the south-east and thence occasionally into France, did more than gipsies or canting rogues to perpetuate fears of the dangerous vagabond.[31]

Native English vagrants, on the other hand, generally travelled only in ones or twos, and for the majority of them it seems to have been the more ordinary characteristics of youth and lack of family or other ties which made them suspect in the first place. We have the ages of 191 vagrants, and two-thirds of them were between 10 and 40, that is in precisely those age-groups which were under-represented in listings of the resident respectable poor. They were distinguished from the latter also in being single and largely male. Of the 3,000 vagrants in our basic sample, slightly more than half were single men and a further quarter were single women. A few apparently solitary vagrants may have had families with them who escaped detection, and the proportion of women and children among those apprehended seems to have been increasing slightly in the early seventeenth century;[32] but mobility militated against permanent attachments. Where they existed, vagrant liaisons were unstable and temporary. There were seventeen couples among the Salisbury vagrants 'living lewdly together, being unmarried'; ten single women were spared punishment because they were pregnant, and another seventeen were sent back to their husbands. Their children felt the consequences. The Salisbury justices twice had to send for mothers of young boys deserted in the town, and a Hertfordshire rogue 'had left a child of his in a barn and forsaken it'.

In some cases the vagrant's physical appearance was enough to make him threatening. There was Elizabeth Taylor in Lancashire, 'having black hair, a green waistcoat, a red petticoat and tall of stature, being great with child'; or the two beggars in Buckinghamshire who had been soldiers: one of them 'had the pox and his face disfigured thereof and the plague and [a] piece of his flesh with a bullet struck off . . .; and the other had a great disease in his head'.[33] When they were not misshapen, 'loathsome and diseased', they might terrify people by pretending to be carriers of plague, or gather in threes and fours for the night in barns, fields, or holes in walls, or flock into towns begging at Christmas.[34]

Vagrants sheltered in one particular barn near Winchester 'to the great affrightment and putting in fear' of the farmer and his household, 'they being a good distance from neighbours'; and they moved in crowds to localities where there might be work, like the saltpans at Yarmouth, where there were great numbers of poor, 'divers of them being apprentices and servants with other the very worst conditioned of people, no better than wandering rogues'.[35] It is easy to see why people thought vagrants 'consorted together as beasts',[36] and why constables picked on the people they did for a whipping. They presented an extraordinary variety. They were not a precisely demarcated social group. But it would be accurate to conclude – with all the room for subjectivity and argument the statement implies – that people knew vagrants when they saw them.

There is one further important point to be made, however. The very process of labelling a man a vagrant helped to make him one. The first punishment was the decisive stage in the downward social spiral which produced a dangerous and incorrigible rogue. When the constables happened to catch people at the respectable end of the vagrant spectrum, they gave them a firm push towards the opposite extreme. Thomas Coxe, his wife and two children, had an apprentice with them when they were whipped as vagrants and sent from Salisbury to Gaddesden, Hertfordshire, in March 1624. They were unlucky not to be expelled without punishment, or asked for sureties, as many people like them were. Eleven months later the family was taken in Salisbury and whipped again, but the apprentice and one of the children had by then disappeared. The household was gradually being fragmented and degraded.

Pretexts were quite often found to force the native poor of a parish, or people who threatened to become such, onto the road. Stephen Poole of Salisbury deserted his sick wife and went to Romsey 'because the parish would not provide more for his wife's maintenance'; she was sent after him with a passport. The justices in Oxford made vagrants distribute their children in the parishes where they happened to have been born and had a settlement, while the parents were ordered elsewhere.[37] They quite deliberately broke up families. In Kent, Jane Jacquet was denied poor relief and shunned by the parishioners after she had nursed victims of plague. She became 'a mere idle vagrant person leading a very loose life', and 'this was the beginning of her ruin and decay'. She got pregnant, her lover fled, and she was moved from one parish to another by constables fearful of the cost of maintaining her bastard. She gave birth 'in a little straw under a tree in the common highway in a cold night ... after a cruel and savage manner, contrary to Christianity, nature and humanity'.[38]

That was an exceptional case, no doubt. People were not always so uncharitable. A deserted child being transported from Essex to Kent in 1594 was taken in by John Brewer who 'made it his adopted son, calling him by the name of John Brewer'. There are also those diseased and disabled wanderers who were sent away without punishment, pushed along 'upon a handbarrow'. One of them, a sick boy of 12, died in his cart, but the minister of the parish had wanted to let him stay until he recovered: he had been overruled by the constable, 'void of all human pity'.[39] Some former or potential vagrants were allowed to remain, if useful to the parish; others, especially women, were spared punishment – 'having the whipping *almost*' – if they seemed less than genuine rogues.[40] As always, local discretion allowed mercy. But it also encouraged a rough and ready justice, which was always socially formative, and sometimes physically so. Corporal punishment by whipping, which was standard after 1531, and boring through the ear and branding, which were inflicted on some offenders, made social labels plainly visible.[41]

Vagrancy legislation thus helped to create the conditions it was directed against. It was self-confirming. From this perspective, it makes little sense to ask whether vagrants were innocents or criminals, for they had no choice. The circumstances of life on the road prevented them being the first; the law and the constable made them the second.

INCORRIGIBLE DISORDERS

From the point of view of the social elite, the identification and punishment of the vagrant fringe constructed a broad defensive rampart between order and plain anarchy. Simple vagrants, even the most sinister of them, were scarcely deviant enough wholly to explain the treatment to which they were subjected. They were the victim rather than the cause of a paranoia which had its roots in what appeared to be more subversive kinds of crime and disorder. We must widen our focus and see how far the poor were involved in those.

According to Francis Bacon, rogues were not only 'a burthen, an eye-sore and a scandal' but also 'a seed of peril and tumult in a state'.[42] There was not very much truth in that. The Rising in the North in 1569 scared many local authorities, forcing them into action both for and against the poor; but the searches for vagrants after it turned up only one potential source of sedition, a beggar in Gloucestershire who claimed to have been a soldier serving Mary Queen of Scots.[43] Vagrants occasionally uttered seditious threats, like another vagrant soldier who said that he would rather fight against his country than with it in 1602. More generally, the group interests of the poor as against the rich were sometimes voiced in circumstances of actual or prospective rebellion. 'Captain Poverty' and 'Lord Poverty' were leaders of the Pilgrimage of Grace in the Lake Counties. 'What can rich men do against poor men, if poor men rise and hold together?', asked an Essex labourer in 1594.[44] But it was not the very poor who were the participants in major risings, let alone the leaders; and after 1569 popular rebellion disappeared for more than a century.

Riots were a little different. More frequent and less dependent on elite leadership, they had a greater social coherence. Poor men and women were heavily involved in food riots, for example. 'A great company of poor people', and 'poor ragged women whereof many of them were very aged', were responsible for stopping carts containing grain outside Newbury in 1630; and a riot against a grain dealer in Hitchin was planned by a widow who was unable to get wheat from overseers of the poor because there was none in the market.[45] Crowd activity tended also to be concentrated where the poor were concentrated. Disturbances occurred in poor parishes and clothing towns in years of dearth; and in forests and fens where royal attempts to stop encroachments and restrict common rights produced an inevitable reaction from growing populations. Enclosure riots had similar features and sometimes similar participants. The Midland Rising of 1607 attracted apprentices, artisans and labourers from towns such as Leicester and from forest areas not themselves directly involved in the dispute.[46]

Disturbances of this kind were instrumental in forming elite attitudes towards social problems and social policies. Even when food riots did not occur, for example, the prospect of them prompted the government to enforce its grain policy and encourage greater local investment in poor relief. Fear of 'the jealous eyes of the watchful poor', as one magistrate put it, was a powerful incentive to action.[47] But riots did not justify the fear of the wandering rogue. Although a vagrant was said to have spread information about a projected corn riot in Kent in 1587, at root popular disturbances were community affairs, not the work of strangers.[48]

Vagabonds were, however, deeply involved in crime. As we have already seen, the deficiencies in the records make it impossible to say precisely how deeply; but petty theft in particular was the activity of the stranger to a village or parish, stealing clothes drying in gardens and almost anything that could be reached through open windows. Moreover, the incidence of crime was rising in the period when vagrancy was probably approaching its peak, that is in the years up to 1600; and it was especially high in years of dearth like the later 1590s, when high prices meant more crimes against property as well as more beggary.[49] The consequence was a growing concern, evident in a statute of 1601, about the petty crimes of 'lewd and mean persons', who broke down hedges and stole wood for fuel, and stepped across the ill-defined dividing line between legitimate gleaning and the theft of corn.[50] The same anxiety can be seen in a report from Hertfordshire in 1637, where

the necessities of labouring men, and of poor people, by reason of the dearth of corn and want of work is so extreme ... that having pawned and sold their goods, many of them do not only break hedges and spoil woods and wander abroad for relief, but also they steal sheep in the night ... and pilfer for provision of victuals.[51]

Equally alarming was the increase in organized crime and the evident development of a criminal underworld in London. Its professional sophistication was probably exaggerated by some observers, but it was not wholly a figment of the imagination of writers such as Robert Greene. There was organized prostitution and large-scale receiving of stolen goods in the capital, and there were real schools for pickpockets. When William Fleetwood, the Recorder, found one in 1585 which was appropriately equipped with verses in canting slang on the walls, it confirmed all his prejudices.[52] We must beware of exaggeration, however. We must not assume that all parts of the stereotype were accurate because some of them were. Not all rogues and vagabonds became semi-professional thieves, any more than all hungry labourers became petty pilferers. Neither was all crime committed by wandering tramps. There is the particular difficulty here that the sources for crime, like many others, are to an unknown extent biased against the vagabond. Criminals native to a village or parish may often have been dealt with informally, through local arbitration. Indictments probably exaggerate the role of the stranger.[53]

There are similar uncertainties involved in investigating another contemporary social concern – bastardy. This too was reaching a peak between 1595 and 1610, and quarter sessions records again leave one in no doubt that the labouring and migrant classes were heavily involved in it. But it is difficult to know how to interpret the phenomenon. It has been suggested that there was a 'bastardy-prone sub-society' of people who repeatedly had illegitimate children. That would nicely fit the stereotype; and if the sub-society was increasing in size around 1600, it would account for rising illegitimacy ratios and for contemporary worries about related and apparently mounting problems such as infanticide. The strongest evidence for the existence of such an identifiable sub-group comes from the eighteenth century, however, not from the early seventeenth. The alternative explanation for the bastardy peak seems more persuasive: that it was the result of courtships being disrupted when falling living standards sharply limited marriage opportunities for the poor. Like vagrancy, high illegitimacy rates may well have been a manifestation less of deliberate deviance from social norms than of stresses within the social and economic structure.[54]

Much the same might be said about the problem of drink. Contemporaries had good reason to be anxious about the growth in the number of alehouses. Recent research suggests that they were multiplying quickly in the later sixteenth and early seventeenth centuries, partly because the occupation of alehouse-keeper was a useful by-employment for the poor, and partly because they provided multiple services for wage-labourers and migrants. It is quite likely that the incidence of public drunkenness increased as a result; and alehouses were obvious centres of disorder, where stolen goods could be disposed of, whores picked up, money wasted and youth corrupted. But it was also the idleness of the underemployed which was conspicuous inside and outside the alehouse door.[55] Here was tangible proof of the 'leisure preference' of people who had little work and not enough money to invest in more respectable pleasures, like drinking at home.

All this provided ample grounds for abhorrence of the idle rogue and for his confusion with the simple vagrant or pauper. The perceived danger lay less in the major problems of rebellion and riot than in petty crimes and misdemeanours which were both more common and more on public display in the years around 1600 than they had once been. They also fed off one another in particular recognizable environments. Alehouses were commonest in suburban parishes, and notable too in areas of woodland and pasture.[56] Thieves and bastard-bearers were to be found among vagrants and in poor tenements. Though not in a majority there, they determined the reputation of the whole. Surveys of inmates in Southwark who might prove chargeable to the parish in 1619 and 1622 uncovered a host of pregnant girls and women out of service, and a few plainly incorrigible rogues whose behaviour justified the expulsion of the others. There were two women who dumped children on the parish, one vagabond who gave birth in the highway, and Elizabeth Winter, 'a vagrant in the street', who 'feigned herself mad and dumb' and so got the parish to take her child into care.[57]

The drive towards a regulation of manners which is such a striking feature of parliamentary activity between 1580 and 1660 is therefore intelligible. So are the increasing efforts made by parish notables as well as justices of the peace in the early seventeenth century to get inmates and strangers out of towns, cottagers off commons and wastes, and to suppress social delinquency generally.[58] But it is important to recognize that the manners being corrected, and the crimes being punished, were not just those of the poor. To think that they were is once again to swallow contemporary propaganda whole. When the Puritan magistrates of Dorchester undertook a cleansing of their town from disorder in the 1620s and 1630s they found themselves combatting a large and varied section of the population. There were citizens stopping carts when grain was short or stealing fuel in winter, alehouse-keepers entertaining schoolboys, petty chapmen who were whipped as vagrants, idlers wandering suspiciously at night who were sent to the house of correction, and householders who abused over-zealous constables. But few of the disorderly were vagabonds, and many of them were not in any sense poor. Of 320 people presented for a variety of disorders in one year, 1629–30, only 34 were vagrants or strangers; and members of the medical profession seem, man for man, to have been as delinquent as apprentices. A physician was found drunk on two successive days, and a surgeon kept a disorderly house.[59] The stigma of drunkenness and disorder was attached to the poor because they were the easiest target, not because they were the only one.

A CULTURE OF POVERTY?

Enough has been said to show that there are great difficulties involved in accepting contemporary stereotypes of the dangerous poor, particularly those created by the rogue literature; and it is time that we attacked the subject directly. For the pamphlets of Harman and his successors have proved influential. They have been taken at face value in some superficial, if entertaining, accounts of the Elizabethan underworld; and, along with continental literature in the same vein, they have been treated seriously by more perceptive historians because they seem to hint at the existence of a distinct culture of poverty, not unlike that which some sociologists have detected in twentieth-century societies.[60]

The literature begins with the German *Liber Vagatorum*, first printed in about 1510, but circulating before then in manuscript, which described the various orders of beggars and their tricks. The model was taken up and adapted to English rogues by John Awdeley in his brief *Fraternity of Vagabonds* (1561). It was then developed at greater length and more successfully by Thomas Harman in his *Caveat for Common Cursitors* of 1566. Harman, a Kentish gentleman, described the various sorts of rogue he claimed to have seen and talked to in his neighbourhood, their language, social hierarchy, tricks and trades, and he added diverting anecdotes about their behaviour. Later writers rushed to exploit what was obviously a popular line, particularly Robert Greene in his descriptions of 'cony-catching' in London. They produced a genre which was not quite social reportage and not quite picaresque novel, but a combination of the two, and which culminated in Richard Head's *The English Rogue* of 1665.[61]

We have already seen that there was some truth in the picture which these authors presented. It was most firmly rooted in fact, though even then not entirely so, in the middle of the sixteenth century. Harman named several vagrants whom he found near his home in Kent, and at least eighteen of them can be found in lists of vagrants in official records. The canting language had a real existence, a little of it coming from Romany; and that means that different kinds – if not quite 'orders' – of rogue were probably distinguished by rogues themselves.[62] It is dangerous to go further than that, however. Although we are groping in the dark in this as in so many areas of popular culture, a reading of Harman leaves little doubt that he selected, shaped and gilded his material, to give it a clear structure and provide amusement for his readers.

Moreover, once the language and the society of rogues had a literary embodiment it became ossified and stereotyped. In the end, in the later seventeenth century, there was even a dictionary of cant.[63] It is impossible to say whether vagabonds ever reversed the process, and borrowed terms and styles of life from literary art. The possibility cannot be ruled out of court. Even leaving aside such means of transmission as canting verses on tavern walls, the literature itself must have circulated well down the social scale, especially in London; and it might just possibly have been carried by pedlars of 'small books' like the one punished in Salisbury. But its content cannot have reached illiterate country rogues quickly or directly.[64] It did, however, fix both elite and popular perceptions of them in a rigid mould. At the same time, the increase in the number of simple vagrants on the roads swamped the gipsies, tricksters and 'upright men' of the early and middle sixteenth century who provided Harman's material. By 1600 the gap between literary convention and social reality was probably becoming very wide.

That did not prevent the literature being popular, however. Quite the reverse. The rogue pamphlets made pressing social problems palatable by both explaining and distancing them. In life, the vagrant was only just distinguishable from other migrants and paupers, as we have seen. In fiction, he became much more easily recognizable, and the perplexing problems of definition were thereby evaded. The stereotype also satisfied the impulse to see the rogue, not as a victim of social forces, but as an unusually free agent, in many ways attractive, if not romantic. The caricature offered all the guilt-ridden fascination of misrule. Like any other literary genre, rogue pamphlets translated reality for the benefit of their audience. They do not demonstrate the existence of a rogue society or counter-culture, but people's determination to believe in one.[65]

A similar scepticism is necessary when we turn to assess the applicability of modern depictions of a 'culture of poverty'. Some of its alleged attributes could almost have been listed by Harman himself: 'lack of privacy, gregariousness, a high incidence of alcoholism, frequent resort to violence, ... free unions or consensual marriages, a relatively high incidence of the abandonment of mothers and children, ... a belief in male superiority, ... a high tolerance for psychological pathology of all sorts'.[66] We have found evidence for much of this behind the dry contents of censuses and the like. But it must be observed that the first four qualities at least would apply to almost the whole of early modern English society, and some of the others only to a proportion of the very poor. Other suggested traits of a culture of poverty – 'a strong present-time orientation with relatively little ability to ... plan for the future, a sense of resignation and fatalism' – are not entirely consistent with the professional rogue's professionalism, with the education which some of the labouring poor invested in for their children, or with the aspirations of those vagrants who wished, like a drummer boy from Devizes, 'to travel until they were settled' somewhere where they could practise a profitable trade. Many of them obviously thought that wealth might come as suddenly as poverty, if they chanced on the right circumstances at the right time; but that view was not unique to the pauper or the vagabond.[67]

The search for a distinct culture of poverty seems doomed to failure, unless we define the term so narrowly that it applies only to a very small group of incorrigible rogues, or so broadly that it becomes synonymous with 'popular culture' as a whole. Where we have some record of the opinions and attitudes of the poor, they appear to be indistinguishable from those of the labouring classes in general, and to be as diverse. They believed in charity as well as good fortune, for example, and thought it more reliable. A ballad of 1630 depicted a pauper who was given gold by the Devil but finally saved from perdition by his good neighbours.[68] Those whose generosity was limited, who gave 'little or nothing' in special collections for the poor, were abused; those who gave alms to wanderers were praised. Several vagrants claimed to live by getting alms at gentlemen's gates, or more often 'by the charity of good people' or 'good folks'.[69]

Poor people naturally defended begging and attacked the laws against it. The Act of 1572 aroused the fury of an Essex husbandman who thought (wrongly) that 'there is no Christian prince that hath such cruel laws as to burn men through their ears as are used in this realm'; and after the statute of 1598 a Kentish man said that 'if the Queen did put down begging' she was worse than a local witch 'which forsook God and all the world'.[70] There is nothing remarkable in this, however. As we shall see, members of the House of Commons were also critical, if in more restrained fashion, of legislation which threatened to destroy some aspects of traditional wayfaring life. Almost everyone would have agreed with the general social criticism in an allegedly seditious verse found in Essex in 1594:

> Now favour hindreth equity, and riches rule the roost.
> In vain the poor cry charity; go help you, say the most.[71]

Yet there was little uniformity among the poor even on the subject of poverty. Some thought beggary a stigma, as we can see from those who were 'ashamed' to engage in it in the early sixteenth century;[72] and the behaviour of individual rogues clearly caused as many problems for the more respectable poor as for magistrates. The neighbours of Elizabeth Mascall, the widow of a highwayman, vehemently complained about her to the Essex quarter sessions in 1665. She used false passes claiming losses by fire, abused her second husband, and often deserted her children in order to go drinking and thieving with her friends in London:

> She lived here lewdly and unpeaceably, often threatening to be the death of her said husband, and threatened in the night season to burn the house

over his children's heads ... in so much that [he] was forced to board out his children at charge and to armour himself from her as fearing she would cut his throat, which she had often threatened in bloody manner. And one great reason of their unquiet living together was because he would not forsake his honest calling and follow her pernicious counsel, which was to accompany her in the highway to take a purse.[73]

There was a good deal of 'psychological pathology' but very little 'male superiority' here; and neither quality can have evoked the sympathy of law-abiding paupers.

The deserving poor probably did not need any encouragement to imbibe some of the attitudes of their superiors, therefore. Even if they did, the machinery of social welfare and the poor law could be powerfully persuasive. It created those deferential almspeople in Christ's Hospital, Abingdon, who would not take the money offered them by Samuel Pepys but insisted he put it in the collecting box; and the poor woman in Wiltshire who was terrified out of her wits by the thought that she would end her days in the local Bridewell.[74] But the law could be manipulated as well as submitted to. John Baldwin and his wife, 'both of them able to work for their living', had nevertheless been able to get the dole in Bocking in 1665: he was 'a very refractory fellow, abusing his superiors, and coming for his allowance in so masterly manner which encourageth others in the same'.[75] Baldwin shows that poverty and the dole did not necessarily mean powerlessness or passivity. He also suggests that the culture as well as the status of the poor was partly shaped by the constraints and loopholes of the law.

Untidy as it is, we must take the poor as a mixed bunch indistinguishable in many respects from the rest of society. Demarcation lines were imposed on them by the poor law and its implementers; they did not exist in reality, however much some commentators might allege that they did. We must also conclude that attitudes always impinged on realities. Even misperceptions of the poor were creative. The concept of the impotent determined the nature of outdoor relief and the people to whom it was given. The image of the vagrant rogue produced laws which manufactured a vagrant class out of an amorphous group of poor migrants. The system made paupers and delinquents by labelling them. Even when realities proved to be different, and some attitudes were reshaped in consequence, the interaction was never a simple one-way affair. The discovery of the labouring poor which came with listings, censuses and surveys was to an extent artificial, an invention. When people looked for poverty, they found it; they shaped its image and produced responses which helped to realize it. In the next two chapters we must look at the development of those responses over time.

NOTES AND REFERENCES

1.   Quoted in **R. Vorspan**, 'Vagrancy and the New Poor Law in late-Victorian and Edwardian England', *Eng.Hist.Rev.*, xcii (1977), 63.

2.   Above, pp. 28–9. Cf. below, pp. 124–8.

3.   Recent work gives a modified picture between the two extremes, but for opinions tending to the softer view, see **A. L. Beier**, 'Vagrants and the Social Order in Elizabethan England', *Past and Present*, 64 (1974), 3–29; **P. A. Slack**, 'Vagrants and Vagrancy in England, 1598–1664', *Econ.Hist.Rev.*, 2 ser., xxvii (1974), 360–79; and for the harsher interpretation, **J. S. Cockburn**, 'The Nature and Incidence of Crime in England 1559–1625: A Preliminary Survey' in **J. S. Cockburn** (ed.), *Crime in England 1550–1800* (Methuen, 1977), pp. 62–3. See also the debate between **Beier** and **J. Pound** in *Past and Present*, 71 (1976), 126–34. **Dr Beier's** *Masterless Men* (Methuen, 1985) is the fullest and most reliable account of the whole subject.

4.   Cf. **C. B. Herrup**, 'Law and Morality in Seventeenth-Century England', *Past and Present*, 106 (1985), 102–23.

5.   Colchester Borough Records, Sessions Book II; Devon RO, C5/102, Exeter Strangers' Book 1621–68. Cf. **P. Styles**, 'The Evolution of the Law of Settlement', in *idem, Studies in Seventeenth-Century West Midlands History* (Roundwood Press, Kineton, 1978), pp. 175–204.

6.   For a good example of the latter, see Chester Borough Records, M/L/5/19.

7.   **J. R. Kent**, 'Population Mobility and Alms: Poor Migrants in the Midlands during the early seventeenth century', *Local Population Studies*, 27 (1981), 35–51; **Slack**, 'Vagrants and Vagrancy', p. 368. For other examples, see Sheffield City Library, Spencer Stanhope MS. 60214; Essex RO, D/B 3/3/211; Dorset RO, Dorchester Records, B/2/16/4, 11 Feb. 1641/2.

8.   **Beier**, 'Vagrants and the Social Order', p. 15.

9.   **Cockburn**, 'Nature and Incidence of Crime', pp. 62–3; **J.S. Cockburn**, 'Early Modern Assize Records as Historical Evidence', *J. Society of Archivists*, v (1975), 223–4; **M. J. Ingram**, 'Communities and Courts: Law and Disorder in Early-Seventeenth-Century Wiltshire', in **Cockburn**, (ed.), *Crime in England*, pp. 130–2. Cf. **J. A. Sharpe**, *Crime in Seventeenth-Century England. A County Study* (Cambridge UP, 1983), pp. 164–5.

10.   **Beier**, 'Vagrants and the Social Order', pp. 5–6.

11.   PRO, SP 12/80, 81, 83, 86 *passim*; **Beier**, *Masterless Men*, p. 16.

12.   *Ibid*. The returns are in PRO, SP 16, vols 188–427, 533–8. Some of these simply give numbers of vagrants.

13.   **A. L. Beier**, 'Social Problems in Elizabethan London', *J. Interdisciplinary Hist.*, ix (1978), 204. I am grateful to Professor Mark Benbow for showing me an unpublished paper on the wider activity of Bridewell.

14.   London Corporation RO, City Cash Accounts, 'Foreign Charges', 1632–3, f. 65, 1633–4, f. 154v. (I owe these references to Dr S. M. Macfarlane.)

15.   Below, pp. 115, 118; **Beier**, *Masterless Men*, pp. 159–60.

16.   Below, p. 124; **Cockburn**, 'Nature and Incidence of Crime', pp. 62–3.

17.   Below, pp. 126–7.

18. **P. Williams,** *The Tudor Regime* (Oxford UP, 1979), pp. 202–3, 212–13; **J. F. Larkin** and **P. L. Hughes** (eds), *Stuart Royal Proclamations* (Oxford UP, 1973–83), i. 361–2. There are some reports of provost marshals' activities in the State Papers for the 1630s: e.g. PRO, SP 16/426/19, 37.

19. The information in the following paragraphs is taken from **Slack,** 'Vagrants and Vagrancy', unless otherwise noted. For other local lists, besides those used there, see Essex RO, D/P 232/8/1, f. 1; West Sussex RO, Par 128/1/1/1, f. 28v; Oxford Corporation Records, N.4.2, ff. 46–9; and for further information, **Beier,** *Masterless Men.*

20. For similar circuits, see the examinations in Essex RO, D/B 3/3/211.

21. The mean distance moved was sometimes quite high, however, because of a few long-distance migrants. Cf. for the later seventeenth century, **D. Souden,** 'Migrants and the Population Structure' in **P. Clark** (ed.), *The Transformation of English Provincial Towns* (Hutchinson, 1984), pp. 142–5.

22. For Exeter, see Devon RO, C5/102; and for comments on vagrancy in dearth years, **R. H. Tawney** and **E. Power** (eds), *Tudor Economic Documents* (Longmans, Green and Co., 1924), ii. 341; HMC, *Various,* i. 84; West Devon RO, Plymouth Receivers' Accounts, 1596–97, f. 114v.

23. **Slack,** 'Vagrants and Vagrancy', pp. 371, 374; **G. Salgado** (ed.), *Cony-Catchers and Bawdy Baskets* (Penguin Books, Harmondsworth, 1972), p. 379.

24. Essex RO, D/B 3/3/211, 28 July 1634.

25. Essex RO, Q/SR 76/57; **Beier,** *Masterless Men,* p. 125.

26. Essex RO, Cal. Assize Files, 35/68/H, 35/69/T, 12 March, 9 July 1627. Cf. **W. Hunt,** *The Puritan Moment* (Harvard UP, Cambridge, Mass., 1983), p. 53; **Beier,** 'Vagrants and the Social Order', p. 8; **Beier,** *Masterless Men*, pp. 58–62.

27. Essex RO, Q/SR 113/40, 40a.

28. **D. H. Smith,** 'A Seventeenth-Century Tinker's Will and Inventory', *J. Gypsy Lore Society,* 4 ser., i (1977), 172–7; **M. Spufford,** *The Great Reclothing of Rural England* (Hambledon Press, 1984), pp. 8–10, 50–4. For other examples of criminal pedlars, see **J. S. Cockburn** (ed.), *Cal. Assize Records: Sussex Indictments, Elizabeth I* (HMSO, 1975), nos 254, 1824, 1978.

29. Essex RO, D/B 3/3/397/9. Cf. the comments in **H. Arthington,** *Provision for the poore* (1597), sig. C2v.

30. Cf. **Williams,** *Tudor Regime,* pp. 212–13.

31. HMC, *13th Report,* App. iv, p. 132 (Rye).

32. **Beier,** *Masterless Men,* p. 56; **Kent,** 'Population Mobility and Alms', p. 42.

33. Bodl., Ashmole MS. 228, f. 22. (I owe this reference to Dr M. MacDonald.)

34. Bristol AO, Q.S.Minutes 1634–47, f. 53r; Hants RO, Q.S. Order Book 1628–49, f. 106r; **P. Slack** (ed.), *Poverty in Early-Stuart Salisbury* (Wilts Record Soc., xxxi, 1975), p. 42; PRO, SP 16/174/17; **W. H. Stevenson** (ed.), *Records of the Borough of Nottingham* (Nottingham, 1882–1914), iv. 347.

35. Hants RO, Q.S. Order Book 1607–28, p. 502; PRO, SP 16/364/50.

36. **R. Younge,** *The Poores Advocate* (1654), Ch. xiv, p. 11.

37. Oxford Corporation Records, N.4.2, ff. 46–9.

38. *Records of Maidstone* (Maidstone, 1926), pp. 257–8.
39. **Slack,** 'Vagrants and Vagrancy', pp. 377–8; Essex RO, D/B 3/3/211, 20 Oct. 1636; BL, Add. MS. 10457, f. 196v; **H. W. Saunders** (ed.), *The Official Papers of Sir Nathaniel Bacon* (Camden Soc., 3 ser., xxvi, 1915), p. 63.
40. **J. Webb** (ed.), *Poor Relief in Elizabethan Ipswich* (Suffolk Records Soc., ix, 1966), p. 86; Essex RO, D/B 3/3/211, 18 Dec., 1635.
41. For branding, see below, p. 127, and, for examples, Essex RO, Cal. Essex Assize Files, 35/22/H: 1580/56; **J. W. Fowkes,** 'The Minute Book of the York Court of Quarter Sessions 1638–62', *Yorks Archaeological J.*, xli (1965), 451.
42. **J. Spedding** (ed.), *The Letters and the Life of Francis Bacon* (Longman, Green, 1861–74), iv. 252. Cf. HMC, *Salisbury*, xxii. 297.
43. PRO, SP 12/81/22; below, p. 124.
44. **J. S. Cockburn** (ed.), *Cal. Assize Records: Hertfordshire Indictments, Elizabeth I* (HMSO, 1975), p. 173; **S. M. Harrison,** *The Pilgrimage of Grace in the Lake Counties 1536–7* (Royal Historical Society, 1981), p. 106; **Hunt,** *Puritan Moment*, p. 61. Cf. **Cockburn** (ed.), *Cal. Assize Records: Kent, Eliz. I* (HMSO, 1979), p. 437; **W. R. D. Jones,** *The Tudor Commonwealth* (Athlone, 1970), p. 108.
45. PRO, SP 16/176/35, 177/4, 52; **P. G. Lawson,** 'Crime and the Administration of Criminal Justice in Hertfordshire 1580–1625', Oxford Univ. D.Phil. thesis, 1982, pp. 244–5 (I am grateful to Dr Lawson for permission to cite his thesis). Cf. **J. Walter,** 'Grain Riots and Popular Attitudes to the Law', in **J. Brewer** and **J. Styles** (eds), *An Ungovernable People* (Hutchinson, 1980), pp. 47–84; **P. Clark,** 'Popular Protest and Disturbance in Kent, 1558–1640', *Econ.Hist.Rev.*, 2 ser., xxix (1976), 365–82.
46. **J. E. Martin,** *Feudalism to Capitalism: Peasant and Landlord in English Agrarian Development* (Macmillan, 1983), pp. 195–203. Cf. **B. Sharp,** *In Contempt of All Authority: Rural Artisans and Riot in the West of England 1586–1660* (California UP, Berkeley, 1980); **K. Lindley,** *Fenland Riots and the English Revolution* (Heinemann, 1982).
47. PRO, SP 16/204/4; below, pp. 144–5.
48. **Clark,** 'Popular Protest', p. 367.
49. **Sharpe,** *Crime*, pp. 101–3, 113–14, 199–200, 209, 214; **Cockburn,** 'Nature and Incidence of Crime', pp. 53, 67. For contemporary comment on dearth and crime, see HMC, *House of Lords*, xi. 38–9; Devon RO, Q.S. Order Book 1603–13, f. 7r.
50. **Sharpe,** *Crime*, pp. 170–1. For examples, see **W. J. Hardy** *et al.*, (eds), *Hertford County Records* (Hertford, 1905–57), i. 32–3; Essex RO, D/P 232/8/1, f/ 4; Dorset RO, B2/16/1, 8 Nov. 1619. Cf. below, p. 151.
51. PRO, SP 16/385/43.
52. *Tudor Economic Documents*, ii. 337–9. For a highly coloured acount of the London underworld, see **G. Salgado,** *The Elizabethan Underworld* (Dent, 1977).
53. **Ingram,** 'Communities and Courts', pp. 131–3.
54. **Wrightson,** *English Society*, pp. 145–6; **P. Laslett,** *Family Life and Illicit Love in Earlier Generations* (Cambridge UP, 1977), Ch. 3; **P. Laslett** *et al.* (eds), *Bastardy and its Comparative History* (Arnold, 1980), Chs 5, 8. For infanticide, see **Sharpe,** *Crime*, pp. 135–7; **K. Wrightson,** 'Infanticide in

earlier seventeenth-century England', *Local Population Studies*, 15 (1975), 10–22.

55. **P. Clark,** *The English Alehouse: A Social History 1200–1830* (Longman, 1983), pp. 47–50, 79, 109–12, 126–31, 145–51.

56. *Ibid.*, pp. 54, 69–71.

57. Greater London Council RO, P92/SAV/1422,1423.

58. **Hunt,** *Puritan Moment*, p. 71; **Lawson,** 'Crime and the Administration of Criminal Justice', pp. 179–87; **K. Wrightson,** 'Two Concepts of Order: justices, constables and jurymen in seventeenth-century England', in **Brewer** and **Styles,** *Ungovernable People*, pp. 21–46. Cf. below, pp. 130, 149–52.

59. Dorset RO, Dorchester Records, B2/8/1, ff. 2–46, 101r, 139v, 142v, 148r, 153r, 156r, 160v, 163r, 169v. Cf. **P. Collinson,** *The Religion of Protestants* (Oxford UP, 1982), pp. 217–20; below, p. 151.

60. For perceptive discussion of the problem, see **P. Burke,** 'Urban History and Urban Anthropology of Early Modern Europe', in **D. Fraser** and **A. Sutcliffe** (eds), *The Pursuit of Urban History* (Arnold, 1983), pp. 78–9; **R. Chartier,** 'Les élites et les gueux', *Revue d'histoire moderne*, 21 (1974), 378–87; **B. Geremek,** 'Criminalité, vagabondage, paupérisme: la marginalité à l'aube des temps modernes', *ibid.*, p. 357.

61. The early literature is printed in **A. V. Judges,** *The Elizabethan Underworld* (Routledge and Kegan Paul, 1930), and **Salgado,** *Cony-Catchers*. See also **H. Sieber,** *The Picaresque* (Methuen, 1977), pp. 40, 51; **A. A. Parker,** *Literature and the Delinquent: The Picaresque Novel in Spain and Europe 1599–1753* (Edinburgh UP, 1967), pp. 11, 17, 100.

62. **F. Aydelotte,** *Elizabethan Rogues and Vagabonds* (Oxford UP, 1913), pp. 150–1, 18–19; **Beier,** *Masterless Men*, pp. 60–1, 117.

63. **B.E.,** *A New Dictionary of the Terms Ancient and Modern of the Canting Crew* (1699). For elite fascination with cant, see PRO, SP 14/118/130; **V. Sackville-West,** *Knole and the Sackvilles* (Lindsay Drummond, 1948), pp. 135–7.

64. Cf. the similar problems involved in the relationship between printed ballads and oral culture: **M. Spufford,** *Small Books and Pleasant Histories* (Methuen, 1981), pp. 13–14.

65. Cf. **P. Deyon,** 'A propos du paupérisme au milieu du XVIIe siècle', *Annales E.S.C.*, 22 (1967), 146–7; above, pp. 24–5. The evidence above is perhaps enough to refute the argument that the increasingly stereotyped representation of vagabonds after 1590 suggests a decline in the severity of the problem: **Aydelotte,** *Elizabethan Rogues*, pp. 74–5.

66. **O. Lewis,** *The Children of Sanchez* (Penguin Books, Harmondsworth, 1964), pp. xxvi–xxvii; *idem, La Vida* (Secker and Warburg, 1967), pp. xlii–xliv. Lewis's culture of poverty has been much criticised: see for example **C. A. Valentine,** *Culture and Poverty* (Chicago UP, 1968), pp. 68–77. Cf. **P. Mathias,** *The Transformation of England* (Methuen, 1979), pp. 140–1.

67. **Slack,** 'Vagrants and Vagrancy', p. 363. Cf. Spufford, *Small Books*, pp. 244–6.

68. *A new Ballad shewing the great misery sustained by a poore man in Essex* [? 1630].

69. Dorset RO, Dorchester Records, B/2/8/1, ff. 78v, 54r; **T. Kemp,** *The Book*

of *John Fisher* (Warwick, n.d.), pp. 29, 123, 185; **Slack,** 'Vagrants and Vagrancy', p. 377; **Beier,** *Masterless Men,* pp. 79–80, 223.

70. **Hunt,** *Puritan Moment,* p. 60; **J. S. Cockburn** (ed.), *Cal.Assize Records: Kent Indictments, Elizabeth I* (HMSO, 1979), p. 423.
71. Essex RO, Cal.Assize Files, 35/36/T: 1594/34. Cf. below, pp. 124–5.
72. Above, p. 27.
73. Essex RO, Q/SBa 2/105, petition from West Bergholt.
74. **R. Latham** and **W. Matthews** (eds), *The Diary of Samuel Pepys* (Bell and Hyman, 1970–83), ix. 227–8; Wilts RO, Q.S.Roll, Easter 1628, doc. 122.
75. Essex RO, Q/SBa 2/104, petition from Bocking. Cf. below, pp. 191–2.

Chapter 6

THE MAKING OF THE POOR LAW 1485–1610

It would be impossible to pretend that the facts so far surveyed explain why there was an English poor law. They are not serious enough to support an argument that that radical response was an obvious reaction to an overwhelming need. There was a need, of course, as contemporaries fully appreciated. 'The kingdom became then much more populous than in former times, and with it the poor also greatly increased', wrote Matthew Hale, looking back from the middle of the seventeenth century to the great poor-relief statute of 1598.[1] In comparison with other countries in Europe, however, poverty in England was shallow rather than deep, and respectable rather than disorderly – though the balance was tipping in the deep and disorderly direction in the years around 1600. We shall see that crisis circumstances often stimulated action: but they were necessary conditions rather than sufficient explanations for the sort of action which ensued.

Much the same might be said about the second reason for the poor law put forward by Hale: the decline of old methods of 'voluntary relief'. It has already been suggested that the English poor law can partly be attributed to the dissolution of the monasteries and other charitable religious institutions.[2] But new departures began before the dissolution, and that event was obviously not unique to England. In Scotland, where poverty and famine were worse than in England, welfare facilities were similarly laid waste; but there was no similar response. Although the Scots copied the first coherent English poor law of 1572 almost word for word, they did not implement it. It had little practical effect north of the border before the end of the seventeenth century. Many reasons for the contrast can be suggested, including different economic conditions and assumptions. But one factor was certainly the unwillingness or inability of the government in Scotland to impose its will on landowners and parishes.[3]

What set England apart, both from Scotland and from other countries, was not the nature of the problem, but the ability first to formulate and then to execute solutions to it. In other words, it was an intellectual and above all a political achievement. The intellectual inheritance was much the same for all governments: Christian charity and civic humanism dictated similar programmes for the welfare of the poor all over Europe. But the political conditions for their implementation were infinitely varied. In England parishes were not autonomous ecclesiastical units largely left to their own devices: they were partly secular authorities, supervised by county commissions of the peace, and their secular responsibilities grew greater through the sixteenth century. English landowners could not give voice to undiluted vested interests, against new forms of taxation, for example: many of them were justices of the peace with other, conflicting, obligations. Both parishes and property-owners were agents of the central government; and that government could communicate a consistent policy to them, and commit them to it. The achievement was gradual; it met with opposition; it was often untidy and inefficient. But by comparison with other countries it was remarkably effective and remarkably uniform.

The stress in what follows will therefore be unashamedly on political relationships and political constraints. It will also be directed towards the centre. Some of the older interpretations of the English poor law emphasized the originality and influence of local experiments;[4] and we shall see the extraordinary fertility and determination of local magistrates in inventing new devices and institutions. But their innovations proved insubstantial and temporary unless they had the support of Crown or parliament. In the end, embellished and adapted as it was to fit local circumstances, the poor law was a poor *law*. The centre called the tune. The centre also composed it.

ORIGINS

One of the chief difficulties in this area of historical inquiry is our ignorance of the base line from which the poor law developed. We know all too little about the size and efficacy of the welfare apparatus as it existed in 1500. There is no doubt that it was large. Fraternities and craft gilds (they were often the same thing) provided alms for their old and needy members. Manorial and leet courts were often as concerned to arrange support for elderly villagers as to keep out disorderly strangers. Many parishes had church-stocks, sometimes called 'town-stocks', in the form of a few cattle or sheep, houses, land or simply cash, which could be lent or given to the poor.[5] They were supplemented by further charitable gifts in the fifteenth century and later, erecting almshouses and financing doles of clothing or bread in villages as well as towns.[6] Besides the ordinary charitable activities of religious orders, there were also hospitals for the infirm and the sick. Mostly founded during the period of demographic growth in the twelfth and thirteenth centuries, many of them were in decay by the later fifteenth century. There were probably rather more than four hundred of them still in existence in the 1530s, on the eve of the dissolution, which further depleted their number. Along with other charitable foundations, however, some of them were protected from total destruction by urban corporations and their benefactors, and they survived to be used as almshouses when population pressure increased again.[7]

Whether these instruments would have sufficed to meet the demands made on them in the later sixteenth century, if there had been no poor law, it is difficult to say. We do not know how many large hospitals there might have been by then, or how many organized parish collections for the poor of the kind which were already beginning before 1520.[8] Since charity and the poor law together failed to prevent people starving in the 1590s, it is unlikely that charity alone would have been enough. But the question is beside the point, as well as hypothetical, since we are not comparing like with like. The charitable machine could not do – or did not set out to do – three things which the poor law aimed at or achieved. It did not suppress begging but encouraged it; it was not as a rule concerned to provide work for the poor; and it did not supply relief strictly according to regularly measured local need. The new welfare strategies of the sixteenth century were intended to do things differently, or to do different things.

There was little sign of this when the Tudors first engaged with the problem of the poor. Their concern was political security and their target the vagabond. At the outset of his reign Henry VII ordered local searches for wanderers and 'suspect persons',[9] and in 1495 a Vagrancy Act provided that they were to be set in the stocks for three days and then sent home. According to its preamble, the Act was intended to provide 'softer means' for repressing vagrants than the legislation of Richard II which ordered their imprisonment. There was, of course, no softening of government attitudes. Stocking was simply more practicable than imprisonment when scores of rogues had to be dealt with, and the new statute insisted more clearly than its predecessor on beggars remaining in the hundred where they were born or where they resided.[10] This set a pattern for the rest of our period: anxiety about domestic security pushed new regimes into action against the mobile, rootless poor right up to the Act of Settlement of 1662.

While security was fundamental, however, there were other, newer impulses directing attention to vagrants and beggars in the early sixteenth century. As population rose, idleness seemed a rampant infection and its suppression a matter of social hygiene as well as political self-interest. It was not mere coincidence that municipal by-laws against beggars and vagabonds were often issued at the same time as orders for cleaning the streets.[11] Town councils wished to purify their communities from every kind of dirt and disorder which threatened the health of the body politic. They received powerful support from humanist writers who used the same analogy of the body politic to underline the dangers of civic and national disease and decay, and the need for prompt treatment. The most influential writer on poor relief of the period, Erasmus's Spanish disciple, Vives, visited England in the 1520s; and even before that Thomas More's *Utopia* (1516) had shown an imagined commonwealth in which idleness was forbidden and where the genuinely impotent were cared for. In England too there was a need, alongside the vagrancy laws, for 'some good provision ... for them that through sickness and age were fallen into poverty'.[12]

By the 1530s such notions were becoming commonplace. Thomas Starkey asserted that 'in France, Italy and Spain the commons without fail are more miserable and poor than they be here with us'. Nevertheless, England was 'more poor than it hath been in time past, and such poverty reigneth now that in no case may stand with a very true and flourishing common weal': 'this multitude of beggars here in our country showeth much poverty ... and ... also much idleness and ill policy'.[13] The remedy was to be found in the policies being implemented in some enlightened European towns in the 1520s and 1530s. Starkey referred in passing to Ypres, and the orders promulgated there were translated by William Marshall in 1535 and presented as a model for what must urgently be done in England.[14] No self-respecting set of governors, least of all one as careful about its international reputation as the Council of Henry VIII, could ignore the challenge. Some public response was inevitable, and we can see the attitudes and circumstances which lay behind it in the three different forms which it took before 1558: in the initiatives sponsored by Cardinal Wolsey, in the legislation of the 1530s, and in the institutions erected in London in the 1540s and 1550s.

If one man can claim to have been the inventor of Tudor paternalism, that man was Thomas Wolsey. His driving energy laid the foundations of the social policies pursued by Tudor and early Stuart governments. He began in 1517, not only with his famous enclosure commission,[15] but also with a more general attack on social problems in London. The occasion was partly the disorders evident in the riots of Evil May Day 1517, and partly epidemics of the sweating sickness and plague which threatened the health of the Court in the same year. In January 1518 the Council interrogated the mayor and aldermen about the state of the city, and told them to act against rogues and beggars.[16] Similar campaigns against the wandering and mendicant poor in Coventry, Lincoln, Leicester and Shrewsbury between 1517 and 1521 suggest that the Cardinal's attention was not confined to the capital.[17]

That was not all. Influenced by humanist physicians such as Linacre, and by their aspiration to apply medical knowledge to the health of the commonweal in general, Wolsey founded the College of Physicians in 1518. In the same year he and More were responsible for the first efforts by an English government to prevent the spread of plague. Infected houses in London and Oxford were to be identified and marked so that people might avoid them. Copied from foreign models, this early step towards the practice of quarantine was gradually developed in London and in provincial cities until the isolation of infected households became a standard public-health procedure.[18] Wolsey brought what we would now call social medicine into the political arena for the first time.

Finally, he turned his attention to the other major cause of social crisis: dearth. There were two periods of disastrous harvests in the 1520s. In 1520 and 1521 several towns for the first time provided stocks of corn for their poor, among them Norwich, Coventry and Exeter, where grain was bought 'for a common weal'.[19] In the next harvest crisis, in 1527, Wolsey instituted searches for grain by local commissioners all over the kingdom. They were to take surveys of the corn held by farmers, to arrange for it to be brought to market, and to report their findings to the Council. These procedures were repeated in later years of dearth.[20] Wolsey's creative and all-consuming political ambition turned crisis circumstances into opportunities to advertize the humanist credentials of the English monarchy and its chief minister.

There was no decline in government interest in social policy after Wolsey's fall; but the means of expressing it changed. Wolsey had acted through proclamations, commissions, letters and personal command. Thomas Cromwell used parliamentary statute. Partly the product of personal predilection, partly of opportunity (since parliament was sitting regularly), this shift brought both limitations and opportunities. On the one hand, it slowed the pace of change, since the vested interests represented in parliament needed a good deal of persuading before they would accept innovations which damaged their pockets or radically extended the interference of government in the lives of its subjects. On the other hand, the use of statute implied the formulation of policies which offered practicable solutions to the long-term problems of beggary and idleness. It directed attention to the organized and regular provision of doles and work for the poor, for example. Such devices were bound to seem intrusive in a world where almsgiving was traditionally a matter for the Church and individual consciences. But the progress of Reformation by statute added extra weight to the argument that lay manipulation of charity was both intellectually defensible and socially necessary.

In 1530 and 1535 two paper projects for the relief and employment of the poor were put forward, the first by a lawyer, Christopher St German, the second probably by the translator of the Ypres regulations, William Marshall. St German proposed a royal commission which, among other things, would set vagabonds at work constructing highways and arrange for local collections of alms in 'common chests'. Complaining again about paupers lying 'in the open streets and fallen to utter desolation', Marshall favoured similar solutions and advocated an income tax to pay for public works organized by a 'council to avoid vagabonds'.[21] Not surprisingly, neither scheme reached fruition, although two statutes dealing with the poor were passed in 1531 and 1536, both of them in origin government measures. The first seems to have owed nothing to St German but much to an increase in vagabondage caused by three bad harvests in a row between 1527 and 1529. The second statute was more innovative but also, and perhaps for that reason, only temporary.

Like its predecessor of 1495, the Act of 1531 simplified the punishment of vagrants and tightened up on the definition of settlement. Vagabonds were now to be whipped, not stocked, and then returned to the place where they were born or where they last lived for at least three years.[22] The qualification for settlement was reduced to one year in 1598, but otherwise this remained the usual medicine for vagrancy throughout the period. The statute also introduced a second procedure: the local licensing of approved beggars. Legislation in 1388 and 1495 had already distinguished between able and impotent mendicants; and badges had been issued to some of the latter in Gloucester in 1504 and in other towns, including London, in the 1520s.[23] The Act of 1531 extended this to the whole kingdom. All beggars were to be punished unless licensed by justices of the peace.

The statute of 1536 went much further, though not as far as originally intended.[24] The bill first introduced into the Commons, and supported in person by Henry VIII as a measure 'for a common weal', may well have followed the lines of Marshall's scheme. It almost certainly included provision for public works, for example. It had to be dropped for lack of support. Even so, the second draft which became the main body of the final Act introduced three elements which were of major importance for the future. First, it retained some emphasis on public employment alongside the usual negative sanctions against vagabonds. There were to be monthly searches, and penalties for persistent vagrancy were increased: a third offence was to be felony. But vagabonds were also to be set to work when they arrived home, and poor children were to be put to service in husbandry or other crafts.

Secondly, the Act provided for organized collections for the impotent poor as Marshall had wished, and laid full responsibility for them on the parish. London had again led the way with an order for regular collections of alms in all parishes in the city in 1533.[25] These were now to occur on Sundays and holy days in every English parish, to be supervised by special collectors, and to be accounted for. Thirdly, as a consequence of the rest, the main body of the Act was able to prohibit begging and indiscriminate almsgiving altogether. 'Common and open doles' were castigated. Alms were not to be given to individuals but to the common boxes in every parish. Here was statutory expression of principles which were common to innovations in social welfare in many parts of the continent: centralized charity and a ban on mendicancy.

They proved too radical for the English parliament. The two Houses added to the Act a series of destructive provisos in defence of almsgiving and the institutions which indulged in or relied upon it. Alms given by monasteries, hospitals, the nobility or their servants were exempted from the statute, and so were casual donations of money or food to prisoners and parishioners, to friars, to shipwrecked sailors, or to any 'lame, blind, or sick, aged or impotent people'. It was an exhaustive list. The Lords also insisted that no one should be constrained to give money to the common box. In effect, the Act was maimed from the start.

In any case, it did not survive. It ought to have been continued in the next parliament, also meeting in 1536, and it was not. It lapsed, perhaps through deliberate neglect, perhaps as a result of oversight.[26] It was the Act of 1531 which remained on the statute book and which was widely enforced in the localities. Between 1531 and 1547 licences, badges or other means of regulating begging were introduced in Norwich, Southampton, Cambridge, Chester, Lincoln, Hull, Beverley, York and Kings Lynn.[27] Yet the Act of 1536 had laid down the guide-lines along which poor-relief mechanisms were to develop. It needed only the dissolution, and the removal of some of the institutions which supported indiscriminate charity, to push local and central authorities further along them. In 1539 Cromwell was again contemplating 'a device in parliament for the poor people of this realm'.[28] Nothing came of it. The corporation of London, however, took up the social challenge and opportunity of the Reformation in decisive manner.

The five London hospitals, St Bartholomew's, St Thomas's, Christ's and Bridewell and Bedlam, founded or remodelled between 1544 and 1557, can be compared only with poor-relief institutions in major cities on the continent. In conception and in reality, flawed as it was, they were unique in England. In effect, they attempted to realize the purposes of the 1536 Act, not through parish collections and distributions, but through the incarceration of different categories of pauper in centrally managed civic institutions funded by private philanthropy. Other English towns copied some features of the London scheme, but the hospitals were larger and more ambitious than any of their provincial imitators. They represented the greatest experiment in social welfare in Tudor England.[29]

The impulses behind them will be familiar by now. The first orders for St Bartholomew's, published in 1552, claimed that in the past five years it had cured 800 poor 'of the pox, fistules, filthy blanes and sores . . . which else might have . . . stunk in the eyes and noses of the city'; and its beadles were enjoined to throw vagrants in gaol and bring in any sick loitering in the streets 'to the noyance and infection of the passers-by'. Christ's Hospital housed foundling children whose 'corrupt nature' arose from the 'dunghills' from which they were taken. But revulsion against dirt and contamination was also combined with positive Christian charity. As 'faithful ministers of God', the lay governors of St Bartholomew's claimed to be furthering 'this most necessary succour of their poor brethren in Christ'. Bishop Ridley wished that 'Christ should lie no more abroad in the streets' when he asked Edward VI for the grant of Bridewell: that former royal palace would 'wonderfully well serve to lodge Christ in'.[30]

Christian charity was to be carefully controlled by a secular central authority: not, it is true, by the civic government, but by a separate body of governors, all of them members of the civic elite. It was charity nonetheless. Most of the hospitals were in buildings which had once belonged to religious orders; all voluntary parish collections for the poor were to be paid to Christ's Hospital for central distribution; and the institutions were chartered corporations, able to receive and hold, sue for and defend, gifts of land as well as money. The famous tax of one half-fifteenth raised for St Bartholomew's in 1547 was a once-for-all levy, and philanthropy was supposed then to take over, as in other European towns. The hospitals attracted nearly one half of the charitable bequests of London testators in the 1550s.

The hospitals resembled some continental schemes also in the broad coalition of city fathers which supported them. It included established aldermen such as Richard Gresham and George Barne, and thrusting younger men who were to be significant in the later history of social welfare in the city, such as Thomas Lodge. The Protestant patrician Rowland Hill was deeply involved, but so also was the famous Catholic philanthropist Thomas White. Although we know less about the intellectual inclinations and educational background of these men than we should like, we may suspect humanist influence on some of them: on the two surgeons who were involved, for example, John Ayliffe and Thomas Vicary, and on the two figures most active in the work: Richard Grafton and Martin Bowes. Grafton, the first treasurer of Christ's, was printer to the Edwardian government and he had travelled on the continent. Bowes, the first 'comptroller general' when the scheme was perfected in 1557, had earlier proposed a 'brotherhood of the poor', a fraternity of charitably minded merchants like those to be found in Venice and elsewhere.

Finally, the London hospitals met with precisely the same coldly suspicious reception in orthodox Catholic circles as continental innovations.[31] There was no wholehearted antipathy in the reaction of the new Marian regime of 1553. Cardinal Pole, for example, who had recently returned from Italy, was naturally a leading advocate of hospitals on Italian lines. But they should be hospitals which did not threaten established ecclesiastical authority or those old traditions of indiscriminate charity which had been defended in the provisos of 1536. Queen Mary's own work of piety was significant: the refoundation of Henry VII's Savoy Hospital, which gave food, alms and a night's lodging to any poor who came to its doors. This was a far cry from the discrimination explicit in the various purposes of the different Edwardian hospitals, and from the punishment of casual vagrants and beggars in Bridewell, to which Edward gave the lands of the old Savoy. The privileges and jurisdiction of the church were also vigorously defended. The Greyfriars tried to destroy Christ's Hospital, which had taken over their premises, and Bishop Bonner challenged Bridewell's open punishment of moral offences normally tried by ecclesiastical courts.

These were not serious obstacles to the success of the hospitals, however, for the Elizabethan Settlement removed them. The roots of their ultimate failure lay rather in civic and economic circumstances. The hospitals did not remove the spectre of poverty from the streets, and they had neither the financial resources nor the physical capacity to do so. Charitable endowments, generous as they were, proved inadequate, and unpopular levies on the city companies and new revenues from cloth sales at Blackwell Hall were not sufficient to make up the deficit. More fundamentally, the confinement of the sick and the old in St Bartholomew's and St Thomas's, and of orphans and rogues in Christ's and Bridewell, still left a vast segment of proverty uncatered for. As one level of poverty was identified and removed, another was uncovered. Bridewell never attempted to absorb more than a tiny fraction of the unemployed, and there remained the problems of casual labour and low wages to force men temporarily onto the streets. These were the respectable 'decayed householders' identified and counted when different kinds of poverty were first clearly distinguished in 1552.[32]

The logic of the situation led ineluctably towards parish responsibility for the poor and the regular provision of outdoor relief, towards the solutions first advanced in 1536. As early as 1547 Bowes had planned a system of parochial collections for this purpose, and in 1552 those who refused to pay or paid little were 'cessed and rated' by the aldermen. Although there was no wholly compulsory poor rate in London before 1572, the aldermen were often exhorted to persuade and cajole parishes and parishioners into giving more.[33] Moreover, this parish activity undermined and in the end destroyed the centralizing function of the hospitals. By the 1560s parishes were retaining in their own hands the money for outdoor relief which ought to have been paid into Christ's. For the moment the hospitals were still the central part of social welfare in the city, but they did not have a monopoly of it and their role, as we shall see, gradually declined.

The twin pressures of civic circumstances and humanist rhetoric thus produced a variety of welfare strategies and elicited different responses from different sources – from the aldermen of London, from parliament under Cromwell, and from the Council under Wolsey. As Miss Leonard pointed out long ago, the three forces of Council, parliament and municipal authorities shaped English social welfare.[34] They necessarily interacted with one another. The central government often had a major hand in legislation, as in 1536. It was also influential in the localities, whether through direct pressure from the Council and its provincial offshoots, as in the cases of London and York,[35] or through the activities of individual councillors. In Elizabeth's reign, for example, the earl of Huntingdon, the earl of Leicester and Sir Francis Walsingham were involved in poor-relief schemes in Oxford, Warwick and Winchester.[36] Local innovations equally helped to shape legislation. We have seen that the beggars' licences and parochial collections in the Acts of 1531 and 1536 had been anticipated in London; and civic magistrates necessarily brought their local experience to bear on the legislation which they discussed as MPs. Martin Bowes, for example, sat in the parliaments of 1552 and 1555 which produced poor laws which we shall shortly consider.

Nevertheless, the three authorities had different ends in view and favoured different strategies. The central government remained largely concerned with domestic security, and hence first with vagabondage and then with immediate responses to particular crises. Municipalities continued to place their faith in centralized institutions rather than parish collections. Parliament, concerned with small villages and townships as well as larger cities, perforce concentrated on the parish. There is something to be said, therefore, for treating the three separately as far as possible. Since parliament's achievement was the most long-lasting and the earliest to be completed, we should consider the shaping of legislation first. Central initiatives and local projects will be discussed in the next chapter.

LEGISLATION

For thirty years after 1536 the history of the poor law was one of false starts, parliamentary compromises and half-measures, in which it is often difficult to see the wood for the trees as statute succeeds statute. The first effort, the famous Vagrancy Act of 1547, was the most spectacular failure. Its central provision, that vagrants could be bound as slaves for two years to masters who would take them on, proved hopelessly impractical. Yet the Act was not a wholly abstract exercise in social engineering imposed by the fiat of a new reforming government. It developed out of several bills presented to parliament, and in its final form it was a comprehensive poor law. Like the statute of 1536, it prescribed weekly collections for the impotent poor; it prohibited all begging without exception; and the slavery provisions were themselves a brutally simple means of employing paupers. However, volunteer slave-owners did not materialize, and this damned the whole statute. When it was repealed in 1550 and the elementary provisions of 1531 restored, little was salvaged beyond a clause, like that of 1536, allowing the compulsory employment of poor children.[37]

The clock could not be put back for long, however, for town councils in the provinces as well as in London were already moving ahead. There were censuses and surveys of the poor in Chester in 1539, Coventry in 1547 and Ipswich in 1551. There were schemes for setting the poor to work in Oxford and Kings Lynn between 1546 and 1548.[38] Most important of all, parochial collections were replaced by compulsory levies for the poor in Norwich in 1549 and York in 1550. The council of Norwich acted in May 1549, on the very eve of Ket's rebellion and no doubt through fear of disorder; and compulsion seems to have been abandoned after a year or two. In York, however, there had already been an experiment with a forced levy for plague victims in 1538, and the assessments for the poor which were begun in 1550, in the middle of another crisis caused by dearth and disease, proved permanent.[39] In the next dearth, a few other towns followed suit, all of them close enough to Norwich to be influenced by its example: there were compulsory poor rates in Colchester, Ipswich and Cambridge in 1556 and 1557.[40]

Parliament began to move in the same direction in 1552. The statute of that year retained the voluntary principle, but it prescribed weekly church collections and condemned begging in words very close to those of the Act of 1536. It also backed up its prescriptions by encouraging the measurement of responsibilities and resources in every parish. There should be local registers of the needy poor, and records of the amounts which parishioners agreed to give towards their support, thus committing themselves in advance to weekly payments. This was an important step towards a national poor rate, and it may be that Northumberland's government had hoped to go the whole way. The first bill on the subject, introduced into the Lords, was entitled 'for taxes and assessments for the relief of poor and impotent persons'. It clearly had a mixed reception, and it was replaced with a new bill simply for 'provision and relief of the poor' which was rushed through all its parliamentary stages at the end of the session. Although it is impossible to be sure of the details, it looks as if the government intervened to save as much as possible in a measure whose taxation provisions had proved controversial.[41]

It was scarcely to be expected that Mary's government would pick up that particular hot potato again. It was no less anxious than its predecessors to repress vagrancy, but it was unlikely to offend Catholic sensibilities by further restricting voluntary charity. Rather, perhaps, the reverse. In the event, a new statute of 1555 repeated the provisions of 1552 almost word for word.[42] The only substantial addition was a clause permitting licensed begging wherever the poor were too numerous to be relieved at home; and the fact that this was repeated in the Elizabethan statute of 1563 suggests that it was less a concession to Catholic principles than a recognition of reality in large towns. When a description of England written in 1556 claimed with some pride that 'the poor do not go begging in England, but alms are given to them in their own houses', it referred to the intention rather than the effect of the statutes of 1552 and 1555.[43]

The first Elizabethan poor law of 1563 scarcely took matters further. It introduced the first hint of compulsion, but only after the persuasions of clergy and bishops had failed. In the end, people refusing to contribute to the poor could be bound over to appear before justices of the peace who might imprison them if they remained obdurate.[44] The Acts of 1552, 1555 and 1563 had some impact in the localities, in a few rural parishes as well as in towns. Lists of people refusing to pay to the poor were drawn up, overseers appointed, and accounts of receipts and expenditure kept.[45] But it was scattered, haphazard activity which might have simmered on for decades. If local developments were to be orchestrated and accelerated, the parliamentary caution which was evident in 1536 and 1552 had to be overcome. The necessary sense of urgency was created by the Rising in the North.

The rebellion of 1569 sent as great a tremor through the propertied classes as the more serious revolts of 1549. The government ordered national searches for suspicious vagabonds, and followed them up by pressing for legislation against vagrants.[46] A new penal law was debated and lost in 1571 but considered again and passed with additions in the next parliament in 1572. The Rising also impelled local activity. In York, for example, it led to a survey of the poor and a revision of parish assessments; and in Norwich an associated political conspiracy pushed the corporation into the most radical municipal revision of social welfare since the founding of the London hospitals. There was the great census of the poor of 1570, a new compulsory assessment for their relief, a Bridewell or house of correction for rogues, and a scheme for regular surveys of poor households and for the employment of able-bodied paupers and poor children.[47] All this attracted the attention of Matthew Parker, who sat on the Lords committee considering the 1572 bill; and the House of Commons in the same year included John Aldrich, who had been Mayor of Norwich in 1570. As a result, perhaps, the 1572 Act had two parts: the first was the penal measure against vagrants, first considered in 1571; the second was an enactment for the relief of the poor, including, at last, a compulsory poor rate.[48]

The importance of the statute is partly reflected in the parliamentary opposition which it aroused. The clauses concerning vagabonds proved controversial. According to the final Act, they were to be whipped and bored through the ear by order of sessions for a first offence, unless masters could be found who would take them on; and for a second offence they should be hung as felons, unless taken into service for two years. The punishments seemed to one member, Miles Sandys, 'oversharp and bloody'. His experience in Worcestershire showed that justices of the peace could relieve the poor in their 'own houses and ... stay them from wandering', if they made the effort. The broad definition of vagabonds in the Act, and in particular the inclusion of such familiar wayfaring figures as minstrels, also troubled many members. Minstrels were included in the end, but only if they were not employed by the nobility or licensed by two justices. Moreover, behind these specific criticisms there was an unspoken but tangible reluctance to abandon casual almsgiving. Supporting the bill, Thomas Wilson had to assert that the 'looseness and lewdness' of the times made harsh penalties and hard-headed discrimination essential: 'He said it was no charity to give to such a one as we know not, being a stranger unto us.'[49]

Wilson won the parliamentary argument. While the list of culpable vagabonds included a multitude of sinners, among them 'loitering' labourers, the second half of the Act made it clear that the money raised by the new poor rates was only to be given to 'impotent persons' after careful examination of their credentials. Justices of the peace were to take surveys of the poor in their county divisions and then to 'tax and assess' all inhabitants to provide for them. Overseers were to be appointed in each parish and to conduct monthly inspections to ensure that strangers were excluded from the dole. This has echoes of 1552. It also sounds very like the action taken in Norwich; and the next statute, passed in 1576 and discussed in a committee which included Aldrich, completed the parallel. There should be work-stocks of wool, flax, hemp, iron or other stuff in every city and town where the justices thought them necessary. Furthermore, houses of correction were to be built in every county for vagabonds and others who refused to do the work provided for them.[50] It had obviously proved as difficult to find masters to take vagrants into service after 1572 as after 1547: justices of the peace had to make good the deficiency.

In almost every particular, in fact, the legislation of the 1570s depended on the energy and initiative of magistrates. In corporate towns with their own commissions of the peace the Acts could readily be enforced. There were surveys of the poor and work-stocks or houses of correction in Chester, York and Hull, for example.[51] London now had its first fully compulsory assessment on the parishes, and the aldermen, prompted by Burghley, were discussing schemes to increase rates and provide work for the poor throughout the 1570s.[52] Rural justices had greater difficulties. They could set up county houses of correction, as in Hampshire, Wiltshire, Kent and Suffolk. They could act still more effectively through divisional meetings, which were just beginning in counties such as Norfolk, where there was a divisional Bridewell at Acle as early as 1574.[53] Yet neither houses of correction, nor gaols, nor quarter sessions could cope with all the vagrants who ought in theory to have been thrust upon them under the terms of the Act of 1572. Neither could county justices effectively survey the poor and institute rates in every single parish. Appointments of overseers and reports of refusals to pay rates necessarily remained haphazard.[54]

In addition, it took time for new orthodoxies to be accepted at the local level. A powerful faction in Warwick opposed taxation for the poor in the years after 1576, for example, and there was resistance to rates in Chester in 1574.[55] The shock of 1569 also wore off with time, thanks to political stability and runs of good harvests in the middle of Elizabeth's reign. By 1593 there were second thoughts about the punishment of vagrants: boring through the ear and the death penalty for a second offence were abolished and the simple whipping of 1531 restored. In the same year there was a large Commons committee considering the laws relating to the poor; the House seems not to have been in any hurry to legislate, however.[56]

The crisis of the later 1590s altered all that. Harvest failures, grain riots and threatened risings, especially one in Oxfordshire in 1596, put poverty once again at the top of the agenda when parliament met in the winter of 1597–98.[57] At least seventeen bills on the subject were introduced, there was prolonged debate, and there was another Commons committee to consider legislation. None of the resulting Acts can therefore be described as a purely government measure. Some of the bills may have come from the 1593 committee, since Miles Sandys proposed it and sat on its successor in 1598.[58] His colleagues in 1598 included Thomas Smith, Francis Bacon and Edward Hext, a Somerset justice who had written a famous letter to Cecil complaining of the growth of vagabondage.[59] A more powerful figure pushing business along may have been Sir Robert Wroth, a man of Puritan inclinations who was becoming a familiar face on committees considering all kinds of social regulation; and there were other, similarly motivated members of the committee, such as George More, Francis Hastings, Nathaniel Bacon, Thomas Hoby and Anthony Cope, who himself invested in projects for the employment of the poor in Lincolnshire.[60] The quantity of legislation passed in 1598, however, testifies to its broad appeal as well as to the determination and careful deliberation of particular committed members.

The first Act, for 'the relief of the poor', was the most important.[61] It placed the responsibility for outdoor relief of the impotent, for the provision of work for the able-bodied and for the apprenticeship of poor children firmly on the shoulders of churchwardens and overseers of the poor in every parish. They were to raise rates for these purposes 'by taxation of every inhabitant and every occupier of lands'. Begging was forbidden, unless licensed by the parish, and it was assumed that this would be rare. Most of this had been anticipated in 1572, but justices were now spared many of the burdens of implementation. They were only to exercise a supervisory role and to hear appeals against parish decisions.

The second Act, for the 'punishment of rogues, vagabonds and sturdy beggars', had similar effect.[62] The definition of a vagrant remained almost exactly as it had been in 1572, but the punishment was now to be only a whipping for a first offence, followed by return to place of birth or dwelling, and this could be carried out by the constable and minister of a parish acting alone. Even the approval of a single justice, as required in the legislation of 1531 and 1593, was no longer necessary. Quarter sessions were involved only in the punishment of 'dangerous and incorrigible rogues', who could be banished.

There were four other relevant Acts in 1598. Two dealt with maimed, idle and disorderly soldiers and sailors returning from the wars, building on an earlier enactment of 1593.[63] Two attacked the equally familiar but more complex problem of endowed charities. The first allowed benefactors to found almshouses, houses of correction or hospitals without the cumbersome and expensive process of obtaining charters or letters patent.[64] The second provided for commissions to investigate breaches of charitable trusts, a mechanism much used in later years to ensure that the wishes of donors were respected. This statute was the basis for the Charitable Uses Act of 1601 which went further in clarifying acceptable charitable purposes. Legal and practical problems remained, however, and if there was ever any hope that private philanthropy might be harnessed to obviate the need for public rates and doles, it was soon disappointed.[65]

Although they had loose ends and inconsistencies of their own, and although parliament often debated additions and revisions, the Vagrancy and Poor-Relief Statutes of 1598 established the three fundamentals of the English poor law. First, there was the summary punishment of vagrants, recorded in those local lists of passports referred to in the last chapter. A statute of 1604 merely added that incorrigible rogues should be branded rather than banished, and imposed the death penalty for a third offence.[66] There continued to be some anxiety about the loose definition of a vagrant. It was apparent in a proclamation of 1602, in the 'judges' resolutions' of the 1620s and 1630s, and in the parliament of 1657 which passed another Vagrancy Statute, designed primarily against wandering Ranters and Quakers. There was even fresh debate about the status of minstrels.[67] But local authorities retained the wide discretion which we saw them exercising in the last chapter.

Secondly, outdoor relief financed by poor rates became commonplace in the generation after 1598. The statute of 1601, which presented the 1598 Relief Act in its final form, did little to alter the essentials, though it reduced the number of overseers required in each parish from four to two.[68] There were disputes about who was liable to be rated, and about whether their liability should be assessed on the basis of 'ability', as the judges suggested, or according to the value of land or houses occupied, as came to be the general practice.[69] There was even some resistance still to the very principle of taxation. The parishioners of part of the West Riding opposed the prohibition of begging and the introduction of rates in 1598 on the grounds that 'many are able to give relief which are not able to give money'; neighbours would support their neighbours with help in kind. As late as 1624 the justices around Ormskirk, Lancashire, agreed that there should be no taxation for poor relief there: provided that they were orderly and did not wander outside the parish, the impotent should be 'at liberty to ask and have reasonable relief ... not troubling any house above once a week'.[70] By then, however, poor rates were universal in the larger towns and increasingly common in more populous rural parishes.

The third pillar of the law, the provision of work for the deserving able-bodied poor, proved to be the weakest. Although there were work-stocks in some parishes, most overseers found it easier to pay cash doles to the unemployed than to supervise their labour. Their enthusiasm for binding out pauper apprentices, which was encouraged both by parliament and Council, proved more long-lasting and more effective, but even that was dampened by the usual difficulty of finding masters to take them on.[71] Rich municipalities were able to invest in workhouses, of course, but their chequered history belongs with the local projects considered in the next chapter; it owed little to parliament.

Related institutions, houses of correction, rested more firmly on legislation, and they tell us more about the interests of members and of the generality of magistrates. There was considerable investment in them, especially after 1610 when a statute ordered their erection in every county for 'the keeping, correcting and setting to work of ... rogues, vagabonds, sturdy beggars and other idle and disorderly persons'.[72] The Essex justices had plans for no less than twenty-three houses, and by 1630 there was at least one in every county for which records survive, as well as in several corporate towns.[73] Sometimes they were combined with workhouses, but the summary punishment of disorderly paupers always took precedence over employment in the end, as it had indeed done in Bridewell itself. Fragile and often mismanaged, the houses of correction which were founded and refounded in the English counties were the characteristic institutional expression of the Elizabethan poor law.[74]

Seventeenth-century practice revealed other limitations in the legislation of 1598. Its dependence on the parish, and on annually assessed parish rates and annually agreed lists of poor pensioners, meant that the machinery of relief could not easily cope with critical circumstances, when extra resources were needed, or easily be manipulated by central direction, whether from the Council, county justices or civic magistrates. The 1598 Relief Act did say that mayors and aldermen should enforce it in corporate towns, and several municipalities responded by centralizing poor relief and transferring funds from one parish to another.[75] A statute of 1604 also allowed justices to raise rates for plague-infected parishes and towns and to punish infected wanderers.[76] But the next chapter will show that action outside and beyond the provisions of the law proved necessary if the deficiencies of parish poor relief were to be made good. There is no doubt that the Poor-Relief Act of 1598 gave power as well as responsibility to the parishes.

The effects of the Act in London show this well enough. It destroyed what remained of central organisation through the hospitals. The statute of 1572 had specifically confirmed their role, and the governors of Christ's Hospital arranged for extra payments to the poor parishes of St Sepulchre and St Giles Cripplegate in 1573 and regularly put pressure on the aldermen to revise parish assessments.[77] The statutes of 1598 and 1601 failed to make any such special provision for London, however. In 1598 and 1599, therefore, the corporation appointed a central treasurer to oversee parish rates and separated them from the collections for Christ's Hospital. The two were formally brought together again in 1602, but the governors of Christ's complained that there were now so many parish pensioners that there was little money left over for them.[78] The Hospital's receipts from parish collections, which had already been declining in the 1560s, fell away almost to nothing. The total was £1,820 in 1554–55, £793 in 1579–80, £215 in 1625–26 and only £38 in 1635–36.[79] In effect the Act of 1598 spelled the end of supervision through Christ's. It encouraged the parishes to control their own finances and their own poor, subject only to the aldermen's orders for rates in aid for the poorest of them.

A poor law had thus been created which was eminently suited to small rural communities, which could be adapted to circumstances in large cities, even if imperfectly, and which imposed uniformity on the whole kingdom. After 1598 there could be no question how the poor should be treated. If vagrant, they had a parish of settlement to which they must be returned. If already settled, they should be set to work or supported by outdoor relief financed by local taxation. Uniform settlement regulations and uniform rates would abolish beggary, both as a condition and as an activity.

There had been many forces ranged against this development. Traditional ideals of neighbourly charity, even to strangers, and the tenacious social and religious ritual of almsgiving, without regard to its practical consequences, impeded change as much as the vested interests of property-owners, whether expressed in parliament or in local vestries. But the forces making for innovation were more powerful. One was the force of circumstances. It was not the long-term background features of demographic growth and rising unemployment which inspired government or parliamentary intervention, but sudden crises, often of a multiple kind: the threat or actuality of popular disturbance (in 1517, 1549, 1569 and 1596), harvest failure (in 1527, 1535, 1550, 1562 and 1596–97), epidemic disease (in 1517 and 1551), or a slump in overseas trade with its impact on domestic employment (in 1551, 1563 and the years after 1568). It was no accident that parliament turned again to a complete reconsideration of the poor law – though without reaching any conclusion – in the hard times of the 1620s and later 1640s.[80]

Motives and attitudes were even more important. Humanist stress on the social responsibilities of governments pointed to an instrument which could be used to satisfy both the instinctive desire to clean up the streets and the guilt-ridden conviction that a replacement must be found for charitable institutions maimed or destroyed by the Reformation. The central government, Crown and parliament, could take care of both. The propertied classes were always wary of untrammelled and indiscriminate government intervention, of course. Late in Elizabeth's reign the House of Commons was suspicious of new attempts to regulate social behaviour, unless they were subjected to strict parliamentary controls.[81] Some people even had scruples about the legality of summary punishments in Bridewell and other houses of correction, and the Act of 1610 may have been intended to answer them.[82]

In general, however, there was little objection so long as experiments in social engineering were directed towards the meaner sort, and not towards their betters. This was one important trend in the later sixteenth century. Parliament had ceased to legislate against covetousness and come to tolerate usury by 1572; its opposition to enclosure was no more than half-hearted, at any rate after the 1590s; and it repealed sumptuary laws regulating the fashions of the elite in 1604. By contrast, measures intended to reform the manners and behaviour of the lower orders enjoyed an increasingly warm parliamentary welcome. Between 1576 and 1610 there were 35 bills on drunkenness, inns and alehouses, 9 against the prophanation of the sabbath, 9 dealing with bastardy and 6 against swearing.[83] Regulation and relief of the poor fitted naturally into that context.

All this suggests that the machinery of the poor law was not designed as an economic regulator, but as a moral, social and political one. It is possible that the first public-employment schemes of the 1530s were prompted by government anxieties that labour would not be available for military works, such as the building of harbours and defences.[84] Rather earlier, in 1511, a proclamation against idleness and vaga-bondage had complained that husbandmen and artificers could not 'get labourers for their money'.[85] Conditions of labour shortage no longer obtained in 1598, however. Neither is it persuasive to argue that the poor law was intended primarily as a means of mopping up surplus labour as population grew. Contemporaries were aware of the problem, of course. The Statute of Artificers of 1563 tried, among other things, to enforce full employment through apprenticeship, and there were private economic projects with the same end in view. Yet we have noted that the most constructive legislative proposals for the employment of the poor failed, either in parliament or in their local implementation. There cannot have been any widespread conviction that they were central or indispensable to the whole effort. Appealing as new economic incentives were to some projectors and legislators, they had less hold on the people who counted at the centre and in the provinces than the simpler assumptions that the poor were getting poorer and potentially more disorderly, and that it was the duty of Christian magistrates to relieve their wants and make them respectable. Provision of work, in so far as it was attempted, was a means to other ends, not an end in itself.

Finally, the nature of English politics and government created precedents, constraints and opportunities which proved formative. Parliament's role as a regular point of contact between central government and the localities, debating new solutions and revising old ones in successive sessions, served to cut ambitious strategies down to size. Suspicious of devices which might entail too much central interference, wary too of any major increase in taxation, parliament's natural recourse in the end was reliance on the parish and on local rates. Major property-owners were thus spared too heavy an administrative or financial burden. They could leave detailed management to their inferiors, to churchwardens and overseers, and rely on the fact that poor rates, like all rates, hit modest occupiers of property, ordinary householders, harder than the rich. For their part, parish elites no doubt thought rates a price worth paying to keep disorderly poverty off the streets.

Reliance on the parish and on rates also had other roots. As an ecclesiastical unit the parish had long had a welfare role, and the civil parish, with its origins in the medieval vill, was developing rapidly in the sixteenth century as Henry VIII and his successors imposed new responsibilities on it: poor relief was only one, though the most important, of them. The alternative organs of local government in hundreds and manors proved less flexible and were therefore pushed into the background.[86] The statute of 1536 first stressed the role of the parish in the relief and settlement of the poor; the Acts of 1598 confirmed it for good. Rates were similarly old devices used for new purposes in the early and mid-sixteenth century. There had been local assessments for the upkeep of churches; municipal rates for such purposes as cleaning the streets were beginning; and there were statutory rates in Henry VIII's reign for the maintenance of bridges and sea defences.[87] Rates for the poor were one further expression of the responsible local community fulfilling its obligations.

Simple household relief paid for by parish rates might therefore seem the obvious solution in English circumstances, first as a temporary expedient, as in Norwich in 1549, and then more permanently at the end of the sixteenth century when poverty seemed to be getting out of hand. It is doubtful, however, whether so much would have been accomplished if there had not been elements continually asking for more: the Privy Council and town corporations, some of whose projects we have already touched on. Both were disappointed by the legislative achievement, seeing it as the least that could be expected; but they obtained some of their ends without parliamentary backing. It is to their endeavours that we must now turn.

NOTES AND REFERENCES

1. M. Hale, *A Discourse Touching Provision for the Poor* (1683), pp. 2–3.
2. Above, p. 13.
3. R. Mitchison, 'The Making of the Old Scottish Poor Law', *Past and Present*, 63 (1974), 58–93.
4. Cf. E. M. Leonard, *The Early History of English Poor Relief* (Cambridge UP, 1900), p. 62.
5. J. J. Scarisbrick, *The Reformation and the English People* (Blackwell, Oxford, 1984), Ch. 2; R. M. Smith (ed.), *Land, Kinship and Life-Cycle* (Cambridge UP, 1984), pp. 82–3; M. K. McIntosh, 'Social Change and Tudor Manorial Leets', in J. A. Guy and H. G. Beale (eds), *Law and Social Change in British History* (Royal Historical Society, 1984), pp. 75–7, 83–4; S. and B. Webb, *The Old Poor Law* (Longmans, Green and Co., 1927), pp. 8–12.
6. W. K. Jordan, *Philanthropy in England 1480–1660* (Allen and Unwin, 1959), pp. 253–74, and for specific examples, see Devon RO, Exeter Corporation Records, Receivers' Account Roll 1500–1501; Hooker's Commonplace Book, f. 152v (Christmas doles); B. R. Masters and E. Ralph (eds), *The Church Book of St. Ewen's, Bristol 1454–1584* (Bristol and Gloucs Arch. Soc., Records Section, vi, 1967), p. 137 (bread).
7. R. M. Clay, *The Medieval Hospitals of England* (Methuen, 1909), p. xviii and app. B; J. Youings, *Sixteenth-Century England* (Penguin Books, Harmondsworth, 1984), p. 256; Scarisbrick, *Reformation and the English People*, pp. 114–16; C. D. Ross (ed.), *Cartulary of St. Mark's Hospital, Bristol* (Bristol Rec. Soc., xxi, 1959), p. xvii.
8. E. M. Hampson, *The Treatment of Poverty in Cambridgeshire 1597–1834* (Cambridge UP, 1934), pp. 1–2; W. O. Ault, 'Manor Court and Parish Church in Fifteenth-Century England: A Study of Village By-Laws', *Speculum*, xlii (1967), 66; H. Littlehales (ed.), *The Medieval Records of a London City Church (St Mary at Hill) 1420–1559* (Early English Text Soc., Old Series, cxxviii, 1905), p. 299. For later problems with parish 'poor boxes' and charities, see C. J. Kitching (ed.), *The Royal Visitation of 1559* (Surtees Soc., clxxxvii, 1975), pp. 66, 68, 69, 70.
9. A. Raine (ed.), *York Civic Records* (Yorks Arch. Soc., Record Ser., 1939–53), i. 139–40; M. Bateson and H. Stocks (eds), *Records of the Borough of Leicester* (Cambridge UP, 1899–1923), ii. 308–9, 310–13; M. D. Harris (ed.), *The Coventry Leet Book* (Early English Text Soc., 1907–13), ii. 538–9; P. L. Hughes and J. F. Larkin (eds), *Tudor Royal Proclamations* (Yale UP, New Haven, 1964–9), i. no. 16.
10. 11 Henry VII, c. 2; P. Williams, *The Tudor Regime* (Oxford UP, 1979), p. 196.
11. E.g., *Coventry Leet Book*, ii. 568; Lincolnshire RO, Lincoln Entries of Common Council 1541–64, f. 42r. On general municipal concern with the health of the body politic, see M. James, 'Ritual, Drama and Social Body in the late Medieval English Town', *Past and Present*, 98 (1983), 6–7 and note 18.
12. J. H. Hexter, *More's Utopia. The Biography of an Idea* (Harper Torchbooks, New York, 1965), p. 61; T. More, *Utopia*, ed. G. Sampson (G.

Bell and Son, 1910), p. 53. Cf. **C. Lis** and **H. Soly**, *Poverty and Capitalism in Pre-industrial Europe* (Harvester, Hassocks, 1979), p. 86; **W. R. D. Jones**, *The Tudor Commonwealth* (Athlone, 1970), Ch. 7; **A. B. Ferguson**, *The Articulate Citizen and the English Renaissance* (Duke UP, Durham, N. Carolina, 1965), Chs viii–xi.

13. **T. Starkey**, *A Dialogue between Reginald Pole and Thomas Lupset*, ed. **K. M. Burton** (Chatto and Windus, 1948), p. 90.

14. *Ibid.*, p. 160; **F. R. Salter**, *Some Early Tracts on Poor Relief* (Methuen, 1926), pp. 37–8, quoted above, p. 23.

15. **J. J. Scarisbrick**, 'Cardinal Wolsey and the Common Weal', in **E. W. Ives, R. J. Knecht** and **J. J. Scarisbrick** (eds), *Wealth and Power in Tudor England. Essays presented to S. T. Bindoff* (Athlone, 1978), pp. 45–67.

16. London Corporation RO, Rep. iii, ff. 189v–190r; Journal xi, ff. 337–8; **R. W. Heinze**, *The Proclamations of the Tudor Kings* (Cambridge UP, 1976), p. 17.

17. *Coventry Leet Book*, iii. 652, 658; **C. Phythian-Adams**, *Desolation of a City* (Cambridge UP, 1979), pp. 64, 287; HMC, *14th Report*, App. viii, pp. 27, 29 (Lincoln); **J. H. Thomas**, *Town Government in the Sixteenth Century* (Allen and Unwin, 1933), p. 115 (Leicester and Shrewsbury). Cf. **V. Parker**, *The Making of Kings Lynn* (Phillimore, 1971), p. 150; *Tudor Royal Proclamations*, i. no. 80.

18. **P. Slack**, *The Impact of Plague in Tudor and Stuart England* (Routledge and Kegan Paul, 1985), Ch. 8.

19. **W. Hudson** and **J. C. Tingey** (eds), *The Records of the City of Norwich* (Jarrold and Sons, Norwich and London, 1906–10), ii. xcvii; *Coventry Leet Book*, iii. 674–5; Exeter Corporation Records, Act Book 1, ff. 91r, 96v; Leonard, *Poor Relief*, pp. 24, 40–1; London Corporation RO, Rep. iv, f. 106v.

20. **Heinze**, *Proclamations of the Tudor Kings*, pp. 99–101; **W. Ashley**, *The Bread of our Forefathers* (Oxford UP, 1928), pp. 187–8; below, pp. 139–40.

21. **J. A. Guy**, *The Public Career of Sir Thomas More* (Harvester, Brighton, 1980), pp. 151–6; **G. R. Elton**, *Studies in Tudor and Stuart Politics and Government* (Cambridge UP, 1974), ii. 137–54.

22. 22 Henry VIII, c. 12. The three-year qualification for settlement had first been introduced in a statute of 1504, and whipping in a proclamation of 1530: 19 Henry VII, c. 12; *Tudor Royal Proclamations*, i. no. 128. There was also a statute against gipsies in 1531: 22 Henry VIII, c. 10.

23. 12 Richard II, c. 7; 11 Henry VII, c. 2; **Thomas**, *Town Government*, p. 115; **Leonard**, *Poor Law*, p. 26.

24. 27 Henry VIII, c. 25; **G. R. Elton**, *Reform and Renewal* (Cambridge UP, 1973), pp. 123–4. Professor Elton's reconstruction of the history of the statute is convincing, though, as will appear, I am not persuaded that the clauses added by the two Houses did not 'seriously affect' the Act.

25. London Corporation RO, Rep. viii, f. 274v.

26. **Elton**, *Reform and Renewal*, pp. 124–5; **S. E. Lehmberg**, *The Later Parliaments of Henry VIII* (Cambridge UP, 1977), p. 18, and cf. **Lehmberg** in *Renaissance Quarterly*, xxvii (1974), 572–3.

27. *Records of Norwich*, ii. 161–2; **A. L. Merson** (ed.), *The Third Book of Remembrance of Southampton* (Southampton Record Ser., ii, iii, viii, 1952–65), i. 52–3; **R. H. Morris**, *Chester in the Plantagenet and Tudor*

Reigns (Chester, 1893), pp. 355–7; HMC, *14th Report*, App. viii, p. 40; **K. Anderson**, 'The treatment of vagrancy and the relief of the poor and destitute in the Tudor period', London Univ., Ph.D. thesis, 1933, pp. 262–3; HMC, *11th Report*, App. iii, p. 174.

28. **Elton**, *Reform and Renewal*, p. 126.
29. The following paragraphs are substantially taken from my 'Social Policy and the Constraints of Government, 1547–1558', in **J. Loach** and **R. Tittler** (eds), *The Mid-Tudor Polity c. 1540–1560* (Macmillan, 1980), pp. 108–13, where full references may be found. Cf. above, pp. 69–71.
30. **R. H. Tawney** and **E. Power** (eds), *Tudor Economic Documents* (Longmans, Green and Co., 1924), ii. 312.
31. Cf. **Salter**, *Early Tracts*, pp. 76–8; **L. Martz**, *Poverty and Welfare in Habsburg Spain* (Cambridge UP, 1983), pp. 22–9.
32. Above, pp. 70–1.
33. London Corporation RO, Journal xvi, f. 256v. For aldermanic pressure later, see Rep. xiii(i), f. 10v; Rep. xvi, f. 112r; Journal xviii, ff. 327v, 328r. As late as 1569 parishes were left to 'assess ... themselves': Journal xix, ff. 173v–174r.
34. **Leonard**, *Poor Relief*, p. 21.
35. Cf. **Slack**, *Impact of Plague*, pp. 202–4; **D. M. Palliser**, *Tudor York* (Oxford UP, 1979), p. 275.
36. *VCH Oxfordshire*, iv. 344; **A. L. Beier**, 'Social problems of ... Warwick' and **A. Rosen**, 'Winchester in Transition 1580–1700', in **P. Clark** (ed.), *Country Towns in Preindustrial England* (Leicester UP, 1981), pp. 75, 158.
37. 1 Edward VI, c. 3; 3 & 4 Edward VI, c. 16; **C. S. L. Davies**, 'Slavery and Protector Somerset: The Vagrancy Act of 1547', *Econ. Hist. Rev.*, 2nd ser., xix (1966), 533–49.
38. Chester Corporation Records, Assembly Book 1, A/B/1, f. 60; *Coventry Leet Book*, iii. 783; **N. Bacon**, *The Annalls of Ipswiche*, ed. **W. H. Richardson** (Ipswich, 1884), p. 235; *VCH Oxfordshire*, iv. 343; **Parker**, *Kings Lynn*, p. 149.
39. **Slack**, 'Social Policy', pp. 107–8; *Records of Norwich*, ii. 126; *York Civic Records*, v. 33–4, 50; **Palliser**, *Tudor York*, p. 81. It seems clear from Norfolk RO, Norwich Assembly Book 1553–83, f. 34r, that by 1557 collections for the poor in Norwich were based on persuasion by the aldermen. The 1549 rising in the West may similarly have produced the 'book for the gathering of the money for the poor' drawn up in Plymouth in 1549–50: **R. N. Worth**, *Calendar of the Plymouth Municipal Records* (Plymouth, 1893), p. 117.
40. **Webb**, *Old Poor Law*, p. 51; **J. Webb** (ed.), *Poor Relief in Elizabethan Ipswich* (Suffolk Records Soc., ix, 1966), p. 18; **E. M. Hampson**, *The Treatment of Poverty in Cambridgeshire 1597–1834* (Cambridge UP, 1934), p. 6. In the first two cases at least, as in Norwich, the innovation was probably temporary: see **Webb**, *Poor Relief in Elizabethan Ipswich*, p. 18; Essex RO, D/Y 2/41, p. 42.
41. 5 & 6 Edward VI, c. 2; **Slack**, 'Social Policy', p. 103.
42. *Ibid.*, pp. 103–4; 2 & 3 Philip and Mary, c. 5. Cf. **Williams**, *Tudor Regime*, pp. 199–200.
43. **G. Rainsford**, 'Ritratto d'Inglitterra', ed. **P. S. Donaldson**, *Camden Misc. XXVII* (Camden Soc., 4th ser., 22, 1979), p. 98.

44. 5 Elizabeth I, c. 3.
45. See, for examples, **A. Hanham** (ed.), *Churchwardens' Accounts of Ashburton 1479–1580* (Devon and Cornwall Record Soc., N.S., xv, 1970), pp. 129, 154, 190; **F. M. Osborne** (ed.), *The Churchwardens' Accounts of St. Michael's Church, Chagford, 1480–1600* (Chagford, 1979), p. 189; **F. G. Emmison**, 'Poor-relief accounts of two rural parishes in Bedfordshire, 1563–1598', *Econ. Hist. Rev.*, iii(1931), 102–16; **F. G. Emmison**, 'The Care of the Poor in Elizabethan Essex', *Essex Review*, lxii (1953), 9–10, 24.
46. Above, p. 93; **T. E. Hartley** (ed.), *Proceedings in the Parliaments of Elizabeth I*, I: 1558–81 (Leicester UP, 1981), p. 339; London Corporation RO, Journal xix, ff. 171v–172r.
47. **Palliser**, *Tudor York*, p. 275; **J. F. Pound** (ed.), *The Norwich Census of the Poor* (Norfolk Record Soc., xl, 1971), pp. 8–9; **J. F. Pound**, 'An Elizabethan Census of the Poor', *Univ. Birmingham Historical Journal*, viii (1962), 135–51; *Tudor Economic Documents*, ii. 316–26. Cf. below, pp. 149–50.
48. **Pound**, 'Elizabethan Census of the Poor', p. 138; **S. D'Ewes**, *Journals of all the Parliaments of Elizabeth* (1682), p. 198; **P. W. Hasler** (ed.), *The House of Commons 1558–1603* (HMSO, 1981), i. 333; 14 Eliz. I, c. 5.
49. **Hartley**, *Proceedings in the Parliaments*, i. 219, 311–13, 366–7, 384–5.
50. 18 Elizabeth I, c. 3. Cf. **Hartley**, *Proceedings*, i. 477, 482.
51. **Morris**, *Chester*, pp. 362–3; **Palliser**, *Tudor York*, pp. 133, 275–6; **Anderson**, 'The treatment of vagrancy and relief of the poor', pp. 376– 7.
52. London Corporation RO, Rep. xvii, ff. 261v, 388v, 425v–426; Journal xx(i), ff. 15v, 32v, 119v; Rep. xviii, ff. 108v–110r, 155v; Rep. xix, f. 25v; Journal xx(ii), ff. 323, 465r, 483r, 499v–503v.
53. Hants RO, Jervoise MSS., box 44M69/010; **J. Hurstfield**, *Freedom, Corruption and Government in Elizabethan England* (Jonathan Cape, 1973), pp. 266–7; **S. A. Peyton**, 'The Houses of Correction at Maidstone and Westminster', *Eng.Hist.Rev.*, xlii (1927), 251–4; **F. M. Eden**, *The State of the Poor* (1797), iii. cxxxvi; **F. A. Youngs**, 'Towards Petty Sessions: Tudor JPs and Divisions of Counties', in **D. J. Guth** and **J. W. McKenna** (eds), *Tudor Rule and Revolution. Essays for G. R. Elton* (Cambridge UP, 1982), pp. 210–12; **H. Ellis**, 'Letter from Secretary Walsingham', *Norfolk Archaeology*, ii (1849), 92–6. Cf. **A. H. Smith** and **G. M. Baker** (eds), *The Papers of Nathaniel Bacon of Stiffkey*, ii (Centre of East Anglian Studies, Norwich, 1983), p. 1.
54. E.g., Essex RO, Q/SR 44/27, 57; 84/67; **H. C. Johnson** (ed.), *Minutes of Proceedings in Sessions 1563 and 1574 to 1592* (Wilts Record Soc., iv, 1949), pp. 58, 64, 67, 121.
55. **A. L. Beier**, 'The Social Problems of an Elizabethan Country Town: Warwick 1580–90', in **Clark**, *Country Towns*, pp. 74–5; Chester Corporation Records, QSF/27/86–93.
56. 35 Elizabeth I, c. 7; **S. Lambert**, 'Procedure in the House of Commons in the early Stuart period', *Eng.Hist. Rev.*, xcv (1980), p. 761.
57. For the impact of the projected Oxfordshire rising, see **J. Walter**, 'A "Rising of the People"? The Oxfordshire Rising of 1596', *Past and Present*, 107 (1985), 138.
58. **Leonard**, *Poor Relief*, pp. 74–6; **D'Ewes**, *Journals*, pp. 499, 561.
59. *Tudor Economic Documents*, ii. 339–46.

60. **J. R. Kent,** 'Attitudes of Members of the House of Commons to the Regulation of "Personal Conduct" in Late Elizabethan and Early Stuart England', *Bull. Institute of Historical Research*, xlvi (1973), 41–2; **Hasler,** *House of Commons*, iii. 658–63 (Wroth) and *passim*; **J. Thirsk,** *Economic Policy and Projects* (Oxford UP, 1978), pp. 21–2.
61. 39 Elizabeth I, c. 3.
62. 39 Elizabeth I, c. 4. Cf. above, pp. 28–9, 94.
63. 39 Elizabeth I, cc. 17, 21. Cf. 35 Elizabeth I, c. 4; 43 Elizabeth I, c. 3.
64. 39 Elizabeth I, c. 5. Cf. 35 Elizabeth I, c. 7; 14 Elizabeth I, c. 14.
65. 39 Elizabeth I, c.6. Cf. **G. Jones,** *History of the Law of Charity 1532–1827* (Cambridge UP, 1969), pp. 13–14, 19, 21–6; **Jordan,** *Philanthropy*, pp. 112–16; below, pp. 152, 164–5.
66. 1 James I, c. 7.
67. Above, pp. 28–9; **C. H. Firth** and **R. S. Rait,** *Acts and Ordinances of the Interregnum*, ii (1911), pp. 1098–9; **J. T. Rutt** (ed.), *Diary of Thomas Burton* (Henry Colburn, 1828), i. 21–4.
68. 43 Elizabeth I, c. 2.
69. **T. G. Barnes** (ed.), *Somerset Assize Orders 1629–40* (Somerset Record Soc., lxv, 1959), pp. 66–7; below, p. 174. For an excellent account of the history of poor rates, see **E. Cannan,** *The History of Local Rates in England* (P. S. King and Son, 1912). Cf. **A. Hassell Smith,** 'Militia Rates and Militia Statutes 1558–1663', in **P. Clark, A. G. R. Smith** and **N. Tyacke** (eds), *The English Commonwealth 1547–1640. Essays presented to Joel Hurstfield* (Leicester UP, 1979), pp. 103–4.
70. **J. Lister** (ed.), *West Riding Sessions Rolls 1597/8–1602* (Yorks Arch. Soc., Record Ser., iii, 1888), p. 84; **R. C. Richardson** and **T. B. James** (eds), *The Urban Experience. A Sourcebook 1450–1700* (Manchester UP, 1983), pp. 116–17. Cf. below, p. 170.
71. 1 James I, c. 25; *Somerset Assize Orders*, pp. xxix–xxx, 64. For examples of work-stocks, see **E. Melling,** *Kentish Sources IV: The Poor* (Kent County Council, Maidstone, 1964), pp. 44, 47–8.
72. 7 James I, c. 4. For comments on the value of this statute, see **E. Coke,** *Institutes*, pt 2 (1671), pp. 728–30.
73. **W. Hunt,** *The Puritan Moment* (Harvard UP, Cambridge, Mass., 1983), pp. 65–6; *Tudor Economic Documents*, ii. 363; information from Joanna Innes, who is engaged on a full study of these institutions. Cf. **A. L. Beier,** *Masterless Men* (Methuen, 1985), pp. 164–9.
74. For examples, see **Hurstfield,** *Freedom, Corruption and Government*, pp. 267–8; *VCH Shropshire*, p. 105; *Kentish Sources: The Poor*, p. 45; **S. and B. Webb,** *Old Poor Law*, pp. 84–5; **W. T. MacCaffrey,** *Exeter 1540–1640* (Harvard UP, Cambridge, Mass., 1958), pp. 114–15; **T. G. Barnes,** *Somerset 1625–1640* (Oxford UP, 1961), pp. 182–3; **A. Fletcher,** *A County Community in Peace and War: Sussex 1600–1660* (Longman, 1975), pp. 167–8; **J. S. Morrill,** *Cheshire 1630–1660* (Oxford UP, 1974), pp. 93, 247.
75. For examples, see Norfolk RO, Norwich Sessions Minute Book 1602–18, July 1616; below, p. 191.
76. 1 James I, c. 31.
77. 14 Elizabeth I, c. 5, sect. xxix; London Corporation RO, Rep. xvii, ff. 425v–426; Rep. xviii, ff. 108v–110r; Journal xx(i), ff. 42, 119v; Rep. xxiii, f. 2r.

78. The complex changes of 1598–1602 can be pieced together from London Corporation RO, Journal xxiv, ff. 289, 306r, 320–3; Rep. xxiv, ff. 198v, 229v, 237v, 252v, 411v, 414v, 448r; Guildhall Library, MS. 12806/3, f. 66r; E. **Freshfield** (ed.), *The Account Books of S. Bartholomew Exchange* (1895), pp. 4–5, 17. Work at present being undertaken by Ian Archer will throw more ample light on them.

79. See the accounts for these years in Guildhall Library, MSS. 12819/1, 2, 5, 6. Cf. **V. Pearl**, 'Puritans and Poor Relief: the London Workhouse, 1649–60', in **D. Pennington** and **K. Thomas** (eds), *Puritans and Revolutionaries. Essays presented to Christopher Hill* (Oxford UP, 1978), pp. 213–14; below, pp. 154–5.

80. *Commons Journals*, i. 699, 714, 800, 833, 853; **D. Underdown**, *Pride's Purge* (Oxford UP, 1971), pp. 282–3.

81. Cf. **Kent**, 'Attitudes of Members of the House of Commons to the Regulation of Personal Conduct', pp. 51–5; below, pp. 141–2.

82. See **J. Spedding, R. L. Ellis** and **D. D. Heath**, *The Works of Francis Bacon* (Longmans, 1889–92), vii. 507–16 for an opinion on the legality of committals to Bridewell.

83. **Kent**, 'Attitudes of Members', pp. 63–71.

84. This point is suggested in **Youings**, *Sixteenth-Century England*, p. 281.

85. *Tudor Royal Proclamations*, i. no. 63.

86. **S. and B. Webb**, *English Local Government: The Parish and the County* (Longmans, Green and Co., 1906), Ch. I; **McIntosh**, 'Social Change and Tudor Manorial Leets', pp. 76–7.

87. **Cannan**, *Local Rates*, Chs I, II.

Chapter 7

PROJECTS AND POLITICS
1570–1660

Cardinal Wolsey's innovative directives between 1517 and 1527 and the London hospitals of 1547 to 1557, described in the last chapter, had successors. The central government and local authorities continued to sponsor more elaborate schemes for regulating and relieving the poor than the law was ever able to provide. Sometimes they succeeded; very often they failed. But their efforts are at least as important in the history of English social welfare as the poor law itself. They also throw a good deal of light on the pressures which created, and those which impeded, public provision for the poor of any kind. They show that poor relief was a matter of political as well as social control, and that it had implications for the distribution of power as well as for the distribution of property and wealth.

CENTRAL DIRECTION

From the later years of Henry VIII to the reign of Charles I, the Council deployed its powers under the royal prerogative in order to limit, and if possible alleviate, the social distress and dislocation caused by plague and dearth. Whenever epidemics or bad harvests occurred, councillors followed Wolsey's example, sending instructions to local authorities, especially in London, sometimes issuing circular letters or proclamations, and in general trying to mobilize a national response. In 1543, for example, the Council wrote to the aldermen of London insisting that they proceed to segregate people infected with plague in the manner adopted in other countries, 'so as we may be seen to have learned that point of civility, and to have among us as charitable a mind for preservation of our neighbours as they have'. In the end such blandishments and more abrupt commands succeeded. By 1563, when there was an epidemic of plague in London which spread through much of the country, several municipalities were trying to prevent contagion by isolating the infected and their families in their own houses, or by moving them to sheds or huts outside the town walls; and they were raising money to support those who were sick and in quarantine.[1]

In the case of grain policy, similarly, central direction proved formative. Town councils often acted independently. Municipal purchases of corn were becoming more common in dearth years, and more or less permanent grain stores had been established in a few towns by the 1550s.[2] But outside corporate towns, local searches for grain and the organized provisioning of markets were responsibilities imposed by royal command: first on special commissioners, in 1527 and 1534, and then, in every year of real or expected dearth from 1544 onwards, on justices of the peace in their county divisions.[3] The evidence suggests that many local authorities responded: lists of corn stocks and orders for their transport to market survive from one part of the country or another in every year of scarcity. There were no statutes to sanction these search procedures, as there were with related controls on the export of grain and the activities of middlemen.[4] Even the proclamations which authorized them gradually lost their original importance. When the necessary detailed regulations grew too long for the usual format of a proclamation, they were first embodied in circular letters, as in 1556,[5] and then printed separately. They became Books of Orders with an authority of their own.

The first printed Book of Orders, published in 1578, was concerned, not with dearth, but with plague. It formalized the public-health procedures which had been developing over the previous half-century. During an epidemic, justices of the peace were to meet every three weeks in towns or county divisions, to receive reports on the progress of infection from every parish, and to impose a 'general taxation' for the relief of the sick. All infected houses should be completely shut up for at least six weeks, with all members of the family, whether sick or healthy, still inside them. Watchmen were to be appointed to enforce this order, and other officers should provide the inmates with food. The book was reprinted in later plague years, in 1592, 1593, 1603, 1625, 1630 and 1636; there was a separate printed book for London beginning in 1583; and the orders were being enforced in all the major towns and in several counties by 1603. They were fundamentally revised only in 1666, when the isolation of the sick in pesthouses was preferred to their incarceration in their own homes. Until then, until the last breath of plague in England, the Book of Orders of 1578 dictated policy from one end of the kingdom to the other.[6]

The second Book of Orders, that concerned with dearth, was equally influential. Published in 1586, and based on a draft corrected by William Cecil in his own hand, it added new details to old policies but did not alter the essentials. Justices' searches for grain were now to be managed through local juries, whose duties were carefully prescribed. There should be restraints on malting, brewing and starch-making in order to safeguard stocks of bread-corn. Grain was to be sold only in open markets, and then in small amounts and first to the poor. It was further recommended that the poor laws should be enforced, paupers set to work and houses of correction established in crisis years. Regular reports on all this activity should be sent to the Council. The orders were again reprinted with only minor alterations in later dearth years, in 1594, 1595, 1608, 1622 and 1630; and they were widely enforced, producing those local surveys of grain and the poor in the 1590s and 1620s which were discussed in Chapter 4.[7]

That was not all. The use of printed books to enforce uniformity in social policy was adopted in other areas too. There were printed regulations for the control of alehouses in 1607 and 1609, for example, and in the latter year a short volume entitled *Four Statutes* included the Vagrancy and Poor-Relief Acts of 1598 and 1601, the book of plague orders, and regulations against new building in London. That composite volume was itself reprinted in 1630 and 1636. Finally, in January 1631, there came the most famous Book of Orders of all – often referred to simply as *the* Book of Orders. Entitled *Orders and Directions*, it contained directions for the relief and regulation of the poor along the lines already established by the poor laws, orders governing divisional meetings of justices of the peace on the same subject, and a royal commission of Privy Councillors which was to watch over the whole effort and receive reports. The result was a flood of certificates to the Council from the counties in the 1630s, nearly one thousand of them in all, recording the number of vagrants punished, alehouses closed down, and poor children apprenticed. Along with more than 300 similar returns on the enforcement of corn policy in 1622–23 and 1630–31, and more occasional descriptions of activity against plague, particularly in 1630, they give a superficial impression both of purposeful direction from the centre and of considerable order in the localities.[8]

The origins of this mounting conciliar drive are easier to determine than its effects. It was partly the product of twin pressures on the Council. Just as Wolsey's policies had been influenced both by European developments in social policy, communicated to him by medical men, and by knowledge of local problems, particularly in London, so too were those of his successors. Projects and circumstances were once again productive partners. William Cecil took advice from an Italian physician, Cesare Adelmare, and from the College of Physicians on how to deal with plague; and in the 1570s he corresponded with London's Recorder, William Fleetwood, about social problems in the capital. In 1630 and 1631 the Council was influenced by the King's French physician, Sir Theodore de Mayerne, who pressed for a new 'political' means to combat plague and the social diseases of vagrancy and poverty which encouraged it. The Council also heard about local problems of grain provision and poor relief, particularly through the letters between a Northamptonshire justice, Edward Montagu, and his brother, Henry Montagu, Earl of Manchester. It was Manchester who was chiefly responsible for drawing up the Caroline Book of Orders of January 1631.

It should be noted that Books of Orders were not invented in the worst crises. It was not the plagues of 1563 and 1603, or the dearths of the mid-1550s and 1590s which inspired innovation. The plague of 1578, the dearth of 1586 and the combination of the two in 1630–31 were minor in comparison. That perhaps encouraged careful reflection rather than a frantic repeat of old remedies. What seems to have been particularly influential, however, was the coincidence of different kinds of problem, all seemingly interrelated. Popular disorder, sweating sickness and plague had pushed Wolsey into action in 1517. Plague, gaol fever and metropolitan poverty similarly impelled Cecil in 1578. Plague, dearth and renewed concern about London prompted the Council in 1630 and 1631. And on top of all this there was a political element: the determination of councillors to exercise new and real political authority.

It is impossible to mistake the increasingly commanding tone of the government's pronouncements in this area, as it sought to remedy the deficiencies in legislation and to invigorate local administration – to 'quicken' it, to use the expressive term often employed in 1630. The plague orders were supported by statutory sanctions in an Act of 1604, but they contained details never approved by parliament. In a similar way, the appointment of paid provost marshals to apprehend vagrants, which the Council promoted vigorously in the early seventeenth century, supplemented inadequate legislation.[9] Lawyers and judges with long experience of the difficulties of enforcing regulatory statutes, like Francis Bacon and Montagu, understandably wanted royal commissions to oversee all commonwealth and prerogative matters.[10] Montagu's commission of Privy Councillors in the *Orders and Directions* had power to appoint deputies to act for it: he intended them as 'spies' to report on the activity of justices of the peace. At the same time, Charles I was trying to make London a 'royal city' fit for an 'imperial' king, through determined use of building regulations; and his physician, Mayerne, was advocating a public-health commission for London which would have 'absolute power' to 'repress all opposition'. Although neither of these latter schemes was realized, they show that social policies were an integral part of the ambitions of king and Council at the start of Charles I's personal rule.

Plainly, such precise central direction could last only as long as the royal prerogative on which it was based lasted; and its efficacy depended on the degree to which the royal prerogative was respected. Not surprisingly, there was opposition. New forms of government interference, whatever their source, could never be popular; and the naked intrusion of the royal prerogative, far from guaranteeing universal obedience, might provide a cloak of principle for self-interested resistance. From the beginning, local efforts to control marketing in dearth years provoked opposition from men of property: there were 'seditious and unseemly words' in Lincoln in 1521.[11] By the 1580s and 1590s some people were disputing the legality of action under the first two books of dearth orders, since they proceeded simply from the 'absolute power' of the monarch. Even the Council was less confident than it sometimes sounded. It invoked common and statute law whenever it could to defend its policy, and it was often reduced to plaintive outbursts of frustration. In 1609 it fulminated against the negligence of justices, even when prodded 'by extraordinary directions derived from the prerogative power of his Majesty by proclamations, letters and commissions, or from us of his Council by orders and letters in his name'.

If the policies embodied in Books of Orders were to be effective, therefore, they needed the consent of the governing and propertied classes. Sometimes it was withheld. The insistence in the Book of Orders of January 1631 that men should be forced to take on pauper apprentices very often failed, for example: people were being asked to do 'more than they were compellable to by law', one victim asserted, 'and . . . the directions of the Lords of the Council could not impose any such thing upon them'. Sometimes consent was given to the ends of government policy but not to the means. The orders against vagrants in the same book were welcomed, but the threat of conciliar supervision was not. In the event, the commission of Privy Councillors was never more than a paper tiger; there were no government spies in the localities. The requirement of regular reports from the counties seemed dangerous enough, however, and several justices deliberately replied in the most general terms, telling the Council what it wanted to hear, that vagrants had been cleared from the roads and the poor relieved.

The deficiencies in these certificates make any judgement about the effects of the Book of Orders of 1631 difficult. There is no doubt that they give a misleading impression of ready compliance and good government. Numerous as they are, they amount to only a tenth of the reports which ought in theory to have been submitted, and they spring in large numbers only from a small sample of counties. One of them was Hertfordshire, Henry Montagu's own territory. Another, in the early years, was Somerset, which explains why the historian of that county's government places such emphasis on the Book's impact. Several counties scarcely reported at all, however. They included those in the far North, where little may have been done, but also some in the Midlands, such as Northamptonshire and Warwickshire, where we know from other sources that justices were diligent.[12] Moreover, while justices and overseers in many parts of the country were certainly busy, raising the level of poor rates or otherwise increasing the pace of activity in 1631 and 1632, some of them had begun before the Book of Orders was issued, at the end of 1630 or even earlier.[13]

They also continued when the Council's guiding hand disappeared. Miss Leonard's opinion that the absence of conciliar direction after 1640 meant the disintegration of ordered relief for the poor was mistaken. It has been shown in the case of Warwickshire that there was no decline in the amount of poor-relief business dealt with by sessions after the Civil War.[14] In fact, it increased. This may not have been the result of greater commitment on the part of the justices: all kinds of sessions business were booming, and the number of orders concerned with the poor was much the same proportion of the total in the later 1640s and 1650s as it had been in the 1630s.[15] But there was continuity not collapse. The machinery continued to function after 1646 without direction from the centre, and it would probably have done so in the 1630s. The evidence suggests that there may have been some 'quickening' of activity under the stimulus of the Caroline Book of Orders. There was no radical transformation.

The case is different with the other two Books of Orders, dealing with plague and dearth, since they imposed policies which were not already part of the poor-law machine. The question of whether or not they were effective is still more difficult to answer, however. It is not so much a problem of enforcement: there is abundant evidence that the books were enforced, and therefore that in these instances conciliar direction was decisive. The question is rather whether the books achieved what they set out to achieve. How instrumental were they in mitigating the crises against which they were directed?

The plague orders were intended to prevent contagion. Controls on public assemblies, the notification of plague cases, and the compulsory isolation of whole families in their own homes once they were infected, were all procedures designed to inhibit transmission of infection from person to person. Unfortunately, they took no account of the fact, unknown to contemporaries, that rats and fleas were carriers of bubonic plague. They could never be wholly effective, therefore. Plague could move unseen from an isolated household to an uninfected one. Moreover, as some contemporaries were quick to point out, the incarceration of whole families, sick and sound together, might well increase mortality rates rather than reduce them – especially, we might add, when people were confined in close proximity to domestic rats. In the seventeenth century the government began to swing to an alternative strategy, advocating the isolation of the sick apart from the healthy in specially built pesthouses, a practice common in Italy and elsewhere. But pesthouses were expensive and they never housed more than a small minority of the infected. Right up to 1665 household quarantine remained the standard policy.[16]

There is some reason to think that in special circumstances, and in the early stages of an epidemic, rigorous action along conventional lines could prevent a major outbreak. Controls on human movement, the apprehension of suspicious wanderers, and the tracing and isolation of the sick and their contacts, could sometimes restrict plague to one or two households and protect the majority. They seem to have worked in York, for example, in 1631, when plague was successfully confined to the extramural suburbs and kept out of the inner city, largely thanks to energetic action taken under the direction of Thomas Wentworth, President of the Council in the North. There may have been similar success stories in Bristol and Exeter in 1665 and 1666. But there are many more examples of such measures failing. They could not be relied upon.[17]

It must have been more than the promise of medical efficacy which commended the plague orders to local authorities, therefore. What they offered most obviously was the potential to control the unruly victims of plague as much as plague itself. The 'severe and strict courses' recommended by Wentworth in York, and enforced in many other towns in the seventeenth century against crowds, public funerals, infected households and vagrants, were all intended to impose order in circumstances of the utmost disorder, and to restore public health, broadly defined. The first printed plague regulations for London of 1583 were significantly endorsed 'for repressing of disorders and relief of the poor', and the term 'order' recurs again and again in the context of plague in early modern England, often with a significantly associated word, 'rule'. The last plague regulations, printed in 1666, were entitled *Rules and Orders*. It was a set of concepts and associations which lay behind much of the poor law itself.[18]

Yet there was an alternative concept of order: not order in the sense of tidiness and command, but order as harmony between the several parts of the body politic, each with reciprocal rights and duties. And the latter concept could be employed in opposition to the plague regulations, with their divisive social implications, just as it had been used in the sixteenth century against proposed statutory restrictions on indiscriminate almsgiving and neighbourly charity. The infected, their families and friends, resisted restraints on their movement, sometimes on the principled grounds that Christian charity and the rules of humanity demanded that neighbours should visit their sick neighbours and attend their funerals. They were trying to assert the need for social solidarity in the face of plague, and they were occasionally supported by people in authority, by a few determined clergymen and the odd eccentric alderman. They failed. 'Rule' and 'order' took precedence with the vast majority of the 'better sort of people' when plague among the 'under sort', among 'divers poor nasty people', threatened their health and security.[19] Some of the imperatives of popular morality and traditional charity were once more pushed aside.

The situation was very different in the case of the third Book of Orders, the dearth orders. Here government policies did not conflict with popular morality. They were consistent with it and even helped to condition it. They showed how legitimate and caring governors should act.[20] 'Wise and careful magistrates' could be distinguished from 'negligent and improvident' ones by their vigour in attacking middlemen and forestallers of the market who were 'more like to wolves and cormorants than to natural men'. The government publicly sided with the poor against some of the rich, against maltsters and regrators in Northamptonshire, for example, who were '(for the most part) aldermen, bailiffs, and men of great wealth ... using all sinister and unlawful means to ... bring a famine amongst the inferiors and poorest sort of people'.[21] In 1596 the Vicar of Barnstaple preached a sermon in which he described the aldermen as unchristian 'fat oxen': an inflammatory remark when many were hungry. He was committed to gaol by the men he offended. But the earl of Bath and other county justices, who were in town to enforce the Book of Orders, had him released. It was a persuasive gesture.[22]

It is not surprising that governors played the 'commonweal' tune for all it was worth in years of dearth. They had little other opportunity, and they knew what they were doing. When the authors of the dearth orders stressed the need for 'Christian charity' and 'deeds of mercy', and when town councils purchased corn for their 'little commonweals', they were prompted by a fear of disorder quite as powerful as that which inspired their plague regulations.[23] They wished to appease 'the tumult of the poor', to repress 'tumultuous disorders', and to satisfy 'the common poor people ... being ready to rise in tumultuous manner'.[24] They may well have succeeded. The evidence suggests that public rhetoric and the prompt promulgation of dearth orders could pacify or prevent riot and disturbance.[25] Whether the orders also lessened the intensity of dearth itself, reducing the amount of malnutrition or the extent of starvation, it is much more difficult to say.

We need to distinguish carefully here between different sorts of corn policy. Legislative controls on the export of grain when prices were high were obviously sensible.[26] There was also a good deal to be said, as we shall see, for the stocks of corn purchased independently by municipal governments, and often sold cheaply to the poor. On the other hand, the real efficacy – as distinct from the propaganda value – of the searches and market regulations provided for in the book of dearth orders is open to doubt.

Many contemporaries were themselves sceptical about them. Farmers evaded the restrictions on private marketing and the long-distance movement of corn, and some local officers aided and abetted them. A preacher in 1609 implied that grain was bound to flow unimpeded down the Severn from Gloucester to Bristol because the people who were supposed to stop it were in no danger of starving themselves.[27] It could also be argued that restraints on the marketing and transport of corn were as counterproductive as the quarantine of households. Although one clause in the book encouraged local justices to negotiate with large cities and towns and arrange their provision, the general effect of the rest

– if they had been fully enforced – would have been to keep corn in the areas where it was grown. Those parts of the country where we know there was malnutrition, if not starvation, found the book working to their disadvantage. There were complaints from towns such as Bristol, and from pastoral and forest areas like Derbyshire and Northamptonshire.[28] The government had to license exceptions to the rules, in order to permit large shipments of grain to London, for example; and the exceptions must have been more attractive to farmers than the rules, and hence more readily complied with.

Critics of the book also alleged that its promulgation created dearth by spreading panic, encouraging hoarding, and thus raising prices. When the orders were enforced for a second time in 1587, one observer in Barnstaple commented: 'What good this order will do the common ... buyers of corn may stand in doubt, because now corn being dear ... they fear this order may take it dearer as it did last year'. There was an insoluble dilemma here. Publication of the book was designed to allay popular fears and suppress rumours of dearth, not inflame them. There was truth nevertheless in the criticism that searches of barns 'doth but discover the want, and thereby enhance the prices, but augments not the store'.[29] Restrictions on malting and brewing may marginally have helped the store of food-grains; but its uneven geographical distribution could hardly be remedied by a Book of Orders which emphasized local self-sufficiency. It is arguable that market forces and free internal trade would have distributed corn more equitably across space and also encouraged economic integration, better communications and greater agricultural productivity, on which the final conquest of dearth depended.

Municipal provision of corn was a different matter. Bulk purchases took advantage of market forces rather than working against them. They brought supplies to places which most needed them rather than confining them to areas which were relatively well endowed. They might even serve to increase the national stock, since towns often imported corn from the Baltic, particularly from Danzig. Above all, by involving subsidies from rich to poor, municipal provision helped to solve the problem of the social as well as the geographical distribution of grain. Where granaries were kept permanently stocked, as in Norwich until the 1640s, corn bought cheaply in good years could be released on to the market to hold down prices in years of dearth. It could also be sold directly to the poor, sometimes below the prevailing market price. Very often, of course, town councils incurred financial losses in the process, but these were met from corporation or charitable funds, from councillors' own pockets, from benevolences from city companies, or from rates levied for the purpose.[30] Whether hidden or open, real transfer payments were made when food was provided for the urban poor in the sixteenth and early seventeenth centuries.

The extent of their impact cannot be precisely measured. We do not have the evidence which would show us how far public corn supplies in towns depressed prices below those in places which were not so favoured. It is only rarely, indeed, that we have any full accounts of the amounts of corn purchased and their distribution. There is no doubt, however, that they were substantial. The council of Norwich arranged for 800 two-penny loaves to be baked every week for the poor in 1631. In the same town, in 1647–48, the granary sold off 250 quarters of corn, enough to supply 1,000 people with bread-corn for 12 or 13 weeks.[31] Very much earlier, in 1562–63, by no means a year of severe crisis, the corporation of Exeter arranged for the purchase of 750 quarters of imported corn for the town. It sold it at 20s. a quarter, about 25 per cent below the then market price. This was enough to supply the whole town with food (though not with drink) for five weeks. Two-thirds of it was sold to private consumers, but one-third – again enough for 1,000 people for twelve weeks – was retained by the corporation for its granary or sold to the city companies for their poorer members. The city laid out almost £900 in expenses and made a loss of £300.[32]

When repeated in major crises, as in 1587 and 1597, such efforts must have alleviated distress in the poorer quarters of many English towns, even if they did not obliterate it.[33] Their value is indicated by the fact that they were copied in small towns and even in some villages in 1630 and 1631.[34] By then, however, the nature of the problem was beginning to change. The threat of wholesale famine was receding with rising agricultural productivity. The poor might still have starved in years of high prices, since they had inadequate exchange entitlements, inadequate purchasing power.[35] But that problem could now be remedied by other means: by insisting, for example, on clothiers maintaining employment even in years of depression, a policy pursued throughout the period and included in the book of dearth orders;[36] and above all, after 1598, by direct transfer payments in the form of poor relief. As a result, town councils were altering their priorities by mid-century. In Norwich, for example, the corn stock was allowed to run down after the crisis of 1647–48 and the granary was sold in 1669. There, as in other towns in the later seventeenth century, the provision of fuel, wood and coal, to help the poor over bad winters, replaced the provision of food.[37]

Economic change and the increase in transfer payments through poor rates similarly helped to undermine the book of dearth orders. It seemed irritating and irrelevant when no great crisis occurred in 1630 or 1631, and when grain prices leapt again, in 1637, it was not reissued. Political change, the decline of the royal prerogative, worked in the same direction. Although parliament expressed an interest in the dearth orders in 1662, and they were then reprinted, they did not have conciliar backing.[38] The Council even hesitated before revising and republishing the book of plague orders in the epidemic of 1665–66, hoping that parliament would supply a solution. The political caution was palpable.[39] Popular attachment to something like the book of dearth orders remained, and the lack of it may have stimulated riots when food prices rose in the 1690s.[40] But it did not cause starvation. Books of Orders were no longer economically necessary or politically welcome.

Impermanent as they were, however, the policies encapsulated in the books had had a permanent effect on attitudes. They persuaded people that the management of crises was as much a matter for government as was day-to-day poor relief. Human action could mitigate the divine punishments of pestilence and famine. There were some who objected to the secularizing implications. One or two of the clergy opposed plague regulations on predestinarian grounds: if God sent plague as a punishment for sin, how could man's actions avert it? Edward Montagu wondered why fasting and prayer were not used against the 'judgements' of famine and sickness in 1630.[41] They were fighting a losing battle. There had been special prayers and fasts against dearth in 1586 and 1596. They seem not to have been repeated in 1622 or later.[42] Special forms of prayer against plague continued from 1563 right up to 1665, but from 1603 onwards they included a sermon explaining its physical causes and how they might be avoided. Archbishop Laud's suspicion of preachers who placed too much stress on the role of providence in plague went hand in hand with his famous statement that the dearth of 1630–31 was 'made by man and not by God'.[43] By 1640 men's confidence in their capacity to manipulate the environment was much greater than it had been in 1500. The strategies of crisis-management pursued by the central government had had a great deal to do with the change.

Not everyone saw the issues as Laud and his fellow councillors did, however, and it would be wholly wrong to think that religious and secular aspirations were necessarily incompatible. On the contrary, we shall see in a moment that outside government circles, in the provinces and especially in towns, religious enthusiasm was itself a powerful motor persuading magistrates to undertake new forms of relief and regulation of the poor. Like Privy Councillors, godly magistrates believed that man's intervention could work wonderful effects, though only with divine help. They shared the same concepts of order and rule, though they set them in a theological framework. They had no less confidence, and even more faith, in social engineering. They also had the same political ambitions and faced similar problems in the exercise of authority.

LOCAL EXPERIMENTS

The embellishment of the machinery of social welfare was a continuous preoccupation of municipal governments in the later sixteenth and early seventeenth centuries. We have noted already municipal corn stocks and granaries. There was often some attempt to care for the health of the poor, by providing medicines, salaried doctors and even small hospitals.[44] Still more common were attempts to employ the able-bodied poor and train pauper children in useful skills, involving investment in workhouses, houses of correction and schools.[45] To some degree provincial towns were simply copying, or adapting to their own purposes, the model of the London hospitals considered in the last chapter. But there was also an intensification of earlier impulses. As poverty increased, particularly in old centres of the cloth industry now in decay, and as evangelical Calvinist Protestantism took firm hold of urban patriciates, the physical relief and moral reform of the poor seemed ever more urgent goals.

Bridewell's attempt to combine the suppression of vagrancy with the punishment of sin therefore had a growing appeal in the later sixteenth century.[46] So did that careful provision of spiritual as well as physical remedies for illness and idleness, which had been embodied in Grafton's first orders for St Bartholomew's and St Thomas's.[47] In the 1570s some of the Norfolk justices met regularly at the new 'Bridewell' at Acle where, after prayers, they punished rogues, drunkards and bastard-bearers: work both 'necessary and ... full of piety', Walsingham reported to Cecil. It was work especially undertaken in towns, and, as Professor Collinson has shown, in towns ruled by godly alliances of ministers and magistrates. One such was Bury St Edmunds, where the justices' orders against a variety of social and moral offences were displayed in the parish churches in 1578.[48] Another, and probably the first, was the Norwich of 1570.

The Norwich reforms have already been referred to more than once. They included the great census of the poor and schemes for the employment and training of poor children which were famous for at least a century.[49] They may well have influenced parliamentary legislation in the 1570s, thanks to the links provided by John Aldrich, mayor in 1570 and M.P. in 1572 and 1576. They also had interesting local roots, some of them in the past. Aldrich had been a councillor in 1549, when the first compulsory assessment for the poor was levied in the city; he had married into the Sotherton family which then dominated the town; and he may well have known about contemporary events in London. By 1570, however, he was a man of Puritan leanings, and Norwich, with its large population of Dutch and Walloon Calvinists and its 'apostle', John More, was becoming a renowned Puritan citadel.[50] The documents relating to the reforms also speak the Puritan language of 'collective paranoia', to use Collinson's vivid phrase. A proclamation of 1571 pictured a society in which the lower orders slid inexorably 'from idleness to drunkenness to whoredom to shameful incest and abominable life, greatly to the dishonour of God and ruin of the commonwealth'. The overseers must therefore search the homes of the poor 'several times in each week' to identify disorders and reform them. One Norwich order provided for 'deacons' in every ward. The model was not London but Geneva.[51]

Several town councils took the same road after the 1570s. In Warwick there was Thomas Cartwright, remodelling poor relief and initiating listings of the poor in the 1580s, for all the world like a Calvinist deacon.[52] There was similar activity in a number of towns in the 1620s and 1630s: Dorchester, Salisbury, Gloucester, Plymouth, Southampton and Colchester were among them, and a determined group of godly magistrates can be clearly identified in the first three and reasonably suspected in the others.[53] There seem in fact to have been two geographical clusters of municipalities engaged in social-welfare enterprises between 1570 and 1640. The first was in East Anglia, between Norwich and Colchester, beginning in the 1570s;[54] the second, emerging between 1610 and 1630, was a group of western towns in the triangle formed by Gloucester, Southampton and Plymouth.

There were obviously close contacts between them. In the case of the south-west, for example, we know that the Puritan patriarch of Dorchester, John White, was an associate of Peter Thatcher, the most influential minister in Salisbury. The Recorder of Salisbury, the Puritan iconoclast Henry Sherfield, was also Recorder of Southampton; and Salisbury's High Steward, the Earl of Pembroke, was also High Steward of Exeter. Sherfield sat in parliament and on parliamentary committees alongside Ignatius Jorden, the notorious Puritan alderman of Exeter; and the mayor of Plymouth corresponded with the Mayor of Exeter in the 1620s urging the need for 'reformation' of the people of both cities to ward off God's judgements – notably the plagues which ravaged all these western towns at some point between 1625 and 1630.[55]

This is not to argue that all innovations in poor relief in English towns in this period were necessarily the achievement of Puritans, however we define them, any more than the legislation of 1598 was solely the work of Sir Robert Wroth and other committed Protestant MPs.[56] The economic depression and epidemics of the 1620s pushed several urban magistrates in the same direction: in Norwich, for example, which was no longer under unquestioned Puritan dominance. Special charitable bequests for setting the poor on work inspired action in individual cases, as Kendrick's gift to Reading did in 1630.[57] It is striking, nevertheless, how often investigation of particular poor-relief projects uncovers avowedly godly magistrates and their aspirations to complete civic reformation. Neither should this surprise us, since godly magistracy and the reconstruction of social welfare had their roots in the same perceptions of civic circumstances.

The latter appear clearly in the new orders issued for the house of correction in the Suffolk town of Sudbury in 1624. It was to be used for the safekeeping, punishing and setting to work of idle poor, vagabonds and any that shall be noisome and offensive to any [of] the inhabitants of this town: being common hedge, pale, gate or stile-breakers ... robbers of orchards and fruit trees, milkers of other men's kine against the will of the owner, and of all such women as have or shall have any bastard ... and of all persons that be not in the book of the subsidy being judged reputed fathers of base children ... and of all such men, women and children as shall refuse and will not be put forth to service or to be apprentices ... and of all artificers, labourers and servants that be common drunkards or alehouse-haunters that will not leave the frequenting of such houses of the sin of drunkenness.

Every morning the inmates of the house of correction were to say the General Confession, the Lord's Prayer, and a special prayer acknowledging that 'the punishment wherewith we be now scourged is much less than our deserts; but we humbly beseech Thee that it may work in us a reformation of our former life and true obedience [to] his Majesty's laws'.[58]

Much the same consciousness of disorder can be found in Gloucester in the 1630s, where there was an 'overseer of the manners of the poor', and in Dorchester rather earlier, where a disastrous fire in 1613 stimulated efforts to create a godly commonwealth.[59] By the 1620s John White and his colleagues had erected a workhouse, a storehouse, and a municipal brewhouse, designed to control and profit from the drink trade; and they were engaged in a vigorous campaign for the reformation of popular manners. One half of the three hundred or so offenders coming before the town court each year were presented for prophane swearing, non-attendance at church, tippling and drunkenness. Magisterial rule of this kind was unpopular, especially when it was concentrated in a few hands and, in Dorchester, largely exercised by a single constable, John Bushrod, son of a Puritan mayor. One offender said she 'would rather believe the drunkards of Chard than the Puritans of Dorchester'. Another attacked the by-laws against swearing as 'Puritan laws'. Although the whole town was divided into regenerate and unregenerate, however, there can be no doubt about whose manners were thought most in need of correction. One benefactor left money only to the 'poor who are godly'.[60]

In Salisbury, similarly, all opponents of the Puritan elite were by definition allies if not members of 'the loose unruly rabble'. Here an outbreak of plague, in 1627, persuaded some of the aldermen that they must copy the welfare institutions and the moral regime of Dorchester. In a speech to the first quarter sessions after the epidemic, Henry Sherfield listed the four 'gross and foul sins' which had brought divine retribution on the city: drunkenness, sabbath-breaking, prophane swearing and idleness. They must be rooted out; and Sherfield went on to give a classic statement of that Puritan social activism which inspired him, and others like him, in the task:

I well know that no good thing can be effected without the hand and blessing of God and it is he that worketh both the will and the deed. Yet I do also know that we must use all the good ways and means which God shall discover unto us to bring to pass even what God hath determined to do.

What God had determined on was, once again, Reformation: Sherfield hoped for a 'reformation, a true and real reformation of this city'.[61]

In the particular sphere of poor relief, the rhetoric of civic reformation had much the same practical effect as the Christian humanism of the founders of the London hospitals. First, it demanded administrative centralization. One characteristic of all these projects was municipal control over parish rates, which allowed the financial burden of outdoor relief to be fairly distributed between parishes of different social composition. Secondly, it gave birth to new institutions, especially workhouses with their regular daily routine and, as in Plymouth, careful supervision 'for avoiding of all prophaneness and vice whatsoever'.[62] Several of the projects also provided employment for people who lived out, at large in the town, however; and there was in general less emphasis on residential institutions than there had been in London in the 1540s and 1550s. The institutional novelties of the 1620s were not hospitals but the municipal storehouses in Dorchester and Salisbury which furnished food and fuel to all the town's poor, and the civic brewhouses in the same cities which stimulated similar projects in Colchester and Wells and somewhat diferent methods of intervention in the drink trade in Bridport and Winchester.[63] There had been a shift of emphasis from the isolation of physical illness to the control of manners and habits of consumption at large.

Thirdly, some of these projects were able to take advantage of charitable bequests, just as the London hospitals had done; and that imposed certain common institutional configurations. Private philanthropy endowed the workhouses in Plymouth and Southampton, and steps were taken to have them incorporated so that they could receive initial gifts of property and attract more.[64] Because the complex laws relating to mortmain and charitable trusts made incorporation advisable, if not essential, the insecurity of institutions which did not have the protection given by charters or letters patent was a prime concern throughout the period. It was significant for the future that there was an attempt to get municipal brewhouses sanctioned by Act of Parliament in 1626.[65]

Finally, the story of the London hospitals was repeated in the failure of these projects to have any major impact on real problems. It could be argued that they never had much of a chance. Dependent on the enthusiasm of committed minorities whose political position was never secure, and faced by opposition from parish officials whose autonomy was threatened, they were always fragile. When the costs of outdoor relief failed to fall quickly, they lost credibility. Many of the workhouses limped on for a decade or more, but they were never large enough to realize the ambitions of their founders. They were often in decay soon after their erection and in several towns they had to be revitalized at regular intervals, whenever a new burst of reforming zeal took hold of councillors. The workhouse founded in Exeter in 1579 had to be refounded or reorganized in 1593, 1613, 1652, 1663, 1667 and 1675.[66]

It is true also, however, that there was a fundamental and damaging lack of fit between Puritan perceptions of poverty and the facts. Censuses of the poor like that in Norwich did not uncover idle rogues, drunk and disorderly thieves and bastard-bearers, but whole households reduced to poverty by depression in the town's worsted industry.[67] Some characteristically Puritan medicines for poverty were therefore misplaced. Efforts to deter the poor from wasteful patterns of consumption and to accustom a few of them to moral and work-discipline did little for the mass of the underemployed and unemployed in the declining textile towns of the 1620s. As we shall see, poor rates continued to rise and 'extraordinary' payments to households temporarily in poverty continued to prevent any measurement, forward planning, or orderly control.

Contemporary appreciation of this mismatch between perception and reality may help to explain the growing emphasis on a more economic approach to the problem of poverty which is evident in the course of the seventeenth century. It had never been entirely absent. From the 1540s onwards, as Joan Thirsk has shown, public and private projects had tried to introduce new products and new skills to the labouring population, and they had had some success. Rowland Vaughan, for example, who proclaimed himself neither Papist nor Puritan, planned to set 2,000 poor to work on flax and hemp in Herefordshire in 1610. Some parish and municipal employment schemes following the statute of 1576 had a similar purpose; and town councils gradually learned to look for workhouse managers who could teach trades which would supplement rather than compete with existing employment opportunities.[68] By the 1670s the aldermen of Exeter were learning from the experience of other boroughs, seeking advice from Taunton, Dorchester and Bridport, and encouraging work on the fashionable new materials of rape and hemp, as well as wool. Bristol similarly turned to linen in the 1670s, after trying stocking-knitting in the 1650s. Flax and hemp, linen thread, canvas and sackcloth were the standard materials for employment projects in the mid- and later seventeenth century.[69]

These were promising import-substitutes and useful trades for the England of the Navigation Acts and Anglo-Dutch wars. Their importance for the English economy cannot be denied. But that is not to say that they made workhouses profitable or secure. Even where there were few institutional overheads, as in a putting-out employment scheme in Bedfordshire, receipts only covered two-thirds of costs.[70]

153

When workhouses had to be maintained too, losses were large. As a result, purely economic incentives rarely had enough weight to carry expensive innovations through. If new municipal projects were to be put into effect, the promise of wider social and moral reform remained essential. So did the right political circumstances.

Both were important in the final and greatest Puritan project which we need to consider: the Corporation of the Poor founded in London between 1647 and 1649.[71] It had many similarities with its provincial predecessors. It was anticipated in a scheme for parish works on hemp and flax, put forward in 1623 by the Puritan Sir Thomas Middleton, President of Bridewell; and it was put into effect by a coalition of Presbyterians and Independents which had control of City government immediately after the Civil War. But it also had strong support from Samuel Hartlib, a man with European contacts and Baconian utopian ambitions, who brought to the millenarian enthusiasm of some English Puritans of the Interregnum a less insular and more utilitarian interest in national improvement.

Hartlib's pamphlets rehearsed some old complaints and old responses. Like the founders of Christ's Hospital, he objected to children who 'lie all day in the streets, playing, cursing [and] swearing'; like Sherfield and his contemporaries, he thought they should be 'kept under a godly government which is an excellent step in reformation'. If he used some of the same vocabulary, however, his tone was much less strident than that employed in the 1620s, partly no doubt because economic growth was already removing the worst manifestations of social distress, partly also because his approach was less bound by purely local considerations. The aim of those who dealt with poor children, he thought, should be 'to civilise and train them up in their books, and so by degrees to trades, that so they may be fit servants for the commonwealth'.[72] Civility and utility were to be chords struck ever more frequently in the later seventeenth century.

In management as well as in motivation the London Corporation looked both backwards and forwards. Its immediate functions were two: children (up to 80 at a time) were taught in workhouses, and another thousand or so poor were set at work throughout the city. The first owed much to Bridewell and Christ's Hospital, and the second followed the pattern of employment schemes in some provincial towns.[73] Ordinances of Parliament, in 1647 and 1649, replaced the charters of the hospitals and settled the problem of charitable and legal status. They also defined the Corporation's governors: in 1649 there were to be 52 assistants, ten of them aldermen and the rest freemen elected from the wards of the city. A separate governing body, like that of the hospitals and also of some provincial institutions such as the Plymouth workhouse, reflected the assumption that proper provision for social welfare was too burdensome a task for existing organs of civic government. Its unprecedented size and representative nature, however, reflected a new requirement: the need for co-operation and consent if the problems of parochial independence and unequal parochial provision for the poor were to be circumvented. Noting the 'difference and dissension' between rich and poor parishes, the parliamentary ordinances empowered the Corporation to employ all the city's poor, and to raise money equitably from all parishes for them. The Common Council of London was instructed to levy such rates as the Corporation demanded.[74]

We shall see that this model of a powerful new civic institution sanctioned by parliament proved influential in other towns at the end of the seventeenth century.[75] It was intended to be so in the 1650s. There was a clause in the ordinance of 1649 permitting similar corporations in the provinces. It seems never to have been acted upon, however, and the powers given to the London Corporation itself were never fully exercised. Despite its expense – the initial cost was put at £12,000 – the Common Council never dared to grasp the nettle of raising regular additional rates from wards and parishes.[76] When the Restoration of Charles II brought the restoration of the royal property which the Corporation occupied, it fell without a struggle. There was no attempt to find alternative accommodation. The Act of Settlement of 1662 included clauses permitting the erection of a Corporation of the Poor in London, and similar bodies in Middlesex and Westminster. There was no response in the City, and although a workhouse was erected in Clerkenwell in the 1660s, there were soon complaints about mis-management and decay.[77] The steam seemed to have gone out of the effort.

In the case of Puritan experiments, as in the case of conciliar direction, therefore, the fate of new welfare strategies depended in large measure on political circumstances. The Restoration clipped the wings of the first just as the demolition of prerogative rule in 1640 crippled the second. Like the Books of Orders, municipal projects were also hampered from the start by resistance from below: from anyone whose independence, property or power was threatened by the activities of busy, arrogant cliques of godly magistrates. In 1659 and 1660 John Ivie was engaged in trying to revive the storehouse which he had founded as Mayor of Salisbury in the 1620s. Along with other justices, he was sued in the Court of Common Pleas by churchwardens and overseers who alleged that he had exceeded his powers. The Restoration ensured that Ivie and his colleagues would lose the case. But this was simply the final Act in a long saga of obstruction which had impeded their efforts from the beginning, forty years before. They were confronted by an unholy alliance of conservative aldermen, brewers opposed to the civic brewhouse, and parish overseers resisting centralization. The latter increased the lists of pensioners without permission of the justices, and continued to pay outdoor relief in cash, ignoring Ivie's plans to introduce payments in kind. They jealously guarded their powers of patronage and their control over parish revenues and disbursements.[78]

In the end, in Salisbury as elsewhere, the machinery erected by the statute of 1598 proved more resilient than the various fashionable projects which were always being superimposed upon it. It persisted, not for want of anything better, but because it seemed adequate to its purpose and preferable to expensive alternatives which were politically controversial. Even the parliaments of the English Republic failed to modify the Elizabethan poor law in any major way. Consideration of new legislation for the employment of the poor in the Rump and Barebones Parliaments came to nothing.[79] When it came to the point, members had more urgent business than the task of tinkering with a machine which was functioning well enough. Precisely how, and how well, it functioned are questions we must consider in the next chapter.

NOTES AND REFERENCES

1. P. Slack, *The Impact of Plague in Tudor and Stuart England* (Routledge and Kegan Paul, 1985), pp. 202–6.
2. Kent AO, Sa/AC4, f. 46v (Sandwich); W. E. Stephens, 'Great Yarmouth under Queen Mary', *Norfolk Archaeology*, xxix (1946), 147, 149; Exeter Corporation Records, Act Book 2, f. 159r; Norfolk RO, Norwich Mayor's Court Book 1540–49, p. 293; Assembly Proceedings 1491–1553, f. 226r; *VCH York*, p. 134.
3. P. L. Hughes and J. F. Larkin (eds), *Tudor Royal Proclamations* (Yale UP, New Haven, 1964–9), i, nos 151, 242, 365, 366; ii, no. 430 (draft; but see also N. S. B. Gras, *The Evolution of the English Corn Market* (Harvard UP, Cambridge, Mass., 1926), pp. 448–9); ii, no. 490. See also R. W. Heinze, *The Proclamations of the Tudor Kings* (Cambridge UP, 1976), pp. 121–2, 226–33; P. Slack, 'Social Policy and the Constraints of Government' in J. Loach and R. Tittler (eds), *The Mid-Tudor Polity* (Macmillan, 1980), pp. 105–6; F. A. Youngs, *The Proclamations of the Tudor Queens* (Cambridge UP, 1976), p. 114; P. Williams, *The Tudor Regime* (Oxford UP, 1979), pp. 190–3.
4. R. B. Outhwaite, 'Dearth and Government Intervention in English Grain Markets, 1590–1700', *Econ.Hist. Rev.*, 2nd ser., xxxiii (1981), 389–90, 396.
5. Gras, *English Corn Market*, pp. 448–9. The same may have happened in 1573 when there were searches but no proclamation: W. Ashley, *The Bread of our Forefathers* (Oxford UP, 1928), p. 186; Essex RO, Q/SR, 39/7, 8; BL, Cotton MS. Vespasian C. xiv, A-J, f. 47.
6. Slack, *Impact of Plague*, pp. 207–11. Unless otherwise indicated, the following account of Books of Orders is based on my 'Books of Orders: The Making of English Social Policy, 1577–1631', *Trans. Roy. Hist.Soc.*, 5th ser., 30 (1980), 1–22, where full references can be found.

7. Above, pp. 65–6. Cf. **Youngs,** *Proclamations of Tudor Queens*, pp. 114–16; **E. M. Leonard,** *The Early History of English Poor Relief* (Cambridge UP, 1900), pp. 318–26.
8. *Ibid.*, pp. 171–8; **B. W. Quintrell,** 'The Making of Charles I's Book of Orders', *Eng.Hist.Rev.*, xcv (1980), 569.
9. E.g. *Acts of the Privy Council 1621–3*, p. 43; BL, Add. MS. 12496, ff. 260–1.
10. **Quintrell,** 'Charles I's Book of Orders', pp. 558–60. Cf. **J. F. Larkin** and **P. L. Hughes** (eds), *Stuart Royal Proclamations* (Oxford UP, 1973–83), ii, no. 128; **D. Hirst,** 'The Privy Council and Problems of Enforcement in the 1620s', *J. British Studies*, xviii (1978), 46–66.
11. Lincolnshire RO, Lincoln Entries of Common Council 1511–41, f. 126v.
12. **Quintrell,** 'Charles I's Book of Orders', p. 569, and the certificates in the State Papers; **T. G. Barnes,** *Somerset 1625–1640* (Oxford UP, 1961), Ch. VII.
13. E.g. **W. L. Sachse** (ed.), *Minutes of the Norwich Court of Mayoralty 1630–31* (Norfolk Record Soc., xv, 1942), p. 106; PRO, SP 16/177/55 (Dec. 1630). For rising rates or relief expenditure from 1620 onwards, see e.g. West Devon RO, W128 Plymouth Overseers' Accounts 1611–42, ff. 113–97 (reversed); Essex RO, D/P264/8/2, ff. 5–23; D/P29/5, *passim*. Cf. **W. Hunt,** *The Puritan Moment* (Harvard UP, Cambridge, Mass., 1983), pp. 248–9.
14. **Leonard,** *English Poor Relief*, pp. 268, 277; **A. L. Beier,** 'Poor Relief in Warwickshire 1630–1660', *Past and Present*, 35 (1966), 77–100. Cf. below, pp. 175–9.
15. Calculation based on the orders in **S. C. Ratcliff** and **H. C. Johnson** (eds), *Warwickshire Quarter Sessions Order Books* (Warwickshire County Records, Warwick, 1935–38), vols i–iv.
16. **Slack,** *Impact of Plague*, pp. 215–16, 218–19, 223–5.
17. *Ibid.*, pp. 313–19.
18. *Ibid.*, pp. 303–7.
19. *Ibid.*, pp. 232–4, 296–301, 305–6.
20. Cf. **E. P. Thompson,** 'The Moral Economy of the English Crowd in the Eighteenth Century', *Past and Present*, 50 (1971), 76–136; **J. Walter** and **K. Wrightson,** 'Dearth and the Social Order in Early Modern England', *Past and Present*, 71 (1976), 22–42.
21. Kent AO, Sa/ZB2/83; York Corporation Records, E40/89; **J. Goring** and **J. Wake** (eds), *Northamptonshire Lieutenancy Papers 1580–1614* (Northants Record Soc., xxvii, 1975), pp. 25–30.
22. **J. R. Chanter,** *Sketches of the Literary History of Barnstaple* (Barnstaple, 1866), p. 104; **J. B. Gribble,** *Memorials of Barnstaple* (Barnstaple, 1830), p. 624.
23. *The renewing of certaine Orders* (1594), p. 12; Kent AO, Sa/AC7, f. 194v; above, p. 101.
24. Norfolk RO, Norwich Mayor's Court Book 1615–24, f. 457v; Hants RO, J. L. Jervoise, Herriard Coll., 44M69/xxxv/30; **J. W. Horrocks** (ed.), *The Assembly Books of Southampton* (Southampton Record Soc., xi, 1917–25), i. 62.
25. **Walter** and **Wrightson,** 'Dearth and the Social Order', pp. 32–4. Cf. above, p. 117.

26. **Outhwaite**, 'Dearth and Government Intervention', pp. 389–92.
27. **W. Woodwall**, *A Sermon upon ... the causes of dearth and famine* (1609), sig. K2.
28. **W. B. Willcox**, *Gloucestershire: A Study in Local Government 1590–1640* (Yale UP, New Haven, 1940), pp. 135–6, 139 (and compare York Corporation Records, E40/85–7); **J. C. Cox**, *Three Centuries of Derbyshire Annals* (1890), ii. 189; *HMC Buccleuch*, iii. 219. For other opinions on the efficacy of the dearth orders, see **J. Thirsk** (ed.), *The Agrarian History of England and Wales, IV* (Cambridge UP, 1967), pp. 581–6; **Gras**, *English Corn Market*, pp. 241–2; **E. Lipson**, *The Economic History of England*, iii (A. and C. Black, 1931), pp. 445–7; **J. A. Chartres**, *Internal Trade in England 1500–1700* (Macmillan, 1977), p. 63.
29. **Gribble**, *Memorials of Barnstaple*, p. 618; BL, Add. MS. 12496, f. 236v. Cf. PRO, SP 16/203/60.
30. E.g., Colchester Borough Records, Assembly Book 1576–99, f. 44r, 1620–46, f. 22r; Exeter Corporation Records, Act Book 5, f. 187r; Act Book 7, f. 385v. Sometimes towns bought too late in a dearth year and then had to sell at a heavy loss: Devon RO, Dartmouth Records, DD 62207.
31. Norfolk RO, Case 10(c), Norwich Corn Stock Accounts 1644–62 *passim*. The estimate of how many people the corn would feed is based on **C. Phythian-Adams**, *Desolation of a City* (Cambridge UP, 1979), p. 194. The calculation is for bread consumption only: consumption of beer and ale doubles the amount of grain required: *ibid.*, p. 59; **Gras**, *English Corn Market*, p. 77n.
32. Exeter Corporation Records, Book 229, Corn Accounts 1562–63. I have assumed the population of the city to be 8,000.
33. Above, p. 49; **Slack**, *Impact of Plague*, pp. 74, 117, 122. On the 1590s, see **P. Clark**, *The European Crisis of the 1590s* (Allen and Unwin, 1985), pp. 57–60.
34. E.g., Essex RO, D/P 50/12/1, 1631–32 acct.; D/P 171/81, 3 April 1631; D/P 75/5/1, f. 31r; D/P 163/8, f. 11v.
35. Above, pp. 49–50.
36. E.g. **E. M. Leonard**, *The Early History of English Poor Relief* (Cambridge UP, 1900), pp. 48, 115; Hants RO, J. L. Jervoise, Herriard Coll., 44M69/012(i); *Northants Lieutenancy Papers*, p. 31.
37. Norfolk RO, Norwich Corn Stock Accounts 1644–62; Norwich Mayor's Court Book 1666–77, f. 110v; **P. J. Corfield**, 'The Social and Economic History of Norwich 1650–1850: A Study in Urban Growth', London Univ., Ph.D. thesis, 1976, p. 252.
38. **Outhwaite**, 'Dearth and Government Intervention', *passim*; **Slack**, 'Books of Orders', pp. 12–13, 21.
39. **Slack**, *Impact of Plague*, pp. 223–4.
40. E.g. Kent AO, Q/SB1, f. 43; **Outhwaite**, 'Dearth and Government Intervention', p. 397.
41. **Slack**, *Impact of Plague*, pp. 232–5; **Slack**, 'Books of Orders', p. 16.
42. **W. K. Clay** (ed.), *Liturgies and Occasional Forms of Prayer* (Parker Soc., 1847), pp. 591–4; **J. Ayre** (ed.), *The Works of John Whitgift* (Parker Soc., 1851–53), iii. 617–19. There were, however, special forms of prayer against drought in 1611 and rain in 1613.
43. **Slack**, *Impact of Plague*, p. 237; **Slack**, 'Books of Orders', p. 16.

44. See, for example, **M. Pelling**, 'Healing the Sick Poor: Social Policy and Disability in Norwich 1550–1640', *Medical History*, 29 (1985), 115–37.
45. **Leonard,** *English Poor Relief*, pp. 223–9.
46. Above, pp. 93–4.
47. Greater London Council RO, H.I./ST/A24/1, f. 39v; *The Ordre of S. Bartholomewes* (1552), sigs. D2v–3v.
48. **H. Ellis**, 'Letter from Secretary Walsingham', *Norfolk Archaeology*, ii (1849), 94; **P. Collinson**, *The Religion of Protestants* (Oxford UP, 1982), Ch. 4.
49. Above, pp. 74, 124; **J. Thirsk** and **J. P. Cooper** (eds), *Seventeenth-Century Economic Documents* (Oxford UP, 1972), pp. 753–4; **R. Dunning**, *A Plain and Easie Method ... How the Office of Overseer ... may be managed* (1685), sig. A3v; **T. Firmin**, *Some Proposals For the imploying of the Poor* (1678), p. 6.
50. Above, pp. 123, 124–5; **P. W. Hasler** (ed.), *The House of Commons 1558–1603* (HMSO, 1981), i. 333; **Collinson**, *Religion of Protestants*, pp. 141–3; **J. F. Pound** (ed.), *The Norwich Census of the Poor 1570* (Norfolk Record Soc., xl, 1971), pp. 7, 19–20.
51. Norfolk RO, Case 20(c), Mayor's Book of the Poore 1571–9 (boards), proclamation of 4 June 1571, orders to overseers 1577, and loose 'Charge given to the Overseers'; **R. H. Tawney** and **E. Power** (eds), *Tudor Economic Documents* (Longmans, Green and Co., 1924), ii. 322.
52. **A. L. Beier**, 'The social problems of an Elizabethan country town: Warwick 1580–90', in **P. Clark** (ed.), *Country Towns in Pre-industrial England* (Leicester UP, 1981), pp. 73–8.
53. **P. Slack**, 'Poverty and Politics in Salisbury 1597–1666', in **P. Clark** and **P. Slack** (eds), *Crisis and Order in English Towns* (Routledge and Kegan Paul, 1972), *passim*; **P. Clark**, '"The Ramoth-Gilead of the Good": Urban Change and Political Radicalism at Gloucester 1540–1640', in **P. Clark**, **A. G. R. Smith** and **N. Tyacke** (eds), *The English Commonwealth 1547–1640. Essays presented to Joel Hurstfield* (Leicester UP, 1979), pp. 175–6. For Dorchester, Plymouth, Southampton and Colchester, see below. Bristol in the 1570s, led by the town lecturer, John Northbrook, presents many similarities: **S. Hoffhaus**, 'The Response to Poverty in Bristol 1558–1597', Oxford Univ., M. Litt. thesis, 1986, Ch. 4.
54. For another East Anglian example, see **J. Webb** (ed.), *Poor Relief in Elizabethan Ipswich* (Suffolk Records Soc, ix, 1966), *passim*; **Collinson**, *Religion of Protestants*, pp. 170–7.
55. **Cotton Mather**, *Magnalia Christi Americana* (1702), Book III, part ii, Ch. 26, sect. 2 (I owe this reference to G. F. Nuttall); Hants RO, J. L. Jervoise, Herriard Coll., 44M69/S6/xxxvi. 12; *Commons Journals*, i. 886; Devon RO, Exeter Corporation Records, letters 282, 288. Contact between towns on matters of social policy was no doubt encouraged by Sir Thomas White's revolving loan fund: **W. K. Jordan**, *The Charities of London 1480–1660* (Allen and Unwin, 1960), pp. 370–1.
56. Above, p. 126.
57. *Minutes of the Norwich Court*, pp. 32–4; Norfolk RO, Norwich Mayor's Court Book 1634–46, f. 219r; **J. T. Evans**, *Seventeenth-Century Norwich* (Oxford UP, 1979), Ch. III; **Jordan**, *Charities of London*, pp. 178–9, 372.
58. West Suffolk RO, Sudbury Town Book D, 1618–34, ff. 121–122r.

59. **Clark,** '"Ramoth-Gilead of the Good"', pp. 175–6. Prof. David Underdown pointed out the importance of the Dorchester fire to me.
60. **C. H. Mayo,** *The Municipal Records of the Borough of Dorchester* (Exeter, 1908), pp. 514–32; Dorset RO, B2/8/1, *passim* and ff. 9v, 139r; B2/16/3, f. 94r; above, pp. 103–4.
61. **Slack,** 'Poverty and Politics', *passim*; Hants RO, J. L. Jervoise, Herriard Coll., 44M69/S6/xxxviii. 54.
62. West Devon RO, GP/2, orders for Plymouth hospital 1630.
63. **Slack,** 'Poverty and Politics', pp. 182–3; **P. Clark,** *The English Alehouse* (Longman, 1983), p. 193, n. 72; **A. Rosen,** 'Winchester in transition', in **Clark** (ed.), *Country Towns*, p. 169.
64. **R. N. Worth,** *History of Plymouth* (Plymouth, 1890), pp. 273–4, 277, 286, 289; Hants RO, J. L. Jervoise, Herriard Coll., 44M69/S6/xxxv. 53, 56, 62. Cf. Colchester Borough Records, Assembly Book 1576–99, 1 Sept. 1590; **P. Morant,** *The History and Antiquities of the County of Essex* (Chelmsford, 1816), i, Appendix to History of Colchester, pp. 17–18.
65. Hants RO, J. L. Jervoise, Herriard Coll., 44M69/S6/xxi. 1, 4. In Southampton's case, it took 43 years to get the bequest for a workhouse from the executors: **W. J. Connor** (ed.), *The Southampton Mayor's Book of 1606–1608* (Southampton Records Series, xxi, 1978), p. 30.
66. **W. T. MacCaffrey,** *Exeter 1540–1640* (Harvard UP, Cambridge, Mass., 1958), pp. 114–15; Exeter Corporation Records, Act Book 10, p. 67; Act Book 11, pp. 4, 8, 141, 225, 315; D1/21/50.
67. Above, pp. 82–5.
68. *Rowland Vaughan His Booke, published 1610* (1897), pp. 35, 43; **J. Thirsk,** *Economic Policy and Projects* (Oxford UP, 1978), espec. pp. 65– 6. Cf. **J. Thirsk,** 'Projects for Gentlemen, Jobs for the Poor: Mutual Aid in the Vale of Tewkesbury, 1600–1630', in **P. McGrath** and **J. Cannon** (eds), *Essays in Bristol and Gloucestershire History* (Bristol and Gloucestershire Archaeological Society, Bristol, 1976), pp. 147–69.
69. Exeter Corporation Records, Act Book 11, pp. 225, 315, 338; D1/21/50; Bristol AO, Common Council Proceedings 1649–59, pp. 59–60; 1670–87, ff. 128v–130r. Cf. **Thirsk,** *Economic Policy and Projects*, pp. 73–4; **M. F. Bond,** 'Windsor's Experiment in Poor-Relief, 1621–1829', *Berks Arch. J.,* 48(1945), 31–42.
70. **D. H. Kennett,** 'A Pauper Cloth-Making Account of the Seventeenth Century', *Textile History*, iv (1973), 125–9.
71. The Corporation is fully discussed in **V. Pearl,** 'Puritans and Poor Relief: The London Workhouse 1649–1660', in **D. Pennington** and **K. Thomas** (eds), *Puritans and Revolutionaries. Essays presented to Christopher Hill* (Oxford UP, 1978), pp. 206–32.
72. *Ibid.*, p. 219. On Hartlib's interests, see **C. Webster** (ed.), *Samuel Hartlib and the Advancement of Learning* (Cambridge UP, 1970); idem, *The Great Instauration* (Duckworth, 1975), pp. 360–9.
73. E.g., **Slack,** 'Poverty and Politics', p. 181; West Devon RO, GP/2, 1630 orders for Plymouth hospital.
74. **C. H. Firth** and **R. S. Rait,** *Acts and Ordinances of the Interregnum* (1911), i. 1042–5, ii. 104–10.
75. Below, pp. 195–8.
76. **Pearl,** 'Puritans and Poor Relief', pp. 227, 229.

77. *Ibid.*, p. 230; 14 Charles II, c. 12, sects. iv–vii; **R. Haines,** *A Method of Government for ... Publick Working Alms-Houses* (1679), p. 6; **S. M. Macfarlane,** 'Studies in Poverty and Poor Relief in London at the end of the Seventeenth Century', Oxford Univ., D.Phil. thesis, 1982, p. 279. (I am grateful to Dr Macfarlane for permission to refer to his thesis.)
78. **P. Slack** (ed.), *Poverty in Early-Stuart Salisbury* (Wiltshire Record Soc., xxxi, 1975), pp. 11, 14, 109–16,133.
79. **A. Woolrych,** *Commonwealth to Protectorate* (Oxford UP, 1982), pp. 41, 44, 299; **M. James,** *Social Problems and Policy during the Puritan Revolution 1640–1660* (Routledge and Kegan Paul, 1930), pp. 284–5.

Chapter 8

THE GROWTH OF SOCIAL WELFARE

In order properly to assess its contribution to the alleviation of poverty, it is necessary to measure the growth of statutory poor relief in the seventeenth century, both in absolute terms and in relation to the available alternatives. The task is not easy, given the many limitations in the available evidence. But we need to arrive at some estimate of how quickly poor rates were adopted throughout the country, how much they raised *in toto* at different points in time, and how many paupers they supported. We also need to set poor rates in context: we must have some idea of the extent of the assistance which was provided outside the limits of the poor law, by private philanthropy of various kinds. Was voluntary philanthropy always greater than relief on the rates, or was private charity gradually eclipsed by public welfare in the course of our period? Since philanthropy came first, it demands prior consideration.

PHILANTHROPY

Of all the various sorts of philanthropy, we know most about endowed charities, thanks to the work of W. K. Jordan. His studies of charitable bequests made by will in ten English counties between 1480 and 1660 were designed to show the rising quantity and changing quality of private benefactions for charitable purposes. Rather more than £3 million was given to charitable uses over the whole period in the ten counties. There was a gradual growth in endowments in the sixteenth century, despite a trough in the 1540s, and then a rise to a great peak between 1610 and 1640. More striking still, Jordan argued, was a 'great, and permanent, change in the structure of men's aspirations': the amounts given for religious purposes declined steeply and 'secular' ends – poor relief and education above all – took their place. Over the whole period a little over £1 million was given for the relief of the poor, the sum rising from 13 per cent of all charitable giving in the period 1480 to 1540 to 44 per cent from 1641 to 1660. 'Taking our whole long period in view, it was the needs of the poor that commanded the bulk of men's benevolence'.[1]

There have been many criticisms of Jordan's findings, both in general and in detail. He has been most often taken to task for failing to allow for inflation. If his figures are adjusted to take account of rising prices, they show that the level of giving did not rise in real terms but fell in the later sixteenth and recovered in the early seventeenth century.[2] The early Stuart recovery is perhaps remarkable enough in an inflationary age, but it was not the massive outpouring of wealth which Jordan's rhetoric often suggests. Evidence from Worcester indicates that charitable gifts may even have fallen over the period if they are measured as a proportion of the total property of testators.[3] The argument for a swing to 'secular' aspirations is similarly open to question. Gifts to the poor and for education were no less pious in intent, no less directed towards saving the souls of donors and recipients, than gifts to churches or religious orders. They were acts of piety and good works.

Distortions also arise from Jordan's method of using the total value of benefactions rather than the number of benefactors in most of his calculations. One or two gifts from rich merchants can dominate his picture to the exclusion of all else. Between 1611 and 1630, for example, ten London donors alone provided 38 per cent of gross endowments, while something like two-thirds of benefactors contributed only one per cent of the total sums given over the whole period.[4] Lesser donors probably moved gradually towards the newer charitable purposes, but they are completely overshadowed in Jordan's account by the great metropolitan philanthropists laying down a giant's causeway of endowments. Then there are the problems raised by probable cases of double-counting, and by questionable extrapolation from fragmentary sources.[5] Hunting Professor Jordan has become so popular and successful a game that it sometimes seems that his labours were fruitless.

Such a conclusion would be unnecessarily dismissive. Further criticisms of his work will be noted later; but it is important first to establish the positive value of Jordan's findings for our purposes. John Hadwin's suggestive reworking of his statistics has been particularly useful in this respect. Concentrating on the problem of inflation, he has pointed out that it is not the value of new benefactions each decade which needs to be measured, but the cumulative yield of both new and old benefactions at various points in time. By this measure, there was indeed a definite growth in philanthropic provision in real terms, at least after the mid-sixteenth century. The yield of endowments for the poor rose ten-fold from the 1550s to the 1650s, and four-fold when we allow for inflation. Over the same century the population roughly doubled. There was therefore a rise in yield *per capita*. By the 1650s these endowments ought to have been producing an income of nearly £50,000 a year in Jordan's ten counties. In England as a whole that implies a total of perhaps £100,000 per annum.[6]

Various qualifications need to be made about that impressive-sounding total. It was the sum that ought to have been available rather than the sum that necessarily was available, since benefactions were often diverted from their original purposes. Even if achieved, £100,000 was a relatively small sum: less than half of one per cent of the national income by Hadwin's calculation. In the middle of the sixteenth century the yield was very much lower, and insignificant if we compare it to what had been provided by religious houses and fraternities before their destruction. In real terms, Hadwin suggests, private endowments did not make good the loss of monastic charity at the dissolution until the 1580s. Indeed, if we take into account rising population, the loss was not made good in *per capita* terms until the 1650s.[7] There was therefore very real reason for complaints about the decline of charity in the mid-Tudor period. Yet there was less cause for complaint in the early seventeenth century, although it continued. 'Since popery was abolished, charity has left the land', said a speaker in parliament in the 1650s.[8] He was wrong: by then charity had revived and produced returns which would stand comparison with those in pre-Reformation England.

There are many different kinds of charity, however, and Jordan's benefactors were relatively uninterested in some charitable purposes. The provision of work for the poor, for example, seems to have had little appeal, despite the emphasis given to it by contemporary writers. Over the period 1480 to 1660, only £30,000 was left for workhouses or workstocks, and funds for pauper apprenticeship attracted little more. Help for the sick poor, whether inside or outside hospitals, was also low on the list of philanthropists' priorities, raising £135,000, half of which went to the new foundations in London in the 1550s. Two purposes above all attracted benefactions: first, the erection of almshouses, 309 being founded in Jordan's ten counties between 1480 and 1660, absorbing £417,000 worth of endowments; and, secondly, the provision of 'outright relief' for the local poor in cash, clothing or food, for which £585,000 was given, more than three-quarters of it in the form of endowments, generally managed by parish officers.[9]

The large number of individual benefactions of this kind, all of them for specific purposes, may partly be explained by legal constraints. In order to be legally secure, charitable uses had to be clearly defined and, after the Act of 1601, clearly within the limits of the statute. Yet there was a further legal problem which was only gradually being clarified by legislation and Chancery decree and which seems nevertheless to have had little influence on the behaviour of benefactors. This was the question of who could legally be vested with property for charitable uses. One solution was to appoint trustees, but there must be careful prescription of who the trustees were and complex provision for their successors. A simpler solution was to vest the property in an existing or new corporation: hence the charitable funds given to town corporations or livery companies, and the charters or letters patent which founded the London hospitals and one or two of their provincial copies. Since obtaining letters patent was a lengthy and expensive business, however, statutes of 1572, 1576 and 1598 tried to encourage the founding of houses of correction, hospitals and almshouses by exempting them from this and similar legal obstacles.[10]

These statutes no doubt help to account for the number of almshouse foundations, but they did not produce hospitals and houses of correction. It is also surprising, given their sound legal foundation, that some of the major existing charitable institutions, like the London hospitals, attracted little in the way of new gifts after their foundation. London testators continued to remember the hospitals in their wills, but only to the extent of small donations; and in general benefactors seem to have been determined to establish their own, separate fund or institution, if they could afford it. In London it might be vested in a livery company, though it retained its separate identity; elsewhere, it was given to a municipal corporation or more usually to a specific parish.[11] Chancery was therefore becoming accustomed to treating parish officers, parson and churchwardens, as if they were a legal corporation, or to using other means to validate such gifts; and Chancery inquisitions and decrees had to solve the problems of a host of legally defective endowments.[12] In the long term Chancery was successful: the trusts survived. But its activity showed how the law had to respond to the wishes of testators and how little statute did to push them in approved directions.

There was thus a considerable measure of deliberation and self-regard in the behaviour of donors. They wished their benefactions to create personal memorials, and memorials which were both locally conspicuous and socially worthy. After the Reformation almshouses no longer had chapels as they had once done, and there could be no provision for prayers for the soul of the founder. But almshouses and parish charities almost always perpetuated the name of the donor in their titles. They were also to a degree discriminatory, and perhaps increasingly so. The movement towards almshouse-foundations and away from indiscriminate doles had begun in the fifteenth century;[13] and its continuation in the sixteenth and early seventeenth centuries testifies to the increasing fastidiousness of many benefactors, who were determined to avoid helping the disreputable, disorderly, disease-ridden poor.

Almshouses were plainly for the deserving pauper, past useful labour. Of the 17 people in almshouses in Chelmsford in 1639, 10 were widows and the others appear to have been old men. Many parish charities concentrated on the respectable, whether destitute or not, providing coats, stockings or shoes, for example, both for parish pensioners and for those slightly above them in the social scale. Some were so managed that they missed the genuine poor altogether. Loan stocks commonly suffered this fate, being used for small tradesmen in need of capital and so, as one Exeter testator complained in 1629, 'much lessened in benefit to the poor people'. A benefactor in York in 1647 tried to avoid this danger, but showed in doing so precisely the sort of selection which was common by then: 'I desire that the poorest and honestest and most frugal and religious to be preferred.'[14]

The speed of the transition from open charity to precisely formulated beneficence should not be exaggerated, however. If discrimination was the mark of many larger benefactions, it could have no place in the casual doles, particularly at funerals, which many testators provided for in their wills. Although such once-for-all distributions amounted to only 17 per cent of the total sums given for outright relief of the poor in Jordan's counties, they were the major charitable activity of the vast majority of benefactors, those giving less than £10 each. In Warwick no less than 80 per cent of all gifts to the poor by will before 1650 took the form of outright doles.[15] Work on administrators' accounts has similarly shown that doles at funerals continued to the very end of our period, though they were rather less common in the later seventeenth century than they had been in the sixteenth, at least in the south. The distribution of 1d. to 4,800 poor who attended one London funeral in 1518 would have seemed monstrously anachronistic and hopelessly indiscriminate in 1700; but modest hand-outs to paupers after a burial remained a customary final act of charity.[16]

Much the same mixture of gradually developing selection alongside continuing, if increasingly small-scale liberality, can be found if we turn away from the wishes of testators to charity *inter vivos*. Gifts to the poor from living donors may well have been more substantial in aggregate than those contained in wills; they were socially at least as important; but they are frustratingly intangible because they are impossible to measure. We do not know how many London citizens kept 'poor boxes' in their houses, as Nehemiah Wallington and Samuel Pepys did; or how many early Stuart gentry, like Sir John Scott of Kent, fasted on Fridays and distributed bread to the poor, as preachers said they should.[17] Only a few perhaps. Then as now, however, individual charitable donations were particularly common at Christmas, even if they were given through an intermediary, as with Sir Robert Cecil's gifts to the London prisons and the alms which Alderman Sir William Cockayne's agent gave to the poor who came to his door in the 1620s.[18] There was also a ready response when charitable collections were centrally or locally approved and directed, usually by means of charitable briefs for communities or individuals suffering losses by fire or other misfortune. One of the earliest briefs, that for Nantwich after the fire of 1578, raised £3,300 throughout the kingdom; and such stimuli to individual philanthropy soon became numerous. One London parish registered 471 of them between 1581 and 1620.[19]

Licensed collections and charitable briefs are not the only indicators of the introduction of greater formality and greater discrimination into voluntary charity in the course of the period. There was probably truth in the frequent complaint at the end of the sixteenth century that hospitality was in decline, as the nobility ceased to keep anything like open house and the gentry spent more time in London. If commensality was being curtailed, however, some absentee landlords salved their consciences and sought to maintain their local reputations by carefully managed cash distributions. Sir Thomas Wentworth, for example, provided regular weekly payments to the poor of Wentworth Woodhouse. He stopped them when he was imprisoned in 1627 only so that they might be better appreciated when he was released. As late as the 1680s the earl of Thanet gave £100 a year to the poor of Craven, casting his charity widely at first, to embrace 20 per cent of the population of Keighley and 37 per cent of that of Giggleswick, but then, after 1699, turning to more selective gifts of clothes and regular pensions.[20]

Much more spontaneous, however, and very much less discriminatory, were straightforward gifts to beggars – in the streets, outside church, in the yards of inns. This is the most difficult kind of philanthropy to quantify, and the most difficult to chart over time. Although each transaction was minuscule, the amounts of money transferred *in toto* must have been large. Sir Christopher Lowther's accounts record his gifts in the early seventeenth century: ½d. to 'a poor man', 4d. to 'a poor man at ... church', 1s. to 'the poor on Easter Sunday', and so on. Beggars could certainly make a living out of that, even if few did as well as the poor woman in Norwich in 1562 who had £44 in cash on her when she was apprehended.[21] It is a reasonable guess – though no more than a guess – that the number of beggars and their total pickings declined in the course of the seventeenth century. Over the years the official condemnation of mendicancy and the availability of alternative forms of poor relief ought to have had some effect. But it is certain that begging did not disappear, far from it. There was a 'vast number of beggars' and 'such begging of beggars' in the streets of Restoration London; and they would not have been there if there had been no response from passers-by.[22]

Local authorities themselves were for long ambivalent, recognizing that mendicancy filled some of the gaps in welfare-provision, while condemning its grosser manifestations. In the 1620s parish authorities in Hampshire were happy to acknowledge that they had a rate for the poor 'besides the relief they have when they come to our houses', and as late as 1647 Maximilian Petty, the Leveller, assumed that many of the poor still received 'alms from door to door'.[23] Licences to beg were occasionally issued to the sick and to inmates of lazarhouses well into the seventeenth century: one reflection, perhaps, of the lack of endowed charities for such people until the very end of our period. For while testators were fastidious in their charitable donations, men and women were easily touched by face-to-face confrontations with the worst symptoms of distress. In 1662 John Graunt questioned, as modern observers might do, 'whether what we give to a wretch that shows us lamentable sores and mutilations be always out of the purest charity, that is, purely for God's sake'. The motives were selfish: 'when we see such objects, we then feel in ourselves a kind of pain . . . of which we ease ourselves, when we think we ease them'.[24] But whatever the motives, the habit of casual alms-giving persisted.

The continuation of philanthropic activities of all kinds shows that the advent of the statutory poor law and of outdoor relief paid for by parish rates did not bring any rapid switch from private charity to public welfare. The new poor law did help to encourage the shift towards discrimination which is evident in some forms of charity, and that shift involved important, if gradual, changes in assumptions and attitudes which were far from painless. There was a perceived tension between old charity and new beneficence, a tension which some historians have seen as responsible for many of the witchcraft accusations of the period. These arose from the suspicions and feelings of guilt which were inevitable when neighbourly charity was denied to old men and women in a 'society which no longer held a clear view as to how or by whom its dependent members should be maintained'.[25] Once again, however, it is doubtful whether behaviour changed very quickly. There had been discrimination and denials of neighbourly charity before the 1550s, just as there was casual almsgiving after the 1650s. It is as easy in the later seventeenth century to find people like Matthew Hale who gave alms to the poor because the statutory machine was not doing enough, as it is to find people who refused to do so because the poor law had made the practice redundant.[26]

There are other reasons for stressing the continuities rather than the contrasts between old and new means of relieving the poor. From one point of view parish relief on the rates was simply an expression of that collective responsibility of the local community for the unfortunate which had been recognized by hundred and manor courts in the fifteenth century. It was a more formal embodiment of that responsibility, but it was not wholly impersonal. The relationship between overseers and poor pensioners was nothing if not face-to-face, and it is significant that the money which was handed over could still be described as 'alms' at the end of our period.[27] There could be quite as much clientage and patronage involved in the bestowal of pensions as in the distribution of charitable doles. There was also a certain ritual, and a concern for matters other than mere bodily need. In the early seventeenth century pensioners were often required to come to church and denied relief if they did not.[28] Parish officers distributed special doles at Christmas and on other festive occasions. In 1606 480 loaves were given to the poor of Ipswich so 'that they may rejoice and give thanks to God for delivery of the parliament' from the Gunpowder Plot. Local authorities in the mid-seventeenth century organized collections at church or from door to door to augment the poor rate in times of special hardship.[29] In comparison with what had gone before, parish poor relief was neither so harsh nor so cold a medicine for poverty as it has sometimes been painted.

Nevertheless, although change was gradual, it was real. Some old methods of relieving the poor disappeared. Religious houses and fraternities had gone by 1550. Large-scale hospitality and small parish festivities with a charitable element, such as church-ales, withered away in the following century.[30] Funeral doles gradually followed suit. While begging continued, it may well have changed its character. Begging from door to door by the local poor, while still tolerated in Hampshire villages in 1622, was probably rare by 1700: in the later seventeenth century the beggar was more likely to be a stranger rather than a neighbour. But if there had been losses from the redirection and control of philanthropic impulses, there had also been gains: endowed charities and public welfare under the poor law. We must now ask which of these was the more important.

PUBLIC AND PRIVATE RELIEF

One estimate of the relationship between publicly and privately funded relief in the middle of the seventeenth century was given by Professor Jordan. In a famous assertion, he stated that 'in no year prior to 1660 was more than 7 per cent of all the vast sums expended on the care of the poor derived from taxation'.[31] This calculation rested on a comparison between, first, the income to be expected from charities established by will, and, second, the relief-payments recorded in surviving overseers' accounts. It was a calculation which was deficient in almost every respect. Most obviously, it compared a maximum figure on the charity side with a minimum figure on the taxation side. While those overseers' accounts which Jordan was able to find recorded a mere fraction (though an unknown fraction) of the sums raised by poor-rates, many of the endowments contained in wills represented intentions rather than immediate achievements. Legal uncertainties about trusts provided ample room for dispute and delay, and it sometimes took decades to obtain charitable bequests from jealous executors. Even then, the trustees – whether private individuals, parish vestries, or town councils – often misused the income. A Chancery inquisition taken in Salisbury in 1599 found that charitable funds with a total capital value of £938 were not being used for the intended purposes, and such misappropriation seems to have been particularly common in urban parishes, where the need was greatest.[32]

It is one thing to criticize Jordan's conclusion, however, and quite another to substitute an alternative. One problem is that income from poor rates and income from endowments were often managed by the same people and used for similar purposes, for the maintenance of a workhouse, for example, or for apprenticing poor children. It is hence somewhat artificial, as well as rather difficult, to disentangle the two. None the less, local studies have shown that taxation for the poor was much more important than Jordan allowed. As early as the 1560s poor rates in Exeter raised more than charitable endowments. In late Elizabethan Warwick rates provided as much for the poor as known charities, and more than twice as much if we exclude from the calculation the income of Leicester's hospital, which benefited only a few. In Salisbury in the 1620s, and even in most of the well-endowed parishes of London in the 1650s, poor rates contributed more than other formal sources of poor relief.[33] In some villages in Essex, in Wivenhoe, for example, in 1622 and in Woodford in 1700, three-quarters of the sums spent on the poor came from taxation.[34]

The national picture is much less clear, since both charities and poor rates were unevenly distributed. We know that at least one third of parishes were badly provided for in terms of endowments, and only one in ten probably had an almshouse.[35] Rates must have been needed in many parishes. But they were not common outside cities and market towns until the middle of the seventeenth century. The larger English towns certainly all had rates by 1600. Rural parishes responded to pressure from justices of the peace and appointed overseers within a decade or two of the Act of 1601, but they did not necessarily have rates as well. The least populous, those best endowed with charitable resources, and those resistant to change, avoided them for as long as they could. In 1647 the vestry of one Norfolk village still thought it 'fitter' to provide for the poor by 'voluntary contributions than by rates and collections'.[36] Nevertheless, there is direct or indirect evidence for rates in one fifth of the parishes in Devon and a quarter of those in Essex and Shropshire by 1660.[37] Taking into account gaps in the documentation, it is unlikely to be an exaggeration if we suggest that at that date one third of all English parishes – and those the most densely populated – were accustomed to raising taxes for the poor. Forty years later the practice was well-nigh universal. A survey of 116 parishes taken in Shropshire in 1696 recorded rates in 82 per cent of them, and there were no returns for some of the remainder.[38]

By 1700 therefore the total income from poor-rates across the kingdom must have been very large, and we can put a more or less definite figure to it thanks to an inquiry into the subject undertaken by the Board of Trade in 1696. The Shropshire survey is one of the few local responses to this inquiry which survive, and the Board itself had information from only one half of all parishes in the country. Even so, it was able by extrapolation to conclude that poor-rates in England and

Wales amounted to £400,000 *per annum*, £40,000 of which was collected in London.[39] Different and sometimes much higher figures were given by some contemporaries and have been repeated by later historians. The only one which needs to be taken seriously is Charles Davenant's estimate for 1685, derived from data provided by Arthur Moore: he put the total raised by poor rates in that year at £ 665,362. We do not know how Moore collected his information, however, and some of the county totals given by Davenant seem suspiciously large. The Shropshire survey of 1696, and similar information from Worcester diocese in the same year, suggest figures very much lower, and there is absolutely no reason to suppose that rates had fallen between the two dates.[40] Underestimate as it may have been, it seems safer to rely on the Board of Trade's conclusion and to take £ 400,000 as the minimum annual value of the poor rate in England and Wales at the end of the seventeenth century.

That is the only national figure in which we can repose much confidence, but at least it gives us a *terminus ad quem* for the poor rate in our period. Unfortunately, we have no estimate of the yield from charitable endowments at the same date with which we can compare it. However, given that income from charities was about £100,000 *per annum* in the 1650s, that inflation had stopped and that the rate of accession of new endowments may have slowed down, the total is unlikely to have been more than £150,000 by 1700.[41] At that date, therefore, taxation probably raised about three times as much as charitable benefactions for the needs of the poor. At the end of the seventeenth century private charity was supplementing public relief, not *vice versa*.

As we move back in time from 1700, the difficulties are reversed. We know more about the yield from endowed charity than the yield from taxation. It has been estimated, however, that in the 1650s the poor rate in the City of London amounted to £15,000, as compared with £ 40,000 in the City and suburbs at the time of the Board of Trade's survey. If the national total bore the same relationship to the total for the City in 1650 as to the total for the metropolis in 1695, then taxation raised £150,000 for the poor *per annum* in the 1650s. That is a figure rather lower than some estimates for the period, though it may need reducing further to take account of parishes which were not raising rates. A cautious and safe minimum figure for 1650 would be £ 100,000: rates can scarcely have raised less than that.[42] That leads us to a conclusion very different from Jordan's: taxation provided as much as charitable endowments in the mid-seventeenth century, and therefore not 7 per cent of the total sums expended on the care of the poor but at least 50 per cent. The proportion was lower at the beginning of the seventeenth century, of course, but even then the two elements may have been more equally balanced than Jordan suggested. Hadwin's calculations indicate that the charitable yield was about £25,000 *per annum* for the whole kingdom

171

in 1610. A contemporary estimate that poor rates brought in between £30,000 and £ 40,000 in 1614 was almost certainly exaggerated; but from what we know of rates in various English towns, it would not be unreasonable to suppose that the national total reached £10,000.[43]

If these estimates are anywhere near the truth, and there is obviously a good deal that is conjectural about them, then public relief from the rates provided nearly half as much for the poor as endowed charity at the beginning of the seventeenth century, at least as much in the middle of the century, and nearly three times as much by the end. More important than the relationship between the two sources, however, is the aggregate effect of the expansion in state provision on transfers of wealth from rich to poor. As we have seen, Hadwin's work suggests that real *per capita* income from private benefactions for the poor rose by 100 per cent between 1550 and 1650, but that that growth merely made up for the losses sustained during the Reformation in the 1530s and 1540s. If we add poor rates to the sum in 1650, however, real provision for the poor per head of population had doubled since the beginning of the sixteenth century. More remarkably still, by 1700 there had been something like a four-fold increase in poor relief relative to total population since the beginning of our period. It has to be said that this leaves out of consideration charity *inter vivos*, and in particular informal charity to the begging poor, that major unquantifiable element which may have been declining, and which might therefore have to be entered on the debit side; but it is impossible to believe that informal, casual philanthropy declined by an amount sufficient to balance the overall account.

It is likely therefore that Englishmen gave more to the poor in 1700 than they had ever done; and that they gave the greater part of it through an organized system of public welfare and not through private charity, of whatever kind. The £400,000 collected from poor rates each year was not a negligible sum to redistribute. It probably amounted to less than one per cent of the national income; it represented only about a fifth of the annual sums raised by land and assessed taxes in England and Wales in the 1690s; but it was a large contribution for a preindustrial society in which the people who counted naturally put the demands of war far above those of the poor.[44] In *per capita* terms, it meant a payment of £73 a year for every thousand of the population.

It also meant that the country was able to support an impressively large proportion of the population on the dole. Since the average pension paid out in 1700 was roughly 15d. a week, relief could be given to about 123,000 people – 2.2 per cent of the population. If we add their dependents, the total would probably double to around 4.4 per cent.[45] Alternatively, we may measure the potential benefit in real terms by translating £400,000 into a quantity of wheat at 1700 prices, and estimating how many mouths could be fed from it for a year. The answer is 266,000 people, about 4.8 per cent of the population.[46] Thanks to the poor law, nearly 5 per cent of the total population of England and Wales could be supported from poor rates at the end of our period. That tells us something about the magnitude of the achievement.

PENSIONERS AND RATE-PAYERS

The expansion of public provision for the poor in the seventeenth century rested on more than the spread of new administrative habits. Only part of it can be explained by the introduction of rates into parishes which had not had them before. At least as important, and in the second half of the century still more important, was an increase in expenditure in places which had long had such assessments, notably in towns. We can therefore see some important aspects of the process of growth through the records of selected towns which happen to provide better documentation than smaller communities, as well as more paupers and a larger investment in their support. The documentation is nowhere perfect, however, and some of the problems of interpreting overseers' papers and ratebooks need to be addressed before we can proceed.

There are essentially three quantities we should like to measure at different points in time and in different places: first, the total outlay on the outdoor relief of the poor; second, the number of paupers – preferably as a percentage of the total population – who were supported; and third, the number and proportion of householders paying for their support through the rates. If we had this information, we could form some impression of the changing impact of rates, both on those who paid and on those who received. Unfortunately, none of these sums can be done very easily.

As far as total outlay is concerned, the sources rarely give a complete picture either of income or of expenditure. Although ratebooks list the weekly or monthly amounts to be collected, these were often fixed accounting units, and income was increased by levying assessments of more than 52 weeks or 12 months in a year. We know that the rate-payers of Crediton paid for 78 months in 1679–80 and those of Tiverton for 500 weeks in 1700, for example; but this vital information is often missing from the record.[47] Records of payments are similarly partial. Many ratebooks and overseers' papers give only the amounts spent on weekly pensions. These were determined in advance, once a year, usually at Easter. They are a useful indicator of inescapable recurrent costs. But it has to be remembered that there were also *ad hoc* payments to the poor in the course of a year, variously termed 'discretionary', 'extraordinary' or 'casual' payments, or 'benevolences'. We shall see that these could be substantial, particularly in the later seventeenth century. For the sake of consistency in what follows, however, we shall initially restrict our attention to weekly pensions.

Haphazardly recorded casual payments also inhibit an accurate calculation of the number of poor supported from local rates. The recipients of these hand-outs, often called 'discretioners', were as numerous as regular pensioners in Norwich in 1633–34, and more numerous in some London parishes at the end of the century.[48] Since we rarely have continuous information about them, however, we have to confine our attention to acknowledged pensioners, those supported throughout the year. There is a further difficulty here. The sources usually record the number of pensions but not the number of people who benefited from them. Listings of the poor suggest that many pensioners were indeed single individuals, particularly widows; but others were men or women with sick spouses or young children to support. As a rule of thumb, we may reasonably double the number of pensions to reach a total of the permanently dependent poor, and this procedure will be followed in the next few pages in calculating proportions of town populations receiving the weekly dole. These estimates are likely to be minima.[49]

In contrast, the figures for the number of households paying the poor rate which are given below are probably maxima. According to the statute of 1601, all inhabitants and all 'occupiers' of land in a parish were liable to be rated. The fact that not all occupiers were living in the parish is a problem which affects rural ratebooks much more than urban ones, and it need not particularly concern us.[50] More troublesome is the fact that a resident householder sometimes paid the rate on more than one property. At the beginning of the seventeenth century most urban overseers seem to have compiled their lists of assessments by household and not by property. They tried to take some account of 'ability', of wealth held in stock, for example, as well as assessing the value of real property occupied. By the end of the century, however, it was the general practice for rates to be 'pound rates' on the value of houses or land, and hence for ratebooks to be in effect lists of properties rather than lists of inhabitants.[51] Although the vast majority of payers in towns seem to have been householders assessed only once, there is therefore some risk of double-counting. Nevertheless, in what follows the number of poor-rate assessments has been assumed to be equivalent to the number of householders paying rates; and that number has been turned into a proportion of all householders either by using the hearth taxes of the 1660s and 1670s, or by applying a standard household size of 4.75 to estimates of urban populations at other dates.

This methodological excursus is intended to show that too much certainty should not be attributed to the hard figures in the following tables. It may also explain why generations of historians working on English poor relief have been reluctant to provide firm answers to important questions concerning the growth and extent of rates in the seventeenth century. Partial as the evidence is, however, it is possible to arrive at conclusions which are both interesting in themselves, at the local level, and indicative of broader, national, developments.

A preliminary picture of the rising cost of relief across the seventeenth century in one of the largest provincial towns can be obtained from Figure 2. This shows the number of pensioners and the total amount spent on them in part of Norwich between 1621 and 1719. The information was collected in 1720 by John Fransham from 14 of the 36 parishes, most of them concentrated in the centre of the town, and he used it to draw attention to the leap in costs which occurred after 1705.[52] That was the product of special circumstances of depression in the Norwich cloth industry. Equally interesting, and more characteristic of trends in other towns, is the increase in expenditure and in the number of pensioners in the middle of the seventeenth century, after the bad harvests of the later 1640s. The proportion of pensioners and their families jumped from around 3 per cent of the population in the 1620s and 1630s to a peak of 5 per cent in 1651; and the average weekly pension also rose, from less than 9d. before 1640 to 10.6d. in 1651. After 1651, the proportion of dependent poor fell back slightly, reaching 5 per cent again only after 1700. There was no fall in the value of pensions, however. They remained stationary for twenty years and then gradually increased: from an average of 10.8d. in 1671 to 16.8d. in 1701. In Norwich the remarkable feature of the later seventeenth century was not an increase in the number of paupers receiving the weekly dole but an increase in its value by 50 per cent.

There was somewhat greater stability but a similar underlying trend in

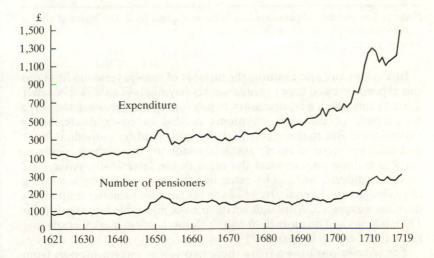

FIGURE 2. Outdoor relief in fourteen Norwich parishes, 1621–1719

York. Complete overseers' accounts permit us to sample the number and average value of pensions over the whole city at five-yearly intervals between 1632 and 1677, and to add data for 1716 (Table 6).[53] The proportion of dependent poor was higher than in the fourteen central parishes of Norwich, but there seems again to have been an increase in the years around 1650 and at some point between 1677 and 1716. Although pensions were lower than in Norwich, presumably because the cost of living was lower, they once more rose in the later 1640s and then again by 50 per cent between 1662 and 1677.

TABLE 6. Poor pensioners in York, 1632–1716

Date	No. of pensions	Pensioners and families as proportion of total population[1] %	Average pension (pence per week)
1632	312	5.2	4.6
1637	332	5.6	5.3
1642	302	5.0	5.1
1647	242	4.0	4.3
1652	338	5.6	5.7
1657	316	5.2	4.5
1662	350	5.8	4.7
1667	385	6.4	5.0
1672	387	6.4	5.6
1677	406	6.8	7.1
1716	490	8.2	8.2

Note: 1. The number of pensions has been multiplied by 2.0 to arrive at the number of pensioners and their families.
Source: see note 53, p. 186.

In York we can also examine the number of rate-payers who financed this expenditure and their average weekly payments (Table 7). The latter are the sums which were necessary to pay for regular pensions: they take no account of the extra payments needed to cover discretionary expenditure. But they suggest that the rates paid by individual York householders were relatively stable throughout the century, rising in marked fashion only to meet the crisis of the later 1640s. After 1652 rising expenditure was met by extending the tax base, not by increasing the average rate. Even so, by 1677 the tax base was smaller than might have been expected. Although we have no comparable information for 1716, it looks as if no more than half the households in York were paying rates at the end of the period.[54]

The conclusions drawn from these two towns receive support from more scattered information collected for other places. Table 8 gives

TABLE 7. Rate-payers in York, 1632–1677

Date	No. of assessments	Estimated proportion of households assessed %	Weekly amount paid by each unit (pence)
1632	541	25	3.7
1637	541	25	3.9
1642	561	26	3.8
1647	442	21	2.9
1652	569	26	4.8
1657	774	36	3.2
1662	659	31	3.7
1667	736	34	3.5
1672	684	32	3.6
1677	919	43	3.1

Source: see note 53, p. 186.

information about pensioners and pensions at various dates in Exeter and Salisbury and in two of the poorer parishes of Bristol (St John Baptist and Temple) in 1696; and it adds data which can be gathered not just for fourteen parishes but for the whole town of Norwich.[55] It shows that there were some relatively high proportions of dependent paupers

TABLE 8. Poor pensioners in selected towns, 1563–*c.*1725

Town	Date	No. of pensions	Pensioners and families as a proportion of total population[1] %	Average pension (in pence per week)
Exeter	1563	160	4.2	3.7
Norwich	1578–9	381	5.1	5.3
Salisbury	1606	141	4.0	4.0
Norwich	1633–4	341	3.8	5.3
Salisbury	1635	134	4.5	8.2
Norwich	1659–60	632	6.4	8.3
Norwich	1679–80	768	7.0	11.2
Exeter	1691	482	7.2	18.7
Bristol (2 parishes)	1696	100	8.0	13.5
Salisbury	*c.*1725	180	5.1	16.9

Note: 1. The number of pensions has been multiplied by 2.0 to arrive at the number of pensioners and their families.
Sources: see note 55, p. 186.

at the end of the century, and that, as one might expect, the proportion was higher over the whole of Norwich than in the central parishes already referred to. But the most obvious feature is again the way in which the value of weekly pensions rose, not least after 1650, when prices were generally stable.

The comparable data about assessments and average rates given in Table 9 provide some further evidence for an increase in the number of rate-payers in the second half of the century.[56] It seems not to have occurred in Norwich, and the high figure for Exeter is suspect because of the likelihood of double-counting; but the very thorough Bristol listings suggest again that rates were being paid by one half of urban households by 1700. It was therefore not the case, in provincial towns at any rate, that all households were either contributing to or receiving pensions: 30 per cent of the total in the two Bristol parishes did neither.[57] There was still some social distance between paupers on the one hand and rate-payers on the other. It was getting narrower, and it could be crossed by rate-payers who ended up on relief in old age. One or two people were even recipients and payers at the same time. In 1696 a widow in Temple

TABLE 9. Rate-payers in selected towns, 1564–1720

Town	Date	No. of assessments	Estimated proportion of households assessed %	Amount paid by each unit[1] (pence per week)
Exeter	1564–5	396	25	1.5
Norwich	1578–9	867	28	2.3
Norwich	1633–4	1137	30	1.6
Salisbury	1635	(300)[2]	24	3.7
Norwich	1659–60	1246	30	4.2
Norwich	1679–80	1186	26	7.3
Exeter	1691	1862	(66)[3]	4.8
Bristol (2 parishes)	1696	253[4]	51	5.3
Salisbury	1720	749	51	3.9

Notes:
1. These are the amounts necessary to produce actual expenditure on pensioners in the given year. More may have been needed to cover 'extraordinary' payments.
2. Estimate based on known number of rate-payers in only one parish.
3. Maximum, since some householders may be counted twice.
4. Only those assessed in the ratebooks who can be identified as residents in the parish from *The Inhabitants of Bristol in 1696* (Bristol Record Society, xxv, 1968).
Source: see note 56, p. 186.

parish, Bristol, paid a rate of ½d a week and received a weekly pension in respect of the poor children she looked after. But such cases support the general point that the poor rate and the parish dole did not create rigid status distinctions, despite their significance for some contemporary social and political commentators.[58]

Behind the flat statistics and raw average in our tables there were, of course, considerable variations, some of which are instructive. Pensions varied from place to place and person to person, and to an extent they were related to need. Generous sums went to orphan children, for example; and an unusual number of them pushed up the average pension in Barking to 23d. a week in the 1690s, compared with 13d. or 14d. in other Essex villages at the same time.[59] At the opposite extreme were the small payments of 3d. or 4d. to male pensioners, supplementary payments in effect, which bridged the gap between inadequate wages and family responsibilities throughout the period. Overseers also took account of moral worth and social standing. Widows often received twice as much as married couples, while people who had once been well-to-do were usually treated generously. In 1684 the Colchester sessions agreed that 2s. a week should be given to an old weaver who had been a rate-payer for years: half as much again as the going rate.[60]

Yet the pension lists show that there was a going rate. It was higher in the south of England than in the north, but it was increasing everywhere over the century: in the south from around 6d. a week in the early seventeenth century to 12d. in the 1670s or 1680s and rather more than that in the 1690s. These increases seem often to have taken place by a sort of ratchet mechanism. Weekly payments were increased in periods of crisis, in the later 1640s, in the bad winters of the 1670s and early 1680s, and again, when severe weather, war and economic dislocation coincided, in the 1690s; and pensions remained at the crisis level when the crisis was over: they were not reduced.[61] The trend was always inflationary.

There were local variations also in the proportions of populations receiving regular relief. Some exceptionally high figures were recorded outside large towns: one third of the households in Aldenham, Hertfordshire, in 1671, for example, and one third of the population of Killington, Westmorland, apparently, in 1695.[62] Much depended on local economic circumstances, and, even more perhaps, on how overseers used discretionary payments. As a rule they tried to keep the number of permanent pensioners small and stable; and they responded to new or temporary demands by making *ad hoc* payments on single occasions or for a week or two. One indication of this is the frequency with which the proportion of the population permanently on relief hovered around 5 per cent in the sixteenth and seventeenth centuries, not only in English towns but elsewhere in western Europe.[63] There appears to have been an accepted ceiling to the number of dependents local communities were willing to tolerate.

That ceiling was difficult to maintain, however, both because it rested on unworkable principles of selection and because it could easily be evaded by large and continuous discretionary payments. The effort to confine pensions to the deserving poor, the old, especially women, and orphan children, is evident throughout the period. In the 1720s as in the 1630s nearly a third of the pensioners in Salisbury were over the age of 60. Women also tended to predominate on annual lists of dependent paupers, although there were variations in special circumstances and from year to year. In Norwich, the reform of poor relief in 1570–71 led to 45 per cent of the payments going to men. But the figure fell to 28 per cent in 1577–79 and it was still no more than 25 per cent in 1659–60 and 1679–80.[64] Men rarely made up more than a third of the pensioners in any of the lists considered here. By contrast, the poor householders who either had no relief or who required more in St Sidwell's, Exeter, in the middle of the century, were overwhelmingly male.[65]

Yet some pensioners were always men, and men benefited more than at first appears. The weekly sums for 'John Smith's wife' or 'John Smith's child', which occur with some frequency in pension lists and overseers' accounts, may well have been payments made to Smith himself in respect of his dependents. Even if the child was being boarded out at the parish charge, that meant lighter family burdens for the father. Like those heads of household who had earlier sent wives and children out begging, able-bodied males were able to turn their sick, disabled or young dependents into marketable assets under the poor law. A large slice of relief therefore went – if sometimes indirectly – to the labouring poor; and it had done so from the beginning, from the 1560s in Exeter and 1570s in Norwich, from at least 1606 in Salisbury and 1632 in York. A still larger slice of casual payments and benevolences naturally went in the same direction.[66] For discretionary payments were the safety valve which enabled the relief machine to respond to real circumstances. When put to continuous use, they blew away the ceiling which conventional criteria of selection sought to impose, adding to the 5, 6 or 7 per cent of urban populations who were pensioners perhaps as many more who were recipients of occasional relief.

Casual payments fluctuated widely according to circumstances. In times of epidemic disease, as in Bristol in 1645 and Chelmsford in 1665, they could form two-thirds of all the sums spent on the poor.[67] Normally they were at much lower levels than that, but in the later seventeenth century it was not uncommon for them to amount to a quarter of the total cost of outdoor relief. It is unfortunate, therefore, that no account could be taken of them in the estimates of the average poor-rate assessments given above. They were certainly an added burden on rate-payers, and where relevant information is available, they seem to have been a substantial one. In Crediton, for example, they led to an increase of 50 per cent in *per capita* rate demands between 1679 and 1691.[68] Elsewhere, although not precisely recorded, they must have greatly increased the pressure to extend the tax-base which was already being exerted by the rising value of pensions.

Some towns were better able to cope with growing relief rolls than others, however, and this is the final local variable which we must consider. In parts of London it was possible to levy rates on many more householders than could be assessed in York or Bristol: in St Katherine Coleman parish virtually all householders were either paying rates or receiving relief at the end of the seventeenth century.[69] Tables 8 and 9 show other variations. Exeter in 1691 was better placed than Norwich in 1679–80, for example. Although both towns supported roughly 7 per cent of their populations with pensions, Exeter was able to pay out sums that were 50 per cent higher than those in Norwich, probably because it was able to tax a larger segment of the population. Some towns could afford to be more generous to the poor than others.

The same point appears if we look at what is perhaps the most useful of all our quantitative indicators of expenditure on the poor in the seventeenth century: the total payments on outdoor relief in selected towns, measured in relation to population size. Figure 3 shows estimated expenditure per thousand people at various dates in the towns already mentioned and in London.[70] Although limited by deficiencies in

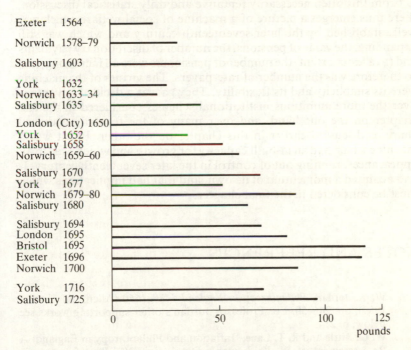

FIGURE 3. Expenditure on outdoor relief in selected towns, 1564–1725 (expenditure per thousand inhabitants)

the records, and in some cases based on the income projected in Easter ratebooks rather than on actual outgoings, the figure gives a suggestive picture of the rate-burden *per capita*. The difference between Exeter and Norwich appears clearly in the profiles for 1696 and 1700. The lower profile for London in 1695 is caused by the inclusion of the populous metropolitan suburbs; if attention had been restricted to the City, as in 1652, it would probably have stood out beyond the rest.[71] More striking than the variations, however, are the general features of the figure which confirm what we have already suggested. Expenditure on the poor increased, perhaps with an initial leap in mid-century, and then more certainly and more gradually over the last decades of the seventeenth century. The profiles give some support to the estimate drawn from the Board of Trade's survey of 1696 that the nation as a whole was spending £73 per thousand population on its poor dependents each year. They also show that, even in towns which had been unusually active in schemes for public welfare before 1640, the financial outlay doubled between then and the end of our period. The mounting expense of poor relief in the later seventeenth century was not simply a matter of other places catching up with the precocious few. It was a general phenomenon of major importance.

From this often necessarily tentative and drily statistical discussion, there thus emerges a picture of a machine of social welfare which was well established by the later seventeenth century and which was still expanding: the value of pensions, the number of discretionary payments and (to a lesser extent) the number of pensioners were all increasing, and so therefore was the number of rate-payers. The virtues of the machine were its simplicity and its flexibility. They gave it a decided advantage over the more ambitious institutional schemes considered in the last chapter on the one hand, and over many of the formally endowed charities discussed earlier in this chapter on the other. But it was a machine which had an in-built capacity for growth and which was, to all appearances, running out of control in the later seventeenth century. It had acquired a momentum of its own, and that had implications which must be considered in the final chapter.

NOTES AND REFERENCES

1. **W. K. Jordan**, *Philanthropy in England 1480–1660* (Allen and Unwin, 1959), pp. 246–50. For Professor Jordan's other supporting works see below, p. 214.
2. **W. G. Bittle** and **R. T. Lane**, 'Inflation and Philanthropy in England: A Re-assessment of W. K. Jordan's Data', *Econ.Hist.Rev.*, 2 ser., xxix (1976), 203–10.

3. **A. D. Dyer,** *Worcester in the Sixteenth Century* (Leicester UP, 1973), p. 241. Jordan also notes a decline in the proportion of estates left to charity by London merchants in the early 17th century: *The Charities of London 1480–1660* (Allen and Unwin, 1960), pp. 54–5.

4. **M. Feingold,** 'Jordan Revisited: Patterns of Charitable Giving in Sixteenth and Seventeenth Century England', *History of Education*, viii (1979), 265; **Jordan,** *Philanthropy*, pp. 339–40. Cf. **S. Brigden,** 'Religion and Social Obligation in early sixteenth-century London', *Past and Present*, 103 (1984), 104–5.

5. **Feingold,** 'Jordan Revisited', p. 267. Cf. **S. Hoffhaus,** 'The Response to Poverty in Bristol 1558–1597', Oxford Univ., M. Litt. thesis, 1986, Ch. 5.

6. **J. F. Hadwin,** 'Deflating Philanthropy', *Econ. Hist. Rev.*, 2 ser., xxxi (1978), 112; *idem*, 'The Problem of Poverty in Early Modern England', in **T. Riis** (ed.), *Aspects of Poverty in Early Modern Europe* (European University Institute, Florence, 1981), p. 237.

7. **Hadwin,** 'Deflating Philanthropy', pp. 113, 117; *idem*, 'Problem of Poverty', p. 240.

8. **J. T. Rutt** (ed.), *Diary of Thomas Burton* (Henry Colburn, 1828), i. 84; above, pp. 13, 19–21.

9. **Jordan,** *Philanthropy*, pp. 255–74, 369, 371.

10. **G. Jones,** *History of the Law of Charity* (Cambridge UP, 1969), pp. 26–30, 37–8, 57–70; **Jordan,** *Philanthropy*, pp. 89, 115–16; above, pp. 127, 152.

11. **Jordan,** *Philanthropy*, pp. 122–3, 273–4; idem, *Charities of London*, pp. 192–3.

12. **Jones,** *Law of Charity*, pp. 66 n. 5, 67–8, 47–56; Jordan, *Philanthropy*, p. 122.

13. **J. A. F. Thompson,** 'Piety and Charity in Late Medieval London', *J. Eccles. Hist.*, xvi (1965), 178–95; **M. G. A. Vale,** *Piety, Charity and Literacy among the Yorkshire Gentry 1370–1480* (Borthwick Paper 50, York, 1976), pp. 26–7.

14. Essex RO, D/P 94/5/1, f. 285v; Exeter Corporation Records, ED/BC/20; York Corporation Records, House Book 36, f. 207r. Cf. **A. Rosen,** 'Winchester in Transition', in **P. Clark** (ed.), *Country Towns in Pre-industrial England* (Leicester UP, 1981), p. 160.

15. **Jordan,** *Philanthropy*, p. 255; **A. L. Beier,** 'The Social problems of an Elizabethan country town: Warwick', in **Clark,** *Country Towns,* p. 72.

16. **C. Gittings,** *Death, Burial and the Individual in Early Modern England* (Croom Helm, 1984), pp. 161–4, 241; **Brigden,** 'Religion and Social Obligation', p. 107.

17. **P. S. Seaver,** *Wallington's World* (Methuen, 1985), p. 237; **R. Latham** and **W. Matthews** (eds), *The Diary of Samuel Pepys* (Bell and Hyman, 1970–83), iii. 230; Exeter College, Oxford, MS. 47.A.6, pp. 244–5.

18. *HMC Salisbury (Cecil),* xxiv. xvi; Northants RO, Cockayne Papers, C. 2714.

19. **C. J. Kitching,** 'Fire Disasters and Fire Relief in Sixteenth-Century England: The Nantwich Fire of 1583', *Bull.Inst.Hist.Res.,* liv (1981), 172–87; Guildhall Library, MS. 4415/1. Cf. **W. A. Bewes,** *Church Briefs* (A. and C. Black, 1896).

20. Above, p. 20; **J. P. Cooper** (ed.), *Wentworth Papers 1597–1628* (Camden Soc., 4 ser., xii, 1973), p. 275; **R. Hoyle** (ed.), *Lord Thanet's Benefaction to*

the Poor of Craven in 1685 (Friends of the Giggleswick Parish Records, 1978), pp. vii–ix, xi.

21. **D. R. Hainsworth** (ed.), *Commercial Papers of Sir Christopher Lowther 1611–44* (Surtees Soc., clxxxix, 1974), pp. 84, 89, 179, 206; **J. Pound**, *Poverty and Vagrancy in Tudor England* (Longman, 1971), p. 100. Cf. **A. L. Beier**, *Masterless Men* (Methuen, 1985), p. 111.

22. **C. H. Hull** (ed.), *The Economic Writings of Sir William Petty* (Cambridge UP, 1899), ii. 353; **Pepys**, *Diary*, vii. 3.

23. Hants RO, J. L. Jervoise, Herriard Coll., 44M69/012; **A. S. P. Woodhouse**, *Puritanism and Liberty* (Dent, 1938), p. 83.

24. **M. Pelling**, 'Healing the Sick Poor', *Medical History*, 29(1985), 118–19, 134; *Economic Writings of Petty*, ii. 353.

25. **K. Thomas**, *Religion and the Decline of Magic* (Weidenfeld and Nicolson, 1971), p. 564. Cf. **A. Macfarlane**, *Witchcraft in Tudor and Stuart England* (Routledge and Kegan Paul, 1970), pp. 205–6, but also *idem, The Origins of English Individualism* (Blackwell, Oxford, 1978), pp. 1–2.

26. Above, p. 21.

27. E.g., **J. Thirsk** and **J. P. Cooper** (eds), *Seventeenth-Century Economic Documents* (Oxford UP, 1972), p. 769; **Marquess of Lansdowne** (ed.), *The Petty Papers* (Constable, 1927), ii. 210.

28. E.g., **C. Bailey**, *Transcripts from the Municipal Archives of Winchester* (Winchester, 1856), p. 73; **P. Slack**, 'Poverty and Politics in Salisbury', in **P. Clark** and **P. Slack** (eds), *Crisis and Order in English Towns 1500–1700* (Routledge and Kegan Paul, 1972), p. 185.

29. **Bacon**, *Annalls of Ipswiche*, p. 428; Norfolk and Norwich RO, Norwich Mayor's Court Book 1654–66, f. 110v; Bristol AO, Common Council Proceedings 1649–59, f. 177, 1659–75, f.7.

30. **C. Hill**, *Society and Puritanism in Pre-Revolutionary England* (Secker and Warburg, 1964), pp. 424–6.

31. **Jordan**, *Philanthropy*, p. 140.

32. Above, p. 160; **Rosen**, 'Winchester in Transition', pp. 159–60; **Webb**, *Poor Relief in Elizabethan Ipswich*, p. 11; **Slack**, 'Poverty and Politics', p. 179.

33. **W. T. MacCaffrey**, *Exeter 1540–1640* (Harvard UP, Cambridge, Mass., 1958), pp. 167–8; **Beier**, 'Social problems of . . . Warwick', pp. 70–1: **Slack**, 'Poverty and Politics', p. 179; **R. W. Herlan**, 'Poor Relief in London during the English Revolution', *J. British Studies*, xviii, (1979), 36.

34. Essex RO, D/P 277/12/1 (1622); D/P 167/8/1, p. 40 (reversed).

35. **Jordan**, *Philanthropy*, pp. 257, 261, 27.

36. **T. Wales**, 'Poverty, poor relief and the life-cycle', in **R. M. Smith**, *Land, Kinship and Life-Cycle* (Cambridge UP, 1984), p. 359.

37. The estimates for Devon and Essex are based on the number of surviving overseers' accounts or ratebooks, together with references to rates in the quarter sessions records before 1660. It may be, of course, that not all these parishes raised rates continuously from year to year, though this was the norm after 1660. For Shropshire, see **J. Hill**, 'A premature welfare state?', *Local Historian*, xiv (1980), 11, and *idem*, 'A Study of Poverty and Poor Relief in Shropshire 1550–1685', Liverpool Univ. M.A. thesis, 1973, Ch. 3. Cf. **A. Fletcher**, *A County Community in Peace and War* (Longman, 1975), p. 156, for Sussex.

38. Bodl., MS. Carte 117, ff. 338–9. Rates were not, however, common in

Wales until the early 18th century. Cf. **A. Fletcher,** *Reform in the Provinces* (Yale UP, New Haven and London, 1986), p. 187.

39.   **S. and B. Webb,** *The Old Poor Law* (Longmans, Green and Co., 1927), pp. 152–3; Bodl., MS. Eng. hist. b. 209, f. 92v; **S. Macfarlane,** 'Social policy and the poor in the later seventeenth century' in **A. L. Beier** and **R. Finlay** (eds), *London 1500–1700. The Making of the Metropolis* (Longman, 1986), p. 255. Dr Macfarlane's current work on the returns in PRO, CO 388/5/194–210, 389/14, may clarify some of the obscurity surrounding this survey and the final total, 'computed' from the £184,735 raised in the parishes which responded.

40.   *Seventeenth-Century Economic Documents,* pp. 803–4. J. P. Cooper kindly informed me of the conclusion of his work on the Worcester returns which survive among the diocesan records. Other estimates for the later seventeenth century are: **W. Petyt,** *Britannia Languens* (1680), p. 132 (£400,000); **H. Mackworth,** *England's Glory* (1694), p. 24 (£700,000).

41.   **Hadwin,** 'Problem of Poverty', p. 237; **C. Wilson,** 'The Other Face of Mercantilism', in **D. C. Coleman** (ed.), *Revisions in Mercantilism* (Methuen, 1969), p. 131.

42.   **V. Pearl,** 'Social Policy in Early Modern London', in **H. Lloyd Jones, V. Pearl** and **B. Worden** (eds), *History and Imagination. Essays in honour of H. R. Trevor-Roper* (Duckworth, 1981), p. 130. Cf. **Hadwin,** 'Problem of Poverty', pp. 239–40. £100,000 is not implausible given the sort of *per capita* payments suggested in Figure 3, p. 181, for the 1650s and assuming that at least a third of parishes (containing more than a third of the population) were paying at that date.

43.   **Hadwin,** 'Problem of Poverty', pp. 237, 250 n. 151; *idem,* 'Deflating Philanthropy', p. 112; **A. Willet,** *Synopsis papismi* (1634), p. 1220. Cf. **Jordan,** *Philanthropy,* p. 141 note.

44.   **Hadwin,** 'Problem of Poverty', pp. 237, 240, 250 n. 156, 251 n. 174; **G. S. Holmes,** 'Gregory King and the Social Structure of pre-industrial England', *Trans.Roy.Hist.Soc.,* 5 ser., xxvii (1977), 61; **J. P. Cooper,** 'In Search of Agrarian Capitalism', in **T. H. Aston** and **C. H. E. Philpin** (eds), *The Brenner Debate* (Cambridge UP, 1985), p. 185.

45.   Cf. below, pp. 177–9.

46.   I have taken the population of England and Wales to be 5.5 million, and assumed that one quarter of wheat would feed a person for a year (cf. above, p. 158, note 31). For prices, see **W. G. Hoskins,** 'Harvest Fluctuations and English Economic History, 1620–1759', *Agricultural History Rev.,* xvi (1968), p. 30.

47.   East Devon RO, R4/2/2/PO3 (1679–80), R4/1/Z/PW3 (1700).

48.   **W. Rye** (ed.), *The Norwich Rate Book 1633–1634* (1903); **S. M. Macfarlane,** 'Studies in Poverty and Poor Relief in London at the end of the 17th Century', Oxford Univ., D. Phil. thesis, 1982, pp. 105–10.

49.   Cf. above, pp. 75–6.

50.   Above, p. 126, and references in note 69, p. 136.

51.   The transition can be seen in Bristol in 1685–86 and in Exeter by the 1690s: Bristol AO, Temple parish Poor Books 1684, 1686; Exeter Corporation Records, D2/159b, Poor Rate Assessments. Cf. **J. V. Beckett,** *Local Taxation. National Legislation and the Problems of Enforcement* (Standing Conference for Local History, 1980), pp. 5–8; **E. Melling** (ed.), *Kentish*

Sources, IV: The Poor (Maidstone, 1964), pp. 50–1; **Macfarlane,** 'Studies in Poverty and Poor Relief', pp. 96–7.

52. **J. Fransham,** *An Exact Account of the Charge for Supporting the Poor of the City of Norwich* (1720). In what follows, population estimates have been based on the information in **C. Parkin,** *The History and Antiquities of the City of Norwich* (1783), p. 178; **P. J. Corfield,** 'A Provincial Capital in the Late Seventeenth Century: The Case of Norwich', in **Clark** and **Slack,** *Crisis and Order in English Towns,* pp. 266–7; and assuming the total population of the city to have been 18,000 in 1621 and 20,000 in 1651, of which about a third was in the 14 parishes.

53. York Corporation Records, E70–74, 74A.

54. For the population of York, see **Palliser,** *Tudor York,* pp. 112–13.

55. The sources used in Table 8 are: Exeter Corporation Records, book 157; D2/159b(2); Salisbury Corporation Records, St Thomas's parish, no. 144 (1606); S165 Overseers' Book 1705–56 (1724 and loose sheet for St Edmund's, 1727); **P. Slack,** *Poverty in Early-Stuart Salisbury* (Wilts Record Soc., xxi, 1975), pp. 75–82; Bristol AO, St John Baptist poor accounts 1695–6; Temple Poor Book 1696; **J. F. Pound,** 'An Elizabethan Census of the Poor', *Univ. Birmingham Hist. J.,* viii (1962), 158, 160; *Norwich Rate Book;* Norfolk and Norwich RO, Poor Rate Books nos 4, 18. For the populations of Exeter and Salisbury, see **MacCaffrey,** *Exeter,* p. 12; **W. B. Stephens,** *Seventeenth-Century Exeter* (Exeter UP, 1958), p. 146; *VCH Wiltshire,* vi. 72; **Slack,** 'Poverty and Politics', *passim.* For Norwich, see note 52: I have taken the population in 1578 to be 15,000. For the two Bristol parishes, see the listings in **E. Ralph** and **M. E. Williams** (eds), *The Inhabitants of Bristol in 1696* (Bristol Rec. Soc., xxv, 1968).

56. Sources for Table 9: as in note 55, plus Salisbury Corporation Records, boxes of poor rates: St Martin's 1635; St Martin, St Thomas and St Edmund, 1720.

57. Cf. **W. Newman Brown,** 'The receipt of poor relief and family situation: Aldenham, Hertfordshire 1630–90', in **Smith,** *Land, Kinship and Life-Cycle,* p. 410. For what it is worth, these figures accord with one of Gregory King's calculations: he estimated that in 1695 45 per cent of occupiers of houses were paying to 'church and poor': *Seventeenth-Century Economic Documents,* p. 787 (and cf. pp. 769–70). He also thought that 25 per cent received alms: perhaps a high estimate, but in York in 1677, Norwich in 1679–80, Exeter in 1691 and the two Bristol parishes in 1696 pensioners formed between 15 and 20 per cent of all householders – and we need to add receivers of discretionary payments. It is not inconceivable that 25 per cent of urban households (though only perhaps half that proportion of urban populations) generally received poor relief at some point in the year at the end of the seventeenth century.

58. For King, for example (note 57 above), and for some Levellers: **D. M. Wolfe,** *Leveller Manifestoes of the Puritan Revolution* (Nelson, 1944), p. 342; **C. B. Macpherson,** *The Political Theory of Possessive Individualism* (Oxford UP, 1962), p. 114. Cf. **K. Thomas,** 'The Levellers and the Franchise' in **G. E. Aylmer** (ed.), *The Interregnum: The Quest for Settlement* (Macmillan, 1972), pp. 64–5, 69.

59. Essex RO, D/P 81/8/1 (1694). Cf. D/P 264/11/2; 321/12/1.

60. **Slack,** 'Poverty and Politics', p. 175; Essex RO, T/A 465/127, Colchester Sessions Order Book 1677–84, p. 122.

61. Cf. **Wales,** 'Poverty, poor relief and the life-cycle', pp. 354–5; **D. Marshall,** *The English Poor in the Eighteenth Century* (Routledge and Kegan Paul, 1926), pp. 93–4.
62. **Newman Brown,** 'Receipt of poor relief', p. 410; **Macfarlane,** *Origins of Individualism,* p. 77. See note 57 above for proportions of urban households on relief.
63. Cf. above, pp. 71–2; 4 (Lyons); and the references in note 49, p. 88.
64. Norfolk and Norwich RO, Norwich Mayor's 'Booke of the Poore' 1571–9 (in boards), lists of 1570–71 and 1577–78; and the sources in note 55.
65. Exeter Corporation Records, Y5, undated list of poor in several parishes.
66. Cf. above, pp. 82–3, and for remarks on the situation at the end of the eighteenth century, **K. Williams,** *From Pauperism to Poverty* (Routledge and Kegan Paul, 1981), pp. 39–42, 147.
67. Bristol AO, Christ Church Overseers' Receipts and Disbursements, 1645–46; Essex RO, D/P 94/12/1–3 (1665).
68. East Devon RO, R4/2/2/PO3, Crediton Overseers' Accounts 1679–94.
69. **Macfarlane,** 'Studies in Poverty and Poor Relief', p. 127.
70. Sources for Figure 3: as in notes 53, 55, 56 and Salisbury Corporation Records, S161 (18 May 1603), S162, Overseers' Accounts 1629–94; **Fransham,** *Exact Account,* p. 14; **E. E. Butcher** (ed.), *Bristol Corporation of the Poor 1696–1834* (Bristol Rec. Soc., iii, 1932), p. 47; Exeter Corporation Records, D2/159b(4), 1696; **Pearl,** 'Social Policy in Early Modern London', p. 130 (and for the population of the City and the metropolis, *ibid.,* p. 117; **Beier** and **Finlay,** *London 1500–1700,* p. 2).
71. See **Macfarlane,** 'Social policy and the poor in the later seventeenth century', p. 255.

Chapter 9

CONTROLLING THE MACHINE
1660–1714

Mounting expenditure on the relief of the poor in later Stuart England raised in novel form issues which have been considered earlier in this book. The paradox that it occurred at a time when standards of living were in some respects improving suggests once more that strategies for social welfare were only distantly related to economic circumstances. Rising expense and the growth in the number of rate-payers also called existing strategies into question. They made the poor laws and their deficiencies a live political issue, and inspired new projects and experiments which resembled those of the past in their quest for more effective and cheaper alternatives. The developments of the later seventeenth century cast fresh light on the relationship between the reality, the perception and the management of poverty.

DEPRIVATION AND ENTITLEMENT

We saw in Chapter 3 that the economic background seemed to imply two changes in the nature of poverty after 1650. First, there was a decline in 'deep' poverty. With the end of population growth and inflation, with rising productivity and rising real wages, the number of people living at the margin of subsistence must have fallen. Bad harvests still caused temporary distress, but it was slight in comparison with what had gone before. Secondly, however, there was probably no decline in the number of people in 'shallow' poverty. It might even have increased, and if it had only stabilised, it had done so at a high level. There was still considerable underemployment, and while new crops and rural industries might be providing jobs for the poor in the countryside, they did not reverse the social polarization of the previous century or remove the insecurity caused by the gradual disappearance of communal rights of gleaning and access to commons and wastes.[1] Most important of all, urbanization increased the proportion of the population dependent on the sale of its labour and on the volatile forces of the market.

In these circumstances the number of people claiming relief was bound to remain high. Trade depressions, cold winters, sickness and disability left people no other recourse but parish doles and parish charities. Half of the poor families in Norfolk villages could expect to have a member on relief at some point in the family cycle, generally at the end of a working life.[2] The varied misfortunes common in towns were rehearsed in bundles of petitions for assistance to the council of Exeter. There were cases of broken legs and arms. Poor weavers had children who were unable to spin because they caught smallpox. There were several references to people thrown out of work by the 'hardness of the times' or 'the badness of trading'. And there were the old again, from couples in their sixties to a man and wife both allegedly 'attaining to the age of 140 years'.[3] In the later seventeenth century, as in the later twentieth, demographic trends made old age a particularly important cause of poverty: 10 per cent of the population was over the age of 60.[4]

Yet it may be doubted whether such factors as urbanization and the changing age-structure of the population can entirely explain the expansion in public welfare which occurred after 1650. Even if the proportion of the population in shallow poverty was rising, and that is not certain, we still have to account for the increase of 50 per cent in the value of individual pensions at a time of stable prices. Part of the explanation for that no doubt lies in the fact that the doles paid before 1650 were far from enough to keep body and soul together. There had to be a 'catching-up' operation if they were to obviate the need for the poor to beg. By 1700, the level of pensions may have been enough to support a single pauper, at least in rural England.[5] If begging and indiscriminate charity were declining at the same time, then rising expenditure on public relief after 1650 simply filled the vacuum.

There must be something in this argument; but again one may doubt whether it can be the whole explanation. We have already seen that informal relief to beggars continued. Moreover, even in 1700, many pensions were still supplementary and were never intended to provide full support for a family. One of the petitioners in Exeter was a sick widow who got 8d. a week from the parish; but she paid 7d. a week in rent, and she was expected to work for the rest of her living. Thomas Firmin noted that many beggars in London were forced onto the streets by inadequate weekly doles.[6] There was still something of a gap between provision and need, and its size depended on a multitude of local decisions about who was to be relieved and how much they were to be paid.

It is necessary to ask, therefore, whether those who managed the poor-relief machine were, consciously or unconsciously, being more generous in the later seventeenth century than they had been before. Some contemporaries certainly thought so; and they attributed the idleness and 'luxury' of the poor to the carefree liberality of parish officers. According to Fransham, the overseers of Norwich were 'very willing to raise to themselves (it being at the public expense) the character of good-natured, merciful, generous men; never [thinking of] the consequences of their over-liberality (as long as 'twas not their own).'[7]

The question is wrongly posed if it is put in terms of more or less generosity or liberality, however. It is a question of perceptions of deprivation. 'Shallow' poverty was defined in Chapter 3 as lying just below the poverty line drawn by contemporaries. It is relative poverty, therefore, and its character is liable to change over time. We must consider the possibility that people were becoming more sensitive to relative deprivation in the later seventeenth century, that they were gradually raising the poverty line and with it both the number of the poor receiving relief and the sums of money paid to them.

There is some reason to suppose that this was happening. It was probably not a conscious shift, despite the moral weight behind reiterated appeals to charity and benevolence.[8] There is too much contrary emphasis in the literature on the need for discrimination, discipline and control. But new perceptions were a likely, if unforeseen, consequence of the poor law itself. In practice, the poor law made the recognition of poverty easier than its denial and the granting of relief easier than its refusal. The machinery of social welfare sharpened appreciations of deprivation and created assumptions about entitlement.

The overseers played the vital role here, and it is important to understand their position. They were often criticized. John Ivie, mayor of Salisbury, drew a caricature of these 'charitable collectors', men 'not two years out of their apprenticeship' but conscious of their 'power' under the law, who gave pensions to their charwomen, refused to assess their friends and neighbours, and forced the justices to consent to exorbitant rates. Overseers were certainly often young men, in their first public position, but that did not make them irresponsible.[9] On the contrary, their overriding concern was to avoid trouble during their year in office. Obliged by statute to raise rates and relieve the poor, and confronted by the sort of hard cases revealed in the Exeter petitions, they naturally tried to give themselves room for manoeuvre. At the start, at Easter, they provided for reasonably adequate pensions and fixed a sufficient rate for the purpose. Yet six or eight months later they were faced with extra claimants and rising casual payments as winter approached, and they needed additional rates before the year was over.[10]

Overseers also had less freedom of action than their critics implied. In cities where the administration of poor relief was centralized, such as York and Salisbury, they had to report regularly to two justices of the peace; and elsewhere they were generally supervised by monthly vestry meetings, chaired by the churchwardens, as the law required. It might be thought that the interests of rate-payers would have been well represented on these occasions and have exercised some restraint. But there is little sign of this. New claims for relief were heard and extra pensions agreed. The atmosphere was a bureaucratic one.[11] The poor law meant that there was business to be done and books to be balanced. Office-holders had the upper hand and rates rose.

Discontented rate-payers had one further recourse: to quarter sessions. Although annual rates were authorized by two justices, acting out of sessions, those assessed had the right of appeal to the whole bench. They exercised it to the full in the later seventeenth century, and there were many sessions orders for the 'abatement' of rates in individual cases.[12] The justices were much more reluctant to overturn a whole parish assessment, however, usually confining themselves to instituting a local inquiry into alleged inequities. They had good reason for caution. In Bristol the parishioners of St James's complained again and again about their rates: the churchwardens and overseers had fixed them in secret and used them for pensions to people 'not fit or qualified', 'under pretence of age and impotency'. But St James's was a notoriously poor parish, and the magistrates had wrestled with its problems for years. They had levied rates in aid for it from other parishes since at least 1615. They had difficulty in finding overseers, since men paid fines rather than serve in St James's.[13] It is not surprising that they turned a deaf ear to the grievances of rate-payers.

Moreover, magistrates also had to listen to the groans of the poor; and they responded to them as positively as monthly meetings. They approved parish levies of extra rates, especially in early winter,[14] and sometimes instigated them. Hard times in Bristol twice prompted a doubling of the rates, in 1658 by order of the Common Council and in 1674 by order of the city sessions.[15] Reductions were less easily achieved. In 1687 the overseers of Norwich were instructed to bring in their accounts to the Mayor's Court so that 'by reason of the cheapness of provision and great plenty of work the collection of the poor of this city may be abated'. No abatement seems to have occurred. The Court had no greater success in its effort to cut down the number of petitions for relief presented to councils and quarter sessions, or the number of petitioners who plagued mayors and individual justices.[16] Overseers were well aware that it was not only rate-payers who could appeal to higher authority against their decisions. Would-be pensioners did so too, and quarter sessions and town councils ordered parishes to provide for them.[17]

Faced with pressure from above as well as from below, overseers were bound to play safe. They kept rates as high as they could, not reducing them much, if at all, in good years, in case hard times returned; and they employed any prospective surplus in casual payments or new pensions to the obviously needy individuals who pestered them. There was never any great surplus on poor-relief accounts, any more than there could for long be a deficit. As a result, people who would once have been forced to be self-sufficient were incorporated among the dependent poor because resources were available. More than that, they naturally began to assume that they were entitled to relief. Practice taught them their rights under the statutes. In 1698 Sir Richard Cockes complained that 'the poor ... thinks the parish is obliged in old age, extremities, and necessities to provide for him, who in plenty and cheap times will either work little or live without saving'.[18]

There were no doubt still some who were ashamed to go on relief, just as there had been some who were ashamed to beg. But access to charitable and public funds, advertised by busy overseers and concerned neighbours, reduced their number. One of the petitioners in Exeter was a poor widow of St Sidwell's who had 'sold and pawned all in her great want because she would not make her condition known'. Her condition was made known in the end. From time to time in the sixteenth century local censuses of the poor had uncovered layers of poverty never previously suspected.[19] The machinery which had been erected by 1700 drew them once and for all into the light of day and permanently altered people's appreciation of what poverty was.

THE LAW QUESTIONED

None of this was intended by the legislators of 1598 and 1601, of course. Neither was it welcome to their successors, who proceeded to question the utility of the Elizabethan statutes. Dudley North pointed out that the poor laws had 'not cleared the streets and land of Beggary'. Sir Richard Cockes would have repealed them altogether, and substituted harsher penalties against idleness, in order to make people 'consider and not get families and children before they had probably got wherewith to maintain them'. Sir Francis Brewster showed how far the reaction had gone by 1695:

> There is no nation I ever read of who by a compulsory law raiseth so much money for the poor as England doth ... Our charity is become a nuisance, and may be thought the greatest mistake of that blessed reign in which that law passed, which is the idle and improvident man's charter.[20]

It was generally appreciated, however, that the chief fault lay not so much in the wording of the 1601 statute as in the failure to implement it to the letter. As Sir Matthew Hale said, the law sanctioned cash payments only to the impotent, not to the poor 'that are able to work if they had it, and had it at reasonable wages'. The latter were not 'within the provision of the law', although Hale conceded that there might legitimately be 'very small' doles to those overburdened with children.[21] For the able-bodied, the statutes provided stocks of raw materials and compulsory employment. It was overseers' reluctance to trouble themselves with these devices which led to swollen relief rolls and new concepts of entitlement.

The remedy seemed plain. There should be more workhouses. 'Above all', John Cary noted in 1695, 'our laws to put the poor at work are short and defective' and 'render the poor more bold, when they know the parish officers are bound either to provide them work, or give them maintenance'. Workhouses had proved their worth in Holland, where there were no poor rates and no beggars.[22] They could not become common in England, however, so long as the poor law rested on so small an administrative unit as the parish; and criticism of that fundamental feature of the Elizabethan legislation was the second common theme of later Stuart commentators. There were too many gross inequalities in rates between parishes, particularly in towns, where rates in aid did little to redress the balance. Vestries were also too set in their ways, too inclined to levy pound rates on property and ignore movables and stocks in trade – a major grievance of landowners.[23]

The extension of rates to something like half of all householders made these issues especially controversial, and by the 1690s, when the Board of Trade was conducting its inquiries, there seemed a real prospect of legislative reform. Between 1694 and 1705 there were at least 14 bills in parliament seeking to overhaul the machinery of relief. Yet no wholesale reconstruction materialized. There were individual statutes for particular towns, founding Corporations of the Poor which took power out of the hands of parish officers and built new workhouses. We shall see shortly, however, that they proved to be financial and political failures. They did not encourage national solutions along the same lines.[24] In effect, the task of reconciling the different needs of town and country, the conflicting interests of parishes and justices, and the inconsistent demands of financial retrenchment and investment in new solutions, proved far too difficult for parliament in wartime. It was not until the return of lasting peace and political stability that there could be a general effort to cut the costs of poor-relief: Knatchbull's Act of 1723 permitted unions of parishes and sanctioned the refusal of relief to paupers who were unwilling to enter a workhouse.[25]

There was some slight tinkering with the law before then. An Act of 1692 reflected prevailing anxieties by seeking to control 'the unlimited power' of overseers and churchwardens, 'who do frequently, upon frivolous pretences (but chiefly for their own private ends) give relief to what persons and number they think fit'. Vestries were to examine lists of pensioners every Easter and to approve only those they thought 'fit to receive collection'; and no casual payments should be permitted except by authority of a justice of the peace. The Act seems to have had little effect. A statute of 1697 tried to reinforce shame sanctions as a deterrent to claimants on relief: pensioners should wear a badge on their shoulder and be refused the dole if they did not comply.[26] Badging the poor was not a new invention. It had been widely attempted in the early sixteenth century and more occasionally since then. But it is an indication of contemporary concerns that the practice was revived in many towns from the 1670s onwards, even before the Act. Constant repetition of the requirement, including its insertion in the Norwich newspapers in 1706, suggests that many overseers found it more trouble than it was worth none the less.[27]

With these minor revisions, the Elizabethan Poor Law remained essentially intact in 1714. There had, however, been one large and crucial addition to it in the later seventeenth century: the law of settlement. This alone made the burden of poor relief tolerable by setting real bounds to it. The fact that the boundaries were parochial ones put further obstacles in the way of any demolition of parish autonomy; but that was a point in their favour as far as rate-payers were concerned. They wished to be reassured that the growth of relief could not be infinite. When they were unable to mount sufficient pressure to deny relief to the resident poor, they naturally turned to the strictest possible definition of who was and who was not resident. Every system of welfare needs some clear demarcation of entitlement; it cannot be open-ended. Since the wording of the 1601 Act proved inadequate, the concept of settlement had to be developed to do the job.[28]

The notion that every man had a place of settlement to which he could be returned was implicit in the vagrancy laws and in the activity of many local authorities against inmates and strangers. But it was not until the statute of 1662 that previous assumptions and practices were codified and applied directly to the problems of poor relief. The Act of Settlement professed itself to be 'for the better relief of the poor of this kingdom', though the preamble made it clear that the real grievance was their 'continual increase' which was 'exceeding burthensome': in fact, it was an Act for Removal. Its central provision authorized two justices of the peace to remove any newcomers who were 'likely to be chargeable' to a parish, provided that complaint was made against them within 40 days of arrival and that they had not rented houses worth £10 a year or more. It was only as an afterthought that a clause was added permitting continued residence in certain circumstances if migrants brought a certificate from their home parishes acknowledging responsibility for them.[29]

If consistently enforced, the Act might have placed a sharp brake on migration, and there were critics who pointed to the damaging economic consequences when labour was scarce in some areas and plentiful in others.[30] In general, public attitudes towards labour mobility seem to have been becoming more relaxed in the later seventeenth century, to judge by the licensing of petty chapmen (once classed as vagabonds) in 1697, and by the lack of anxiety about vagrants themselves.[31] There were new vagrancy statutes in 1700 and 1713, improving procedures for passing them from parish to parish, but it may be that by then local authorities were more concerned about who should pay for their removal than about the need to inflict a bloody deterrent punishment.[32] As time went on, the Act of Settlement must have seemed anachronistically restrictive, especially after 1685 when the limit of 40 days was declared to begin after new arrivals had given notice of their address; if there was no notice, they could be removed at any time.[33]

The law was therefore amended, first with various new provisos in 1692, and then slightly more radically in 1697. Anyone who had a certificate could now be removed only after he became chargeable, and not until then: the 'certificate man' was given a conditional security he had not clearly had before. In consequence, it was hoped that migrants would not be deterred from moving to places 'where sufficient employment is to be had' and where 'the increase of manufactures would employ more hands'.[34] By comparison with the Act of 1662, this was a striking change of tune. Yet the settlement laws were not dismantled altogether. Migrants had to give notice of their arrival, parishes to keep bundles of settlement certificates, and justices to respond to requests for removal orders for another century and longer. The heavyweight bureaucracy of settlement was a price which had to be paid: by justices, overseers and rate-payers in return for the promise of a limit to expenditure on the poor; by the poor themselves in return for recognition of their entitlement to relief.

Endless absurdities ensued in practice. Justices removed chargeable migrants with one hand, while ordering extra rates for the overburdened parishes to which they were returned with the other. There was obviously little point in the settlement disputes which occurred between neighbouring parishes within a town. But the only alternative was to override the parochial system altogether, by means of centralized direction and centralized institutions in larger units of local government. We have seen already that experiments along these lines had failed in the sixteenth and early seventeenth centuries. The Corporations of the Poor in the reigns of William III and Anne showed once more why root-and-branch reform of the poor law was impossible.

CORPORATIONS OF THE POOR

Between 1696 and 1712 Corporations of the Poor became all the rage. The London Corporation of 1647 was revived and others were established by Act of Parliament in fourteen towns: Bristol, Tiverton, Crediton, Hereford, Exeter, Colchester, Hull, Shaftesbury, Kings Lynn, Gloucester, Sudbury, Worcester, Plymouth and Norwich.[35] It was an unprecedented explosion of local activity, and it had several origins.

The list itself shows that there were connections with the past, with the

Puritan projects undertaken in many of these towns of south-west England and East Anglia. Although the Restoration brought a temporary lull in that sort of reform, interest in it did not entirely die. In 1667 the aldermen of Norwich set up a committee to investigate the management of workhouses in Holland and Flanders in order to see what might be done at home. Seven years later their colleagues in Exeter contemplated following the example of the Devon justices and getting an Act of Parliament to give their workhouse full security at law.[36] Matthew Hale and Josiah Child also noted the utility of formal incorporation if new institutions were to be well established and attract benefactions. Hale argued that charity was better focused on such single large projects than squandered in 'doles and little yearly pensions, which consume and come to nothing, but are swallowed up in the present necessity of the poor'. Child hinted at the need to harness the philanthropic and social energies of Nonconformists which were denied public outlet by the Clarendon Code and the Test Act: they should be permitted to govern new welfare institutions, particularly workhouses.[37]

It took the Revolution of 1688 and its aftermath to turn flickers of interest and fertile suggestions into concrete realities, however. Like their predecessor in London, the Corporations rested on the hopes and fears raised by war and political revolution. Regular parliaments provided a basic opportunity for debate and legislation at the centre. But the political will came from elsewhere: from the revived political ambitions of old Dissent after the Toleration Act and the new confidence of its representatives in the localities; and, more generally, from the movement for national regeneration, both moral and religious, which strove to erect collective defences for the war against Popery and France, which spawned voluntary religious societies, including Societies for the Reformation of Manners, and which was sponsored by William III and Anne.[38] The economic context was also important: bad harvests, harsh winters and the disruptive effects of war in the 1690s contributed to anxiety about the condition and productivity of the labouring classes. It stimulated the inquiries of the Board of Trade in 1695–96; and the Board received advice from figures of importance in the history of the Corporations, such as Thomas Firmin of London and John Cary of Bristol.[39]

Bristol's Corporation, founded in 1696, was in fact the model for the rest, and Cary was its instigator and chief propagandist. His aims were similar to those of Hartlib in the 1640s. A new corporate body providing compulsory employment, a vast new workhouse, and central control of parish relief would 'civilise such as had been bred up in all the vices that want of education could expose them to', purge the poor generally of 'a great deal of foulness', and win them 'into civility and a love to their labour'.[40] As a leading Whig, Cary naturally had support from others in the same camp, including Robert Yate, MP for the city, whose father had been involved in a workhouse scheme in the 1650s; and his

Corporation offered particular opportunities to Dissenters. The founding Act exempted its officers and governors from the penalties of the Test Act, and three of the first four treasurers were Quakers. It is probably no accident that the Society of Friends was erecting its own workhouse in Bristol in the 1690s.[41] Yet the Corporation was not narrowly sectarian. It had no High Church or High Tory backing, but several of its governors (called Guardians) were members of the local Society for the Reformation of Manners, and that gave it contacts with moderate Anglicans, like Sir John Duddlestone and John Bachelor.[42] In its early days the Bristol Corporation was founded on a broad alliance of Whig, Dissenting and Latitudinarian interests.

Several other Corporations had similar political and religious inclinations. Quakers were closely involved in Colchester in 1698, again in a financial capacity, and the leaders of the project, Ralph Creffield and Nathaniel Lawrence, were Whigs and second-generation Dissenters, like Yate in Bristol.[43] In Exeter the town council was largely Tory, and the bishop refused to allow a Society for the Reformation of Manners; but a Corporation of the Poor was pushed through parliament in 1698 by the city's Whig MP, Sir Edward Seaward, and its management committee of Guardians, elected by rate-payers in the wards, was a Dissenting faction from the beginning, opposed to the municipal council. Of the city fathers, only the leading Whig, Sir John Elwill, regularly attended meetings of the Corporation of the Poor.[44] The revival of the Corporation in London, again in 1698, rested similarly on the efforts of a Whig, the banker Sir Robert Clayton; it had links with Quakers, through John Bellers, for example, and with Latitudinarians through the alleged Socinian, Thomas Firmin; and its members hoped to be able to obtain dispensation from the requirements of the Test Act. Their ambitions were also the same as Cary's: to repress 'idleness, theft, debauchery, prophaneness and other immoralities in children', to sow 'the early seeds of industry, honesty, sobriety, piety and virtue in them', and to achieve 'the reformation, happiness and welfare of the nation'.[45]

It makes sense, therefore, to see the Corporations as lineal descendants of the Puritan municipal projects of the early seventeenth century. That is not to say, however, that they were necessarily or consistently Whig in political alignment. Times changed, and new forms of centralization were as useful to Tories in power in the localities in Anne's reign as to Dissenters finding their feet in politics again in the 1690s. The Tories of Norwich were responsible for founding the last of the Corporations, in 1712. They took care to avoid the problems of Exeter by having the Guardians elected by the municipal corporation and not by a rate-payer franchise; and they never had much enthusiasm for the exercise. They were contemplating dissolving the Corporation in 1714 when the death of Anne brought the Whigs back into power and perpetuated the institution.[46] Yet they had not thought it against their principles in the first place. In Bristol political fortunes shifted the other way. From being Whig, the Corporation had become firmly Tory by 1714, when the Guardians were again obliged to take the sacraments according to the rites of the Church of England; and it was a High Tory institution, opposed by the Whigs, in the middle of the eighteenth century.[47]

It was not only a question of shifts in power politics, however. Some Tories demonstrated a real commitment to what had once been Puritan and Dissenting causes. Although it had no Corporation of the Poor, the council of Salisbury set up a 'new workhouse' in 1709 with its own 'Directors': Ivie and Sherfield would have approved, but the new scheme had Tory support and it was established with the help of the SPCK. In Plymouth the new Corporation of the Poor of 1708 occupied the premises of the 1630 workhouse, but the project was carried into effect under a Tory Governor, James Yonge.[48] Like Societies for the Reformation of Manners or the SPCK, Corporations were in fact one of the vehicles by which the social and moral aspirations of early seventeenth-century Puritans were conveyed to the Anglican Church of the eighteenth century. It was a moderated Puritanism, of course, shorn of some earlier Calvinist characteristics by the religious developments of the later seventeenth century. It has been well said that Puritanism transmitted to later generations 'its sense of moral duty and feeling of sin more effectively than its doctrines of grace'.[49] But it was a real transmission, providing continuity and guaranteeing the same sort of broad support for welfare reform among civic elites in the years around 1700 as there had been in the 1620s.

Both new and old tones can be heard in two sermons preached by Anglican clergymen before the Bristol Corporation of the Poor soon after its foundation, in 1699 and 1704. They expatiated on good works, and on their spiritual and material rewards, in language which no early seventeenth-century Calvinist would have found congenial. Benefactors of the Corporation, it was said, would enjoy a tangible return, for God would 'bless and prosper them in their affairs: bless them at home and bless them abroad; bless them in their shops and bless them in their ships; and at last give them a comfortable enjoyment of the works of their own hands'. The purpose of the Corporation was still defined in seventeenth-century terms, however. It was directed against 'the habits of idleness and debauchery wherewith the youth among the poorer sort are miserably infected'. They were to be accustomed to 'labour and industry' and made 'useful instruments of society'. The youthful poor had been found 'lousing like swarms of locusts in every corner of the streets'; they should be made to look 'neat and wholesome'.[50]

The sermons preached in Bristol reiterated two other familiar themes: they referred to the local opposition which the Corporation had encountered, and they tried to excuse its failure to keep the cost of poor relief down. In their management, all the Corporations raised precisely the same political and practical problems as earlier projects. In the first place, despite overlapping membership, they were in effect rival authorities posing a challenge to the municipal corporations, the town councils, which had sponsored them. The tension was greatest in Exeter, where the Corporation of the Poor was thought to cast 'an envious eye upon the present government by the civil magistrate of the city', and where the two bodies were at loggerheads for years.[51] The Corporation in London was similarly attacked because it set itself up as a 'new magistracy'. It was also detested by its targets as much as the Puritan magistracy of Dorchester had been in the 1620s. According to one critic, the Assistants of the London Corporation were 'presbyterian dogs and rogues that cheat the poor'.[52]

The greatest opposition naturally came from the parishes. The Corporations managed workhouses, usually for poor children, and several of them tried at the same time to provide employment for paupers who lived out, in the town. This involved a large initial outlay for buildings (£1,000 in the cases of Norwich and Exeter) and extra rates.[53] Most of the Corporations were also made responsible for the whole of outdoor relief in their cities – supervising overseers, and hence rates and doles, much as Christ's Hospital had been intended to do. Like the original London hospitals again, they were supposed to act as central receivers and managers of endowments: in Bristol the Corporation even had authority to take over all existing charitable funds held by the parishes. It was an impossible agenda, and passive resistance and positive obstruction were the inevitable response of parish elites. They appealed against the rates authorised by Corporations, refused to collect them, and failed to report what charities they held and how many pensioners they supported.[54] As a result, municipal justices of the peace in quarter sessions were often caught in a hopeless quandary, between Corporations who instructed them to raise rates, and parishes and rate-payers who challenged every assessment.

London's Corporation never had the same rights and duties *vis à vis* the parishes as the Corporations in Norwich, Bristol and Exeter, although it very much wanted them. It faced the same parochial opposition nevertheless. It could make little headway. As early as 1700 it had dropped its plan to provide employment outside the workhouse and by 1713 the latter was degenerating into a house of correction.[55] Provincial Corporations were rather more successful, because their parishes had neither the wealth nor the political weight of those in London. Some of the Corporations were able to survive as central institutions responsible for outdoor relief over whole cities, and they prevented costly settlement disputes between parishes. Even so, they had to compromise with parochial interests, and they became supervisory rather than directing bodies. In Bristol, for example, the Corporation's capitulation was signalled in 1714 when all church-wardens were made *ex officio* Guardians of the Poor.[56]

Political failure necessarily meant financial failure. Since parishes could not be ruled, pensions and casual doles could not be strictly limited. Far from reducing costs, the provision of employment merely added substantially to them. Rates rose by 50 per cent in Bristol between 1696 and 1714, and the workhouse lost £1,980 in the first seven years of its operation. It turned to unskilled occupations, such as pinmaking, ceased to teach skilled trades, and finally became a hospital.[57] It was the old story of the triumph of outdoor relief; and it was a story which was repeated for more than a century, despite the Workhouse Test Act of 1723, through Speenhamland up to the Poor Law Amendment Act of 1834.[58] Even then, when the political problem of local autonomy could be more easily overcome, the introduction of new methods of institutional deterrence proved expensive, slow and piece-meal.

Despite good intentions and powerful ambitions, therefore, the machine turned out to be uncontrollable. Firmly entrenched, running in well-worn grooves, it shaped the character of English poor relief. Those quests for labour discipline and moral reform which acquired new momentum in the 1690s lost all coherence in the impenetrable sands of parish administration. The practice of poor relief in England, as distinct from its rhetoric, was much more a matter of local benevolence than of social control exercised at a distance and from the top.

NOTES AND REFERENCES

1. **R. B. Outhwaite,** 'Dearth and Government Intervention in English Grain Markets', *Econ.Hist.Rev.*, 2 ser., xxxiii (1981), 401–2; **D. C. Coleman,** 'Labour in the English Economy of the Seventeenth Century', in **E. M. Carus-Wilson** (ed.), *Essays in Economic History,* ii (Arnold, 1962), pp. 291–308; **J. Thirsk** (ed.), *The Agrarian History of England and Wales,* V.ii (Cambridge UP, 1985),pp. 382–3, 385.
2. **T. Wales,** 'Poverty, poor relief and the life-cycle', in **R. M. Smith** (ed.), *Land, Kinship and Life-Cycle* (Cambridge UP, 1984), pp. 382, 384–5.
3. Exeter Corporation Records, Y5, petitions of the poor: many undated, but a large number from 1683–84.
4. Above, p. 44, and see **R. M. Smith,** 'The Structured Dependency of the Elderly', *Bull. Soc. for the Social History of Medicine,* 34 (1984), 37.
5. Wales, 'Poverty, poor relief and the life-cycle', p. 356. Cf. **R. Haines,** *England's Weal and Prosperity* (1681), p. 11, for a different estimate.
6. **T. Firmin,** *Some Proposals For the imploying of the Poor* (1678), p. 14.
7. **J. Fransham,** *An Exact Account of the Charge for Supporting the Poor of . . . Norwich* (1720), p. 6.
8. **D. A. Baugh,** 'Poverty, Protestantism and Political Economy: English Attitudes toward the Poor 1660–1800', in **S. B. Baxter** (ed.), *England's Rise to Greatness 1660–1763* (California UP, Berkeley, 1983), p. 75.
9. **P. Slack,** *Poverty in Early-Stuart Salisbury* (Wilts Record Soc., xxxi, 1975), pp. 114–15, 130–2; above, p. 155, **W. Newman Brown,** 'The receipt

of poor relief and family situation', in **Smith** (ed.), *Land, Kinship and Life-Cycle,* p. 420.

10. E.g., Bristol AO, Q.S.Minutes 1681–1705, ff. 28v–29r; St James's Vestry Minutes 1692–1729, 13 Aug. 1661, 13 Feb. 1672.

11. See, for example, Essex RO, D/P 167/8/1, Woodford Vestry Minutes 1679–1760; Bristol AO, St James's Vestry Minutes 1692–1729, 22 May 1694, 23 July 1694; **F. G. Emmison** (ed.), *Early Essex Town Meetings* (Phillimore, 1970), pp. 61, 99, 101, 106, 113, 119, 134.

12. E.g., Exeter Corporation Records, Q.S.Minutes 1688–1706, ff. 188v, 192r; West Devon RO, Plymouth Borough Sessions Book, W52, 1704–26, f. 44v; Colchester Borough Records, Sessions Book 1677–84, pp. 79, 121–2; Norfolk and Norwich RO, Norwich Q.S.Minute Book 1702–13, 13 July 1703. For the activities of justices out of sessions, see **N. Landau**, *The Justices of the Peace 1679–1760* (California UP, Berkeley, 1984), pp. 27–8, 214–18; **E. M. Hampson,** *The Treatment of Poverty in Cambridgeshire 1597–1834* (Cambridge UP, 1934), pp. 224–9.

13. Bristol AO, Q.S.Minutes 1681–1705, ff. 28v–29r, 62; 1634–47, ff. 133v–134r; 1653–71, f. lv; 1672–81, f. 85; St James's Vestry Minutes 1692–1729, 13 Oct. 1696.

14. E.g., Exeter Corporation Records, Q.S.Minutes 1688–1706, ff. 25v, 34r, 36v. Cf. Norfolk and Norwich RO, Mayor's Court Book 1677–95, f. 56r.

15. Bristol AO, Common Council Proceedings 1649–59, p. 160; Q.S.Minutes 1672–81, ff. 81r, 97v. Cf. Norfolk and Norwich RO, Mayor's Court Book 1654–66, f. 86v; 1666–77, ff. 259v, 260v.

16. Norfolk and Norwich RO, Mayor's Court Book 1677–85, ff. 215v, 56r; 1709–19, f. 52r.

17. E.g., Colchester Borough Records, Sessions Book 1693–5, 30 July 1694; 1677–84, pp. 23, 117, 120; **S. C. Ratcliff** and **H. C. Johnson** (eds), *Warwick County Records* (Warwick, 1935–53), i. 4–6, v. 2–3, 107, viii. 77, 88. Cf. E. **Melling,** *Kentish Sources: The Poor* (Maidstone, 1964), pp. 118–19.

18. **J. Thirsk** and **J. P. Cooper** (eds), *Seventeenth-Century Economic Documents* (Oxford UP, 1972), p. 103. Cf. above, p. 107; **K. D. M. Snell,** *Annals of the Labouring Poor* (Cambridge UP, 1985), pp. 72–3.

19. Above, pp. 27–8, 65–6.

20. **D. North,** 'Some Notes concerning the Laws for the Poor', BM Add. MS. 32512, ff. 124v–125r; Bodl. MS. Eng. hist. b. 209, f. 81r; **S. Macfarlane,** 'Social policy and the poor', in **A. L. Beier** and **R. Finlay,** *London 1500–1700* (Longman, 1986), p. 253.

21. **M. Hale,** *A Discourse Touching Provision for the Poor* (1683), pp. 6–7.

22. **J. Cary,** *An Essay on the State of England in Relation to its Trade* (Bristol, 1695), pp. 156, 159. Cf. **R. Dunning,** *A Plain and Easie Method* (1685), sig. A2v; **R. Haines,** *Provision for the Poor* (1678), p. 8.

23. **Cary,** *Essay,* p. 167; **J. Child,** *A New Discourse on Trade* (1693), p. 61; **Hale,** *Discourse,* pp. 7, 8.

24. **Macfarlane,** 'Social policy and the poor', p. 252; **H. Horwitz,** *Parliament, Policy and Politics in the reign of William III* (Manchester UP, 1977), p. 269. By 1704 there was also the powerful dissentient voice of Defoe, critical of workhouses (though not of moral reformation) on economic grounds: *Giving Alms No Charity* (1704).

25. 9 George I, c. 7; **S. and B. Webb,** *The Old Poor Law* (Longmans, Green and Co., 1927), pp. 243–5.

26. 3 William and Mary, c. 11, sect. xi; 8 and 9 William III, c. 30, sect. ii.

27. Above, pp. 118–19; Colchester Borough Records, Sessions Book 1677–84, p. 10; Exeter Corporation Records, Q.S.Minutes 1688–1706, f. 104v; Norfolk and Norwich RO, Mayor's Court Book 1677–95, ff. 44v–45r, 56r; 1695–1709, f. 226v. Cf. **Slack,** *Poverty in Early-Stuart Salisbury,* p. 83; *Warwick County Records,* ix. 115.

28. The best study of the law is **P. Styles,** 'Evolution of the Law of Settlement', in *idem, Studies in Seventeenth-Century West Midlands History* (Round-wood Press, Kineton, 1978), and of its purpose and effects, **J. S. Taylor,** 'The Impact of Pauper Settlement 1691–1834', *Past and Present,* 73(1976), 42–74.

29. 13 and 14 Charles II, c. 12.

30. **North,** 'Notes', ff. 124v–130v; **Child,** *New Discourse,* pp. 62, 64.

31. **M. Spufford,** *The Great Reclothing of Rural England* (Hambledon Press, 1984), pp. 13–14.

32. 11 William III, c. 18; 12 Anne, c. 23. I owe this suggestion to Joanna Innes, who points out that women were much more heavily represented among vagrants in the early eighteenth century than in the early seventeenth.

33. 1 James II, c. 17.

34. 3 William and Mary, c. 11; 8 and 9 William III, c. 30. Cf. **K. D. M. Snell,** *Annals of the Labouring Poor* (Cambridge UP, 1985), p. 17.

35. The revival of the London Corporation is described in **Macfarlane,** 'Social policy and the poor', and the founding of other Corporations in **T. V. Hitchcock,** 'The English Workhouse: a Study in Institutional Poor Relief in Selected Counties, 1696–1750', Oxford Univ. D. Phil. thesis, 1985, Ch. 2. Other towns, Dorchester among them, petitioned parliament for Corporations but failed to obtain Acts.

36. Norfolk and Norwich RO, Mayor's Court Book 1666–77, f. 46v; Exeter Corporation Records, Act Book 11, p. 278; 18 and 19 Charles II, c. 9, sect. iv. The Devon county institution was in practice a house of correction rather than a workhouse: **S. K. Roberts,** *Recovery and Restoration in an English County: Devon Local Administration 1646–70* (Exeter UP, 1985), pp. 195–7.

37. **Hale,** *Discourse,* pp. 10, 11, 21; **Child,** *New Discourse,* pp. 65, 68.

38. **D. W. R. Bahlman,** *The Moral Revolution of 1688* (Yale UP, New Haven, 1957) and **A. G. Craig,** 'The Movement for the Reformation of Manners 1688–1715', Edinburgh Univ. Ph.D. thesis, 1980, describe this activity.

39. **Macfarlane,** 'Social policy and the poor', p. 261.

40. **J. Cary,** *An Account of the Proceedings of the Corporation of Bristol* (1700), pp. 4, 11, 12. Cf. **Cary,** *Essay,* pp. 154–5. The early history of the Bristol Corporation can be pieced together from **E. E. Butcher** (ed.), *Bristol Corporation of the Poor* (Bristol Record Soc., iii, 1932) and Bristol AO, Common Council Proceedings 1687–1702.

41. Bristol AO, Common Council Proceedings 1649–59, f. 99; **P. McGrath** (ed.), *Merchants and Merchandise in Seventeenth-Century Bristol* (Bristol Record Soc., xix, 1955), pp. 161–3; 7 and 8 William III, c. xxxii (private); **R. Mortimer** (ed.), *Minute Book of Men's Meeting of the Society of Friends 1686–1704* (Bristol Record Soc., xxx, 1977), pp. xxviii–xxx, xxxviii, 109. The first Assistants of the Corporation even included Nathaniel Wade, who had been implicated in the Rye House Plot. The Whig bias of the

early institution was attacked in *Some Considerations Offer'd to the Citizens of Bristol Relating to the Corporation for the Poor* (Bristol, 1711), pp. 8–9.

42. Bristol Reference Library, Braikenridge Collection, B10162, *passim.* At least two Quakers were also attenders at the first meeting of the Society for the Reformation of Manners.

43. Colchester Borough Records, Assembly Book 1693–1712, pp. 146–7; Essex RO, T/A 424/7/1, Colchester Monthly Meeting Book, pp. 166, 190; **S. H. G. Fitch,** *Colchester Quakers* (Colchester, n.d.), p. 181; **T. C. Gline,** 'Politics and Government in the Borough of Colchester 1660–93', Wisconsin Univ. Ph.D. thesis, 1974, pp. 106–7, 220. Quakers seem also to have been involved in the Corporation at Sudbury (1702): West Suffolk RO, FK 6.501/1/1, p. 56; Sudbury Records, Minutes of Guardians of the Poor 1771–1892, statute of 1 Anne (at beginning).

44. **Bahlman,** *Moral Revolution,* p. 40; Exeter Corporation Records, Act Book 13, 1684–1730, p. 246; Corporation of the Poor Court Book 1698–1702, *passim;* **L. Colley,** *In Defiance of Oligarchy* (Cambridge UP, 1982), p. 171. On Seaward and Elwill, see **Horwitz,** *Parliament, Policy and Politics,* p. 354; **B. D. Henning,** *The House of Commons 1660–1690* (Secker and Warburg, 1983), i. 198, ii. 265–6; **L. Glassey,** *Politics and the Appointment of Justices of the Peace 1675–1720* (Oxford UP, 1979), p. 207.

45. **Macfarlane,** 'Social policy and the poor', pp. 258–9, 266; *idem,* 'Studies in Poverty and Poor Relief in London at the end of the 17th Century', Oxford Univ., D.Phil. thesis, 1982, pp. 314–15. Cf. **F. T. Melton,** *Sir Robert Clayton and the origins of English deposit banking* (Cambridge UP, 1986), p. 4.

46. Norfolk and Norwich RO, Assembly Book 7, ff. 196r, 200v, 219r; Assembly Book 8, p. 19; Court of Guardians of the Poor Minute Book 1712–15, *passim;* **B. Cozens-Hardy** and **E. A. Kent,** *The Mayors of Norwich 1403 to 1835* (Norwich, 1938), pp. 111–12; **W. Speck,** *Tory and Whig* (Macmillan, 1970), pp. 77–8. The Norwich Workhouse Committee visited Colchester and Sudbury to take advice: Chamberlain's Accounts, 1711–12.

47. 13 Anne, c. 32; **Colley,** *In Defiance of Oligarchy,* p. 135; **J. Johnson,** *Transactions of the Corporation of the Poor in the City of Bristol* (Bristol, 1826), p. 137.

48. Salisbury Corporation Records, Ledger D, ff. 375r, 379r; SPCK, Abstract Letter Book 1708–9, p. 263 (I owe this reference to T. Hitchcock); **J. Yonge,** *Plymouth Memoirs,* ed. **J. J. Beckerlegge** (Plymouth Institution, 1951), p. 56; **F. N. L. Poynter** (ed.), *The Journal of James Yonge* (Longman, 1963), pp. 206–8, 228.

49. **J. D. Walsh,** 'Elie Halévy and the Birth of Methodism', *Trans. Roy. Hist. Soc.,* 5 ser., xxv (1975), 5.

50. **H. Waterman,** *A Sermon Preached before the Court of Guardians of the Poor in the City of Bristol* (Bristol, 1699), pp 11, 23–4, 35–6, 39; **C. Brent,** *Persuasions to a Publick Spirit* (1704), pp. 11, 13, 18–19, 21, 22.

51. **H. Lloyd Parry,** *The Exeter Civic Seals* (Exeter, 1909), p. 31; Exeter Corporation Records, Corporation of the Poor Court Book 1698–1702, ff. 27r, 35r, 36r, 40 and *passim.*

52. **Macfarlane,** 'Social policy and the poor', pp. 265, 267.

53. Norfolk and Norwich RO, Court of Guardians of the Poor Minute Book 1712–15, ff. 6v, 11r; Exeter Corporation Records, Corporation of the Poor Court Book 1698–1702, f. 8r.
54. For examples, see Colchester Borough Records, Sessions Book 1695–99, 21 April, 1 June 1699; West Devon RO, Plymouth Borough Sessions Book 1704–26, f. 44v; Norfolk and Norwich RO, Court of Guardians of the Poor Minute Book 1712–15, f. 28v; Bristol AO, Common Council Proceedings 1702–22, pp. 190, 213; **Johnson,** *Transactions,* pp. 8, 10–11.
55. **Macfarlane,** 'Social policy and the poor', pp. 258, 262–3, 265–70.
56. **Butcher,** *Bristol Corporation,* p. 3; **Johnson,** *Transactions,* p. 7. For the later history of other Corporations, see **W. G. Hoskins,** *Industry, Trade and People in Exeter 1688–1800* (Manchester UP, 1935), pp. 144–5; **P. Morant,** *The History and Antiquities of the County of Essex* (Chelmsford, 1816), i. 181–2; West Suffolk RO, Sudbury Records, Minutes of Guardians of the Poor 1771–1892.
57. **Butcher,** *Bristol Corporation,* pp. 5, 7, 10, 32; Bristol AO, Common Council Proceedings 1702–22, pp. 258–9; **Johnson,** *Transactions,* p. 21.
58. Similar conflicts and consequences can be seen in Philadelphia in the eighteenth century: **J. K. Alexander,** *Render Them Submissive* (Massachusetts UP, Amherst, 1980), p. 101.

CONCLUSION

The responses to poverty described in the second half of this book were the product of a multiplicity of factors. They rested to an extent on the changes in intellectual approach and modes of thought surveyed in Chapter 2: on the slow shifts in attitude which meant that the poor came to be seen as a threat to be controlled, or as an opportunity for social and economic engineering, rather than as an object of charity. Under the impetus of civic ideals, first of a humanist and then of a Puritan hue, broad notions of hospitality gave way to narrower and more precisely defined responses – to hospitals and workhouses. Charity to 'Christ in the streets' was replaced by discriminatory doles and the social controls of settlement and removal. The drive to use new methods of social welfare to achieve a moral and social reformation was powerful throughout the period. Yet there were also other influences at work which prevented the realization of these imperatives.

The most important of them were political and administrative. Parliament produced solutions which, while regulatory on paper and imposed with remarkable uniformity by justices of the peace, left considerable latitude in the hands of the managers of the machine; and those managers were parish officials in face-to-face contact with the poor. We have seen again and again how tenaciously parishes clung to their poor-law powers once they had them; and from the 1530s, from the poor law of 1536 and the introduction of parish registers in 1538, parishes were in the front line of English local government. Most of them were not large enough or rich enough for their officers to treat the poor as a distinct social group ripe for manipulation. They responded to them as individuals. The benevolence of parish authorities therefore replaced the charity of neighbours, and the poor laws had less of an impact than their authors had intended. Neighbourly charity was formalized and made compulsory; it became bureaucratic and often automatic. It was expressed in thousands of carefully recorded small payments every week, amounting in aggregate to a very large transfer of resources from rich to poor. But it was not erected into a wholly impersonal disciplinary machine.

The parochial basis of the poor law accounts for many of the peculiarities of English poor relief. We have seen that it explains why efforts to erect large institutions, hospitals and workhouses like those in continental cities, had little lasting success. Parish doles may also have made unnecessary those projects for pawnshops and cheap loans for the poor, based on the Italian *Monti di Pietà,* which many Englishmen favoured, but which had little result before the short-lived Charitable Corporation of 1708.[1] A related distinction between English and continental forms of social welfare was the lack of any collective impetus in English philanthropy, at least until the 'associated philanthropy' of the eighteenth century.[2] Individual benefactors founded individual charities, very often for a single parish.

In the latter case, the English Reformation doubtless played a significant role. It destroyed those fraternities and religious orders which might have encouraged collective initiatives. It also created a vacuum in social welfare and it was contemporary appreciation of that which helped to put the poor laws on the statute book in the first place. Yet no other Protestant country had a welfare apparatus paid for by taxation. The unusual centralization of English government, its ability to ensure local obedience through Assize judges and justices of the peace, and its success in moulding parishes into effective units of administration, created a unique English institution. And as the last chapters have suggested, it is not a total anachronism to call that institution, as it had developed by 1700, a welfare state.

This emphasis on political factors pushes the reality of poverty into the background. Economic circumstances were, of course, important, particularly in the years around 1600. They were a stimulus to action as powerful as the Reformation; and the legislation of 1598 would have been inconceivable without them. But legislation could have taken many different forms and had many different outcomes. Moreover, it will be obvious by now that circumstances often counted less than the ways in which they were perceived. If vagrant, disorderly paupers thrust themselves on the attention of contemporaries, the respectable poor in shallow poverty did not: they had to be deliberately identified. We saw in the last chapter that sensitivity to their condition, and an appreciation of their entitlements, may well have followed on from the very existence of a welfare apparatus. But there was an earlier stage: as the pamphleteer who described them in 1601 appreciated, Tudor searches, censuses and listings of the poor were voyages of discovery with a similar effect.[3]

One motive for the search was certainly the desire to identify and repress disorder. But perhaps there was more to it than that. It may not be going too far to suggest that in looking for the poor, Englishmen were also exhibiting a refusal to tolerate misery and deprivation. We have seen one indication of this in Starkey's comment that poor-relief was necessary in England in the 1530s, despite the fact that the English were better-off than the inhabitants of many other countries.[4] There were still paupers to be found, beggars to be relieved and reformed, standards of living to be restored to those of some past golden age. From this perspective, the English poor law may be thought of alongside other reactions to deteriorating economic conditions in the sixteenth and early seventeenth centuries: projects for new crops and new trades, for example, and later ages at marriage and lower fertility, which produced real returns in the end. All these were arguably signs that English society's threshold of tolerance of deprivation was always low. It may well be that we should put such deep-seated attitudes alongside political possibilities when we explain why the English state intervened to provide welfare in the form that it did.

Economic change requires more attention when we turn to consider the consequences of the English poor law. So far as the alleviation of poverty is concerned, the impact of statutory relief was probably marginal, at least until the middle of the seventeenth century. Until then the redistribution of wealth by the formal means we have described was slight: in 1610 the total, including endowed charity, may have been no more than £40,000, compared with £200,000 in 1650 and £550,000 in 1700. At the margin of subsistence, and in crisis years, public measures probably had an effect: control of markets, subsidized sales of grain, and increases in outdoor relief must have done something to save some people from starvation, especially in towns and in the more favoured parts of lowland England. But we have seen that corn policies had their counterproductive features, and many of the poorer parts of rural England had no formally organized outdoor relief before the 1620s. Public welfare plainly did not overcome the critical circumstances for the English poor between 1580 and 1620, and it probably mitigated them only slightly.

It had more to offer in the later seventeenth century. Although economic growth gradually banished deep poverty, there was still work for the welfare machine. There was structural underemployment and seasonal unemployment, quite apart from the permanent problems of disease and old age. The public provision of relief to five per cent of the population cannot have been without its effects – in taking people out of shallow poverty, in preventing malnutrition and destitution. All this was important. Even here, however, economic growth played a crucial role: it enabled the country to afford substantial transfers of wealth from large numbers of respectable householders to the poor. Economic change was primary, welfare secondary.

It is necessary to exercise caution also before we attribute the social stability of seventeenth-century England – as compared with France, for instance – to the poor law. On the punitive side, the law scarcely provided adequate curbs on vagrancy; and poor relief was largely confined to social groups who would not have been major threats to public order anyway: widows, the old, broken families and only a few of the labouring poor.[5] Welfare payments cannot have bought off many potential rioters or rebels directly. The issue is not quite as simple as that, however. Social policies may have supported the social order indirectly, through their impact on popular attitudes. Just as the dearth orders helped to prevent grain riots by calming anxieties, so the whole apparatus of the poor law may well have persuaded subjects that their rulers shared their view of the common weal. Cash doles were a reminder in every parish and every week that there was justice and charity in the social and political *status quo*. As Keith Wrightson has argued, the poor law provided, 'in its balance of communal identification and social differentiation, a powerful reinforcement of habits of deference and subordination'.[6]

Wrightson's reference to social differentiation directs our attention to another important topic in this regard. The poor law necessarily had an impact on the attitudes of those who paid for it, as well as on the attitudes of those who benefited or might expect to benefit from it. The simple fact of paying the poor rate made one half of all householders members of respectable society and distanced them from the destitute and disorderly. They had a vested interest in maintaining settlement rules, enforcing the laws against bastardy and unruly alehouses, and restricting relief to the evidently deserving. Yet people moved into and out of ratebooks, just as they moved onto and off lists of pensioners, and the gulf between the two was not unbridgeable. The welfare machine certainly gave rate-payers a sense of group identity and a consciousness of social superiority, just as it created a recognizable category of the dependent poor. But it also provided a safety net which even rate-payers might at some point need. As individuals, they might welcome its charity as well as its confirmation of social hierarchy. That was perhaps another reason why, in practice, the bark of the English poor law was so much worse than its bite.

Like all social policies, therefore, the English system of poor relief served several purposes at once by the end of the seventeenth century. It held out the prospect of closer social control, even if it did not deliver the strict social disciplines which its architects hoped for. It alleviated poverty for a sizable section of the population. It demonstrated the benevolence of the powers that be and to that extent encouraged deference. All in all, it was a major, if in many respects inadvertent, achievement. Few people saw its benefits in 1700. The achievement was then too recent, and its expense and unpremeditated growth were too obvious. But when Dr Johnson remarked that 'a decent provision for the poor is the true test of civilization', he was passing favourable judgement on the early modern Englishmen who had accomplished it.[7]

NOTES AND REFERENCES

1. **W. R. Scott,** *The Constitution and Finance of English, Scottish and Irish Joint-Stock Companies to 1720* (Cambridge UP, 1910–12), iii. 380. For earlier projects, see *Cal.Patent Rolls 1548–9,* pp. 9–10; *Cal.S.P.Dom. 1547–80,* p. 410; **E. Chamberlayne,** *Englands Wants* (1667), p. 7; **T. Firmin,** *Some Proposals For the imploying of the Poor* (1678), p. 21.
2. There are a few exceptions: see the subscriptions taken up for an almshouse at Strood in 1605: **W. K. Jordan,** *Social Institutions in Kent 1480–1660* (Kent Arch. Soc., 1961), p. 50.
3. Above, p. 27.
4. Above, p. 116.
5. For the activity of some of these groups in food riots, however, see above, p. 101.
6. **K. Wrightson,** *English Society 1580–1680* (Hutchinson, 1982), p. 181. Cf. **K. D. M. Snell,** *Annals of the Labouring Poor* (Cambridge UP, 1985), pp. 104–5.
7. Quoted in **G. Himmelfarb,** *The Idea of Poverty* (Faber and Faber, 1984), p. 3.

SELECT BIBLIOGRAPHY

(Place of publication is London unless otherwise stated. UP = University Press.)

General Surveys

1. **A. L. Beier,** *The Problem of the Poor in Tudor and Stuart England* (Methuen 1983).
2. **E. M. Leonard,** *The Early History of English Poor Relief* (Cambridge UP 1900). Still the best account for the period before 1640.
3. **G. W. Oxley,** *Poor Relief in England and Wales 1601–1834* (David and Charles, Newton Abbot 1974).
4. **Ivy Pinchbeck** and **Margaret Hewitt,** *Children in English Society,* volume I (Routledge & Kegan Paul 1969), Chs VI, VII.
5. **John Pound,** *Poverty and Vagrancy in Tudor England* (Longman 1971).
6. **Geoffrey Taylor,** *The Problem of Poverty 1660–1834* (Longman 1969).
7. **Sidney** and **Beatrice Webb,** *English Local Government: English Poor Law History: Part I. The Old Poor Law* (Longmans, Green and Co. 1927). Essential for post-1660.

European Comparisons

A selection of works which may be used for comparative purposes. (20) is of special interest.

8. **Emanuel Chill,** 'Religion and Mendicity in Seventeenth-Century France', *International Review of Social History,* vii (1962).
9. **Natalie Zemon Davis,** *Society and Culture in Early Modern France* (Duckworth 1975), Ch 2.
10. **Cissie C. Fairchilds,** *Poverty and Charity in Aix-en-Provence 1640–1789* (Johns Hopkins UP, Baltimore and London 1976).

210

11. Jean-Pierre Gutton, *La société et les pauvres: L'exemple de la généralité de Lyon 1534–1789* ('Les Belles Lettres', Paris 1971).
12. Jeane-Pierre Gutton, *La société et les pauvres en Europe (XVIe-XVIIIe siècles)* (Presses Universitaires de France, Paris 1974).
13. Olwen H. Hufton, *The Poor of Eighteenth-Century France 1750–1789* (Oxford UP 1974).
14. Robert M. Kingdon, 'Social Welfare in Calvin's Geneva', *American Historical Review*, lxxvi (1971).
15. Catharina Lis and Hugo Soly, *Poverty and Capitalism in Pre-industrial Europe* (Harvester, Hassocks 1979).
16. Linda Martz, *Poverty and Welfare in Habsburg Spain* (Cambridge UP 1983).
17. Rosalind Mitchison, 'The Making of the Old Scottish Poor Law', *Past and Present,* 63 (1974).
18. Michel Mollat (ed.), *Études sur l'Histoire de la Pauvreté (Moyen Age-XVIe siècle),* 2 vols (Publications de la Sorbonne, Paris 1974).
19. Brian Pullan, *Rich and Poor in Renaissance Venice* (Blackwell, Oxford 1971).
20. Brian Pullan, 'Catholics and the Poor in Early Modern Europe', *Transactions of the Royal Historical Society,* 5 ser., xxvi (1976).
21. Thomas Riis (ed.), *Aspects of Poverty in Early Modern Europe* (Le Monnier, Florence 1981).

Economy and Society

The literature is huge but the following is a selection of fundamental authorities and stimulating surveys.

22. Peter Clark and Paul Slack (eds), *Crisis and Order in English Towns 1500–1700* (Routledge and Kegan Paul 1972).
23. Peter Clark (ed.), *The Transformation of English Provincial Towns* (Hutchinson 1984).
24. C. G. A Clay, *Economic Expansion and Social Change: England 1500–1700,* 2 vols (Cambridge UP 1984).
25. D. C. Coleman, *The Economy of England 1450–1750* (Oxford UP 1977).
26. W. G. Hoskins, *The Age of Plunder. The England of Henry VIII 1500–1547* (Longman 1976).
27. D. M. Palliser, *The Age of Elizabeth. England under the later Tudors 1547–1603* (Longman 1983).
28. Joan Thirsk (ed.), *The Agrarian History of England and Wales,* vol. IV *1500–1640,* vol. V, parts i and ii, *1640–1750* (Cambridge UP 1967, 1985).
29. Charles Wilson, *England's Apprenticeship 1603–1763* (Longman 1965).
30. Keith Wrightson, *English Society 1580–1680* (Hutchinson 1982).
31. E. A. Wrigley and R. S. Schofield, *The Population History of England 1541–1871. A Reconstruction* (Arnold 1981).
32. Joyce Youings, *Sixteenth-Century England* (Penguin Books, Harmondsworth 1984).

Dearth and Disease

See also **Outhwaite** (93), **Slack** (95).

33. **Andrew B. Appleby**, 'Nutrition and Disease: The Case of London 1550–1750', *Journal of Interdisciplinary History,* vi (1975).

34. **Andrew B. Appleby**, *Famine in Tudor and Stuart England* (Liverpool UP 1978).

35. **David Dymond**, 'The famine of 1527 in Essex', *Local Population Studies,* 26 (1981).

36. **Margaret Pelling**, 'Healing the Sick Poor: Social Policy and Disability in Norwich 1550–1640', *Medical History,* 29 (1985).

37. **Amartya Sen**, *Poverty and Famines. An Essay in Entitlement and Deprivation* (Oxford UP 1981). On modern famines, but important comparatively.

38. **Paul Slack**, *The Impact of Plague in Tudor and Stuart England* (Routledge and Kegan Paul 1985).

39. **John Walter** and **Keith Wrightson**, 'Dearth and the Social Order in Early Modern England', *Past and Present,* 71 (1976).

40. **John Walter**, 'Grain riots and popular attitudes to the law: Maldon and the crisis of 1629', in **John Brewer** and **John Styles** (eds), *An Ungovernable People. The English and the law in the seventeenth and eighteenth centuries* (Hutchinson 1980).

Vagrancy and Migration

41. **Frank Aydelotte**, *Elizabethan Rogues and Vagabonds* (Oxford UP 1913).

42. **A. L. Beier**, 'Vagrants and the Social Order in Elizabethan England', *Past and Present,* 64 (1974).

43. **A. L. Beier**, *Masterless Men. The Vagrancy Problem in England 1560–1640* (Methuen 1985).

44. **Peter Clark**, 'The Migrant in Kentish Towns 1580–1640', in **Clark** and **Slack** (22).

45. **Peter Clark**, 'Migration in England during the late seventeenth and early eighteenth centuries', *Past and Present,* 83 (1979).

46. **Joan R. Kent**, 'Population Mobility and Alms: Poor Migrants in the Midlands during the early seventeenth century', *Local Population Studies,* 27 (1981).

47. **Paul A. Slack**, 'Vagrants and Vagrancy in England 1598–1664', *Economic History Review,* 2 ser., xxvii (1974).

48. **David Souden**, 'Migrants and the population structure of later seventeenth-century provincial cities and market towns', in **Clark** (23).

Household and Family

See also **Slack** (109), **Newman Brown** (112).

49. **A. L. Beier,** 'The social problems of an Elizabethan country town: Warwick 1580–90', in **Peter Clark** (ed.), *Country Towns in Pre-industrial England* (Leicester UP 1981).

50. **Peter** and **Jennifer Clark,** 'The social economy of the Canterbury suburbs: The evidence of the census of 1563', in **Alec Detsicas** and **Nigel Yates** (eds), *Studies in Modern Kentish History presented to Felix Hull and Elizabeth Melling* (Kent Archaeological Society, Maidstone 1983).

51. **Nigel Goose,** 'Household size and structure in early-Stuart Cambridge', *Social History,* 5 (1980).

52. **Richard M. Smith,** 'The Structured Dependence of the Elderly as a Recent Development: Some Sceptical Historical Thoughts', *Ageing and Society*, 4 (1984).

53. **Richard M. Smith** (ed.), *Land, Kinship and Life-cycle* (Cambridge UP 1984), Ch 1.

54. **Tim Wales,** 'Poverty, poor relief and the life-cycle: some evidence from seventeenth-century Norfolk', in **Smith** (53).

Public Attitudes

See also **Brigden** (68), **Heal** (71).

55. **Joyce O. Appleby,** *Economic Thought and Ideology in Seventeenth-Century England* (Princeton UP 1978).

56. **Patrick Collinson,** *The Religion of Protestants. The Church in English Society 1559–1629* (Oxford UP 1982), Ch 4.

57. **Arthur B. Ferguson,** *The Articulate Citizen and the English Renaissance* (Duke UP, Durham, N. Carolina 1965).

58. **E. S. Furniss,** *The Position of the Laborer in a System of Nationalism* (Houghton Mifflin, Boston and New York 1920).

59. **Whitney R. D. Jones,** *The Tudor Commonwealth 1529–1559* (Athlone 1970).

60. **Joan R. Kent,** 'Attitudes of members of the house of commons to the regulation of "personal conduct" in late Elizabethan and early Stuart England', *Bulletin of the Institute of Historical Research,* xlvi (1973).

61. **Joan Thirsk,** 'Projects for Gentlemen, Jobs for the Poor: Mutual Aid in the Vale of Tewkesbury 1600–1630', in **Patrick McGrath** and **John Cannon** (eds), *Essays in Bristol and Gloucestershire History* (Bristol and Gloucestershire Archaeological Society, Bristol 1976).

62. **Joan Thirsk,** *Economic Policy and Projects. The Development of a Consumer Society in Early Modern England* (Oxford UP 1978).

63. **Brian Tierney,** *Medieval Poor-Law: A Sketch of Canonical Theory and its Application in England* (California UP, Berkeley 1959).

64. **John Walter,** 'A "Rising of the People"? The Oxfordshire Rising of 1596',

Past and Present, 107 (1985). Useful on the background to the legislation of 1598.

65. **Charles Webster,** *The Great Instauration. Science, Medicine and Reform 1626–1660* (Duckworth 1975), Chs IV, V.

66. **Siegfried Wenzel,** *The Sin of Sloth: Acedia in Medieval Thought and Literature* (North Carolina UP, Chapel Hill 1960).

Charity and Philanthropy

67. **William G. Bittle** and **R. Todd Lane,** 'Inflation and Philanthropy in England: A Re-Assessment of W. K. Jordan's Data', *Economic History Review,* 2 ser., xxix (1976).

68. **Susan Brigden,** 'Religion and Social Obligation in Early Sixteenth-Century London', *Past and Present,* 103 (1984).

69. **B. Clarke,** 'Norfolk Licences to Beg: an unpublished collection', *Norfolk Archaeology,* xxxv (1970–73).

70. **J. F. Hadwin,** 'Deflating Philanthropy', *Economic History Review,* 2 ser., xxxi (1978).

71. **Felicity Heal,** 'The Idea of Hospitality in Early Modern England', *Past and Present,* 102 (1984).

72. **Gareth Jones,** *History of the Law of Charity 1532–1827* (Cambridge UP 1969).

73. **W. K. Jordan,** *Philanthropy in England 1480–1660* (Allen and Unwin 1959). The summary work, based on the following local studies.

74. **W. K. Jordan,** *The Charities of London 1480–1660* (Allen and Unwin 1960).

75. **W. K. Jordan,** 'The Forming of the Charitable Institutions of the West of England', *Transactions of the American Philosophical Society,* new series, 50 (1960).

76. **W. K. Jordan,** *The Charities of Rural England 1480–1660* (Allen and Unwin 1961).

77. **W. K. Jordan,** *Social Institutions in Kent 1480–1660* (Kent Archaeological Society, Ashford 1961).

78. **W. K. Jordan,** *Social Institutions of Lancashire* (Chetham Society, Manchester, 3 ser., xi 1962).

79. **C. J. Kitching,** 'Fire Disasters and Fire Relief in Sixteenth-Century England: The Nantwich Fire of 1583', *Bulletin of the Institute of Historical Research,* liv (1981).

80. **David Owen,** *English Philanthropy 1660–1960* (Harvard UP, Cambridge, Mass. 1964).

81. **J. J. Scarisbrick,** *The Reformation and the English People* (Blackwell, Oxford 1984), Ch 2 (on gilds and fraternities).

82. **J. A. F. Thompson,** 'Piety and Charity in Late Medieval London', *Journal of Ecclesiastical History,* xvi (1965).

83. **Charles Wilson,** 'The Other Face of Mercantilism', in **D. C. Coleman** (ed.), *Revisions in Mercantilism* (Methuen 1969).

The Poor Law

See also **Leonard** (2), **Kent** (60), **Tierney** (63), **Walter** (64).
84. **Edwin Cannan,** *The History of Local Rates in England* (P. S. King and Son 1912).
85. **C. S. L. Davies,** 'Slavery and Protector Somerset: The Vagrancy Act of 1547', *Economic History Review,* 2 ser., xix (1966).
86. **G. R. Elton,** 'An Early Tudor Poor Law', in **G. R. Elton,** *Studies in Tudor and Stuart Politics and Government,* vol. ii (Cambridge UP 1974).
87. **Paul Slack,** 'Social Policy and the Constraints of Government 1547–58', in **Jennifer Loach** and **Robert Tittler** (eds), *The Mid-Tudor Polity c. 1540–1560* (Macmillan 1980).
88. **Paul Slack,** 'Poverty and Social Regulation in Elizabethan England', in **Christopher Haigh** (ed.), *The Reign of Elizabeth I* (Macmillan 1984).
89. **Philip Styles,** 'The Evolution of the Law of Settlement', in **Philip Styles,** *Studies in Seventeenth-Century West Midlands History* (Roundwood Press, Kineton 1978).
90. **James Stephen Taylor,** 'The Impact of Pauper Settlement 1691–1834', *Past and Present,* 73 (1976).
91. **Penry Williams,** *The Tudor Regime* (Oxford UP 1979). Sets the poor law firmly in its context in Tudor government.

Conciliar Intervention

See also **Slack** (38), **Barnes** (110).
92. **R. W. Heinze,** *The Proclamations of the Tudor Kings* (Cambridge UP 1976).
93. **R. B. Outhwaite,** 'Dearth and Government Intervention in English Grain Markets, 1590–1700', *Economic History Review,* 2 ser., xxxiii (1981).
94. **B. W. Quintrell,** 'The Making of Charles I's Book of Orders', *English Historical Review,* xcv (1980).
95. **Paul Slack,** 'Books of Orders: The Making of English Social Policy, 1577–1631', *Transactions of the Royal Historical Society,* 5 ser., xxx (1980).
96. **Frederic A. Youngs,** *The Proclamations of the Tudor Queens* (Cambridge UP 1976).

Local Enforcement

See also **Leonard** (2), **Williams** (91). (97) is the most recent summary and a stimulating survey. (98) to (117) are selected local studies of importance.
97. **Anthony Fletcher,** *Reform in the Provinces. The Government of Stuart England* (Yale UP, New Haven and London 1986), Ch 7.

London

See also **Slack** (87), **Thompson** (82).

98.   **A. L. Beier**, 'Social Problems in Elizabethan London', *Journal of Interdisciplinary History*, ix (1978).

99.   **Ronald W. Herlan**, 'Poor Relief in the London Parish of Antholin's Budge Row 1638–1664', *Guildhall Studies in London History*, 2 (1977).

100.   **Ronald W. Herlan**, 'Poor Relief in London during the English Revolution', *Journal of British Studies*, xviii (1979).

101.   **Stephen Macfarlane**, 'Social policy and the poor in the later seventeenth century', in **A. L. Beier** and **R. Finlay** (eds), *London 1500–1700: The Making of the Metropolis* (Longman 1986).

102.   **Valerie Pearl**, 'Puritans and Poor Relief: The London Workhouse 1649–1660', in **Donald Pennington** and **Keith Thomas** (eds), *Puritans and Revolutionaries. Essays presented to Christopher Hill* (Oxford UP 1978).

103.   **Valerie Pearl**, 'Social Policy in Early Modern London', in **H. Lloyd-Jones, V. Pearl** and **B. Worden** (eds), *History and Imagination. Essays in honour of H. R. Trevor-Roper* (Duckworth 1981).

Provincial Towns

See also **Pelling** (36), **Beier** (49), **Pound** (128), **Slack** (131), **Webb** (133).

104.   **M. F. Bond**, 'Windsor's Experiment in Poor-Relief, 1621–1829', *Berkshire Archaeological Journal*, 48 (1945).

105.   **E. E. Butcher** (ed.), *Bristol Corporation of the Poor 1696–1834* (Bristol Record Society, iii, 1932).

106.   **S. A. Peyton**, 'The Houses of Correction at Maidstone and Westminster', *English Historical Review*, xlii (1927).

107.   **Charles Phythian-Adams**, *Desolation of a City. Coventry and the Urban Crisis of the Late Middle Ages* (Cambridge UP 1979).

108.   **J. F. Pound**, 'An Elizabethan Census of the Poor', *University of Birmingham Historical Journal*, viii (1962). On Norwich.

109.   **Paul Slack**, 'Poverty and Politics in Salisbury 1597–1666', in **Clark** and **Slack** (22).

County and Village Studies

See also **Wales** (54).

110.   **Thomas Garden Barnes**, *Somerset 1625–1640. A County's Government During the 'Personal Rule'* (Oxford UP 1961), Ch VII.

111.   **A. L. Beier**, 'Poor Relief in Warwickshire 1630–60', *Past and Present*, 35 (1966).

112. **W. Newman Brown,** 'The receipt of poor relief and family situation: Aldenham, Hertfordshire 1630–90', in **Smith** (53).
113. **F. G. Emmison,** 'Poor-relief Accounts of two rural Parishes in Bedfordshire 1563–98', *Economic History Review,* iii (1931).
114. **F. G. Emmison,** 'The Care of the Poor in Elizabethan Essex', *Essex Review,* lxii (1953).
115. **E. M. Hampson,** *The Treatment of Poverty in Cambridgeshire 1597–1834* (Cambridge UP 1934).
116. **Julian Hill,** 'A Premature Welfare State?', *Local Historian,* xiv (1980). On Shropshire.
117. **Keith Wrightson** and **David Levine,** *Poverty and Piety in an English Village. Terling 1525–1700* (Academic Press, New York and London 1979).

Developments after 1714

118. **Ian R. Christie,** *Stress and Stability in Late Eighteenth Century Britain* (Oxford UP 1986), Ch 4.
119. **A. W. Coats,** 'Economic Thought and Poor Law Policy in the Eighteenth Century', *Economic History Review,* 2 ser., xiii (1960–61).
120. **Gertrude Himmelfarb,** *The Idea of Poverty. England in the Early Industrial Age* (Faber and Faber 1984).
121. **Dorothy Marshall,** *The English Poor in the Eighteenth Century* (Routledge and Kegan Paul 1926).
122. **J. R. Poynter,** *Society and Pauperism. English Ideas on Poor Relief, 1795–1834* (Routledge and Kegan Paul 1969).
123. **K. D. M. Snell,** *Annals of the Labouring Poor. Social Change and Agrarian England 1660–1900* (Cambridge UP 1985), Ch 3.
124. **Karel Williams,** *From Pauperism to Poverty* (Routledge and Kegan Paul 1981).

Some Printed Sources

See also **Pound** (5), **Taylor** (6).
125. **A. V. Judges,** *The Elizabethan Underworld. A Collection of Tudor and Early Stuart Tracts and Ballads* (Routledge and Kegan Paul 1930).
126. **Thomas Kemp** (ed.), *The Book of John Fisher 1580–1588* (Henry T. Cooke and Son, Warwick n.d.).
127. **Elizabeth Melling** (ed.), *Kentish Sources: IV. The Poor* (Kent County Council, Maidstone 1964).
128. **John F. Pound** (ed.), *The Norwich Census of the Poor 1570* (Norfolk Record Society, Norwich, xl 1971).
129. **Gamini Salgado,** *Cony-Catchers and Bawdy Baskets. An Anthology of Elizabethan Low Life* (Penguin Books, Harmondsworth 1972).

130. **F. R. Salter** (ed.), *Some Early Tracts on Poor Relief* (Methuen 1926).
131. **Paul Slack** (ed.), *Poverty in Early-Stuart Salisbury* (Wiltshire Record Society, Devizes, xxxi 1975).
132. **R. H. Tawney** and **Eileen Power** (eds), *Tudor Economic Documents* (Longmans, Green and Co. 1924), vol. II sect. VII; vol. III sect. IV.
133. **John Webb** (ed.), *Poor Relief in Elizabethan Ipswich* (Suffolk Records Society, Ipswich, ix 1966).

INDEX

Bradford, Yorks, 75
Braintree, Essex, 43
Brandenburg, 9
branding, *see* corporal punishment
bread, provision of for poor, 64, 147
  see also corn
Brewer, John, 99–100
brewhouse, municipal, 151, 152, 155
Brewster, Sir Francis, 192
Bridewell, *see* houses of correction;
  London; workhouses
Bridport, Dors., 152, 153
briefs, charitable, 166
Bristol, 49, 67, 95, 144
  corn supplies, 145, 146
  Corporations of the Poor, 195–200
  hearth tax, 43
  pensions, 177–81, 186 n57
  poor rates, 200
  poor-relief in, 153, 159 n53
  St James, 191
  St John Baptist, 177
  St Mary Redcliffe, 51, 69
  Temple, 177, 178–9
Broune, Rowland, 77
Buckinghamshire, 38
bureau de charité, 11–12
Burghley, *see* Cecil, William
Burton, Samuel, 62
Bury St Edmunds, Suff., 149
Bushrod, John, 151

Cambridge, 68, 69, 72, 97, 119, 123
Cambridgeshire, 42
canon law, 22
cant, of rogues, 96, 102, 104–5
Canterbury, Kent, 68, 69
'Captain Poverty', 100
Cartwright, Thomas, 150
Cary, John, 193, 196–7
Castile, 9
Catholic attitudes, 8–10, 22–3, 120–1, 123
Cecil, Sir Robert, 126, 166
Cecil, William, Lord Burghley, 19, 125,
  139, 140, 149
censuses, *see* poor: listings of
Chancery, 12, 164–5, 169
Chard, Dors., 151
Charitable Corporation (1708), 206
charity
  alleged decline of, 19–20, 21, 164, 167
  bequests for, 120, 150, 151, 160 n65,
    162–6
  centralized, 9, 118, 199
  collective, 16 n26, 206
  criticized, 192, 196

endowments, 11–12, 69, 114–15, 127,
  152, 162–6
  ideal of, 19–22, 84, 119–20, 190
  informal, 12, 21, 49, 62, 165, 166–8, 172
  law relating to, 127, 152, 164–5
  neighbourly, 62, 83–4, 127–8, 129, 144,
    168, 192, 205
  poor's view of, 106
  value of, 13, 162–4, 169–73, 207
  see also alms; begging; briefs
Chamberlen, Peter, 26, 30
Charles I, 141
Chatham, Kent, 64, 65
Chelmsford, Essex, 165, 180
Chester, 68, 119, 123, 125, 126
Chichester, Suss., 95
Child, Sir Josiah, 28, 30, 31, 196
children
  among poor, 65, 66, 68–71, 75, 78, 80
  among vagrants, 97, 98, 99
  begging, 83, 154
  burden of, 27, 44, 192
  family responsibilities of, 84–5
  provision of work for, 82–3, 118, 122,
    199
  training of, 29–30, 82, 105, 149, 154
  see also apprentices; foundlings;
    orphans
Christmas, 62, 69, 98, 166, 168
church-ales, 169
church-rates, 41
church-stocks, 114
Civil War, 51, 72, 143, 154
civility, 24, 154, 196
Clarendon Code, 196
Clark, P., 44
Clayton, Sir Robert, 197
clergy, 38, 100, 126–7, 144, 148
Cockayne, William, 166
Cockes, Sir Richard, 192
Colchester, Essex
  Corporation of the Poor, 195, 197,
    203 n46
  poor-relief in, 123, 150, 152, 179
  vagrants in, 95, 96, 98
collections, *see* alms; briefs; poor rates
College of Physicians, *see* physicians
Collinson, P., 149
Colyton, Devon, 98
common weal, 30, 117, 118, 141, 145, 149,
  208
commons, 30, 52, 63, 101, 103, 188
constables, 92, 93, 94, 99, 100, 103, 126–7,
  151
Cope, Anthony, 126
corn